Christ the Liturgy

Christ the Liturgy

WILLIAM DANIEL

Angelico Press

For information, address:
Angelico Press, Ltd.
169 Monitor St.
Brooklyn, NY 11222
www.angelicopress.com

978-1-62138-555-4 pb
978-1-62138-556-1 cloth
978-1-62138-557-8 ebook

Book and cover design
by Michael Schrauzer

For Amanda, Wyles and Aydah —
being inhabited by Christ with you has shown me
the true nature of liturgical action.

CONTENTS

ABBREVIATIONS viii

INTRODUCTION ix

1   FOR THE SAKE OF THE MANY 1
Introduction 1—*Leitourgia*: Translation in Context 3—Lost in
Translation 6—Giver and Receiver are One 12—Prefiguring
the Gift 20—To Receive is to Give 24—The Liturgical
Economy 30—Only God Can Suffer 34—Conclusion 38

2   APPREHENDING GOD 41
Introduction 41—The Secret Disposition 44—Go Toward
Yourself 49—The Sense-able God 55—Can God Have
Friends? 71—Conclusion 82

3   THE ARCHITECTURE OF FAITH 87
Introduction 87—The Porosity of Space 91—Liturgical
Habitation 99—Spaces of Conviviality 107—*Terroir* and
Leitourgia 118—Conclusion 120

4   THE GRAMMAR OF GOD 121
Introduction 121—Language and Perception 123—The Middle
Voice 125—The Linguistic Subject 133—Agency, Action,
Participation 142—Our Only Mediator and Advocate 146
—An Active-Passivity 153—Conclusion 158

5   CONCLUSION: TOWARD A METAXOLOGICAL LITURGY . . . 161

BIBLIOGRAPHY 167

ACKNOWLEDGEMENTS 179

INDEX OF SCRIPTURE REFERENCES 181

SUBJECT INDEX 183

ABBREVIATIONS

ANF   *The Ante-Nicene Fathers. Translations of the Writings of the Fathers Down to A.D. 325.* Edited by Alexander Roberts and James Donaldson. Edinburgh, 1866–1872. 10 vols. Peabody, MA: Hendrickson Publishers, 1999.

NPNF *The Nicene and Post-Nicene Fathers of the Christian Church.* Edited by Philip Schaff and Henry Wace. Buffalo and New York, 1886–90. First Series: 14 vols. Second Series: 14 vols. Peabody, MA: Hendrickson Publishers, 1999.

PG   *Patrologiae cursus completus. Series graeca.* Edited by J. P. Migne. Paris, 1857–66. 161 vols.

PL   *Patrolgiae cursus completus. Series latina.* Edited by J. P. Migne. Paris, 1844–64. 221 vols.

INTRODUCTION

Jesus does not take us to the Father by going on that journey as our representative and carrying us along with him by throwing out sacramental lifelines. Jesus goes to the Father in our experience of him as victim, which is our experience of ourselves as forgiven and cut loose from our self-made world.

Sebastian Moore

If you humble yourself, God comes down from above and enters into you.

Meister Eckhart

JACK FINNEY'S SHORT STORY, *WHERE THE CLUETTS ARE*,[1] tells the story of Sam and Ellie Cluett and the building of their new vacation home. Sam had become a successful boat builder and his company was doing so well that he was making more money than he and Ellie could spend. So they decided to build their dream house. The only problem was, they couldn't figure out what kind of house they wanted to build nor where they should build it.

After several meetings with an architect, giving the architect no direction, and turning down numerous proposals along the way, Ellie stumbles upon a set of hundred-year-old blueprints for a house, unlike anything they had seen or imagined. While the architect is talking about their options, Sam and Ellie become captivated by the old plans for this 1885 home, and Sam says to his architect, "Can you build it?" "Well," he responds, "it would take some reconfiguring to install the plumbing and wiring, but sure, it can be done." "Let's build it," says Sam, "and I want it just like it is in the blueprints, spare no expense."

As construction begins on the house and the supplies are ordered, strange things begin to happen. For starters, the carpenters hired for the job love the work. It required all the artisanal skills that made them want to become carpenters in the first place, skills for which

1 Jack Finney, *About Time: 12 Short Stories* (New York: Scribner Paperback Fiction, 1986), 112–29.

a society of efficiency no longer had time or money. As the house begins to come together, small, almost unnoticeable things begin to happen to the workers. The workers building the house begin to grow facial hair as would have been customary in the 19th century — wide mustaches, burnsides, muttonchops, and more, and some even begin wearing workman's clothes that seemed to be period dress of the same era as the house's blueprints.

The most interesting transformation occurs, however, after the home is built and Sam and Ellie begin to inhabit it. The 1885 house was intended to be a vacation home, a place the Cluetts could escape to for three, maybe four months a year. However, after Sam and Ellie move into their new home they end up never leaving. Sam begins spending less and less time at the office, and Ellie begins doing things around the house she's never dreamed of doing, like making all of her and Sam's clothing. Sam and Ellie's grammar even begins to shift, as if they had suddenly become Victorian. The house that was intended to be a retreat home had come to re-habituate their sensibilities. If it weren't for the date on the calendar, walking into the Cluett home one might think she had stepped back in time.

Where the Cluetts Are is not your typical time-travel fiction. Sam and Ellie do not walk through a portal or jump into a spacecraft; rather, the home they inhabit comes to inhabit them in unexpected ways. Additionally, they begin to inhabit time as if outside of time, for they come to inhabit and to be inhabited by another age. How the Cluetts came to be inhabited by that which they inhabited is analogous to the dynamic experienced by the worshipper inhabiting sacred liturgy. For the participant involved in the liturgical action of prayer, Eucharistic celebration, baptism, and so on, space and time are not simply occupied by the participant; rather, the movement of the liturgy draws out from the worshipper, like water from a well, a time otherwise unknown, as she is caught up in a space only thereby inhabitable. To put this as simply and clearly as possible, what occurs in the life of the worshipper who gives herself to the liturgical action of making offering *by* Christ, and *with* Christ, and *in* Christ, is a transformation of sensibilities, such that the worshipper begins to resemble, even down to the clothes she wears, the *habitus*[2] of the New Jerusalem. This occurrence does not take place overnight. It happens only through continual participation in the breaking of bread and in the prayers. Gradually, as in the case of Sam and Ellie Cluett, the worshipper's language begins to shift, one's bodily comportment is reconditioned, and the liturgical participant begins to think as they move, inhabiting the world as one who mutually inhabits and is inhabited by the Liturgy—Christ.

The following is an exploration in liturgical habituation. More than this, it is an examination of how language, environments, habits, and other people are bound up together with a person's understanding of what it means to be human, relative to divine action as disclosed in Jesus of Nazareth, and how the early church recognized that the singular, liturgical action of God in Christ makes manifest the truth of human nature. Chapter one is a genealogy of liturgy, unpacking the term *leitourgia* and how it has been used throughout history, especially by St. Paul. This first chapter provides the necessary background for the chapters that follow. Far too much scholarship in modern liturgical studies is built upon the false notion that liturgy is "the work of the people." This particular translation of *leitourgia* is introduced in the late nineteenth century and is decidedly Protestant in tone, reinforcing a post-Enlightenment division between the temporal and celestial realms. I offer, therefore, a robust analysis of its usage in Ancient, Classical and Hellenistic Greek, showing how the Apostle Paul carries forth its historical meaning in his epistles, while also transforming its association to extend the meaning of the word. *Leitourgia* is better translated as "the work of one for the sake of the many." Working with this grounded translation of *leitourgia*, I go on to show how vital is Paul's usage of *leitourgia* for understanding the worshipper's involvement in Christian liturgy and why the modern mistranslation falsifies her participation in divine action and denigrates the worshipper's involvement in liturgical action.

This genealogy of *leitourgia* clarifies how the early church understood liturgy as participatory in nature. In chapter two, I bring Gregory of

---

2 More will be said about *habitus* later on. Briefly, however, *habitus* refers to the whole of one's bodily comportment: the habits, habitat, the mutual inhabiting with others in a habitat, as well as the habituations involved as one relates to their environment.

Nyssa and Maximus Confessor into conversation with phenomenology, especially Maurice Merleau-Ponty, to show how one's bodily comportment through habitual actions creates certain conditions of possibility for perceiving oneself as a participant in divine action. As Gregory and Maximus articulate, the worshipper becomes aware of her *natural nature*[3] in proportion to her devotion through liturgical habituation. Human perception of God, self, and others is an embodied affair relative to one's particular environment and background. Knowledge of God, self and others is acquired through habits of the body, and Gregory and Maximus are exemplary in how this is understood within the context of liturgical action. Liturgy for Gregory is about placing oneself as a mirror before Christ in prayer, whereby we take on the movement of God in Christ and Christ in turn draws out from us the image in which we are created — draws out his own image. We come into contact with this image, says Maximus, through habituation in the likeness of Christ, an ascetical way of life that attunes our sensibilities in the way of humility. All of which is participatory; none of which originates with humans.

In chapter three, "The Architecture of Faith," I show further how the habits and practices described in chapter two relate to our environments and how our habitats are inseparable from how we perceive God and others. Engaging with psychogeographic and cognitive studies, I show how buildings, their external facades and internal designs, influence how we make our way in the world. Extending the work of James K. A. Smith and others who have named *that* it occurs, I unpack *how* this occurs. I use examples of the modern workspace to show how memory is affected and directed by the colors, textures, and materials of the spaces where we dwell. Certain spaces create a feeling of belonging and creativity, whereas "boring spaces" diminish camaraderie and stifle inspiration, even affecting a person's posture and countenance, not unlike the description found in Jack Finney's *Where the Cluetts Are*. I also bring Ivan Illich into conversation with modern architectural studies to show how these tools of society might be refashioned as convivial tools that are life-giving, rather than life-inhibiting.

---

3 Maximus uses the phrase "natural nature" to refer to a person's true, human nature revealed in Christ. This will be unpacked below in chapter 2.

Introduction

In the final chapter, "The Grammar of God," I deal explicitly with the middle voice as a hermeneutic key for faithfully understanding the nature of Christian liturgy as the *work of One for the sake of the many*. Utilizing Émile Benveniste's critical study of the middle voice in linguistics and David Jones's seminal explorations in *poiesis*, I argue that human action is an involvement in divine action that transcends the categories of subject and object. In the middle voice, the subject exists within the process of the verb. As such, the verbal action does not originate with the subject, and neither is there a clear object; rather, there are mutually involved subjects participating in an agency that cannot be neatly ascribed to the subject of the sentence. With the arrival of Latin, the middle voice slowly fades away, eventually giving way to the active-passive binary of modern languages today. This linguistic bifurcation fights against everyday human sensibilities, whereby our environments and the actions of others continually affect human action. In problematizing this linguistic divide, I show how the notion of subjectivity, and thereby objectivity, seeps into human speech over time and has, therefore, made accounting for the worshipper's involvement in liturgy reducible to a transactional relationship with God, whereby the worshipper offers to God something that God lacks. Delving into the medial nature of liturgical action, however, and revealing the breakdown of language over time, I show how liturgy properly understood throws the worshipper into an action that is not her own, a particular relationship of cooperation in an agency that *precedes* and *proceeds from* the worshipper as a participant in the action of Christ who is *action qua action*. As I argue in the final chapter, this paradoxically elevates the action of the worshipper because it is never reducible to her own action; rather, she becomes complicit, as it were, in divinity—the *donum* of the Spirit.

The purpose of this book is to challenge the reader to reimagine liturgy as it is and is to be *experienced* by the worshipper, namely as transcendent. Transcendent, however, in a way that gathers the temporal in the celestial through participation in the eternal liturgy who is Jesus the Christ. I thank all who, along the way, have contributed to this work, especially John Milbank my dissertation advisor, and Catherine

Pickstock, whose encouragement has helped me refine how to articulate liturgy as a medial act. I am grateful to the innumerable parishioners along the way who have asked faithful questions of my project and whose involvement in the liturgies of the church have made this writing worthwhile. I am especially thankful to the Calvin Seminars in Christian Worship at Calvin College, Grand Rapids, Michigan, where much of this research began, as well as Nashotah House Theological Seminary where I was truly habituated in faithful, transcendent liturgy that charges the sensibilities. I offer special thanks to my friends, mentors, and colleagues whose conversations with me are woven throughout this work, especially Harris Bechtol, Kyle Bennett, Mark Wastler, Isaac (John) Slater, Mike Sauter, Tom Holtzen, Garwood Anderson, Stanley Hauerwas, Steven Hoskins, Conor Cunningham, Bishop Prince Singh, Frank Valdez, Hugh Cruse, Elizabeth Bass, James K. A. Smith, Michael Budde, D. Stephen Long, and a whole host of others I know I am forgetting. As this book intends to show, life is always being mediated, and it is mediated with the people, places, and things with which we engage most. I am grateful to all who have inhabited these conversations with me in the many places they have occurred, all in the grace of our Lord.

1

For the Sake of the Many

There is really no action without Jesus Christ.
Dietrich Bonhoeffer

God, by whom all things are being made, is the real doer of all that is here done.
Evelyn Underhill

INTRODUCTION

In *The Mother Tongue*, Bill Bryson describes a Japanese driver's manual that has been translated into English for expatriates who need to take the driving test in Japan. In the section discussing the right of way for pedestrians, it reads: "When a passenger of the foot heave in sight, tootle the horn, trumpet at him melodiously at first, but if he still obstacles your passage, tootle him with vigor...." I don't know about you, but I've never heard anyone "trumpet at me melodiously," although I have had people "tootle me with vigor." There are obvious flaws in the translation. And it is evidenced here that the translator does not live in a place where English is the native tongue.

Alasdair MacIntyre argues that, "A language cannot be translated; it can only be learned." Obviously, we *can* translate a language — we can especially translate it badly. However, what MacIntyre presses us to understand is that to really know what we're saying requires a mastery acquired only by enculturation. Understanding involves being assimilated to the people and geographical space where a language is used, because *language is use*. How we *use* our words is what we mean by them.

The following is, in fact, a translation. It is the translation of the word λειτουργια, from which we English speakers derive "liturgy." Specifically it is a retranslation of a word that has been mistranslated, the first instance of which appears to have been at *The Fourth General Council* of the Alliance of The Reformed Churches holding The Presbyterian

1

System (London, 1888), whereby liturgy is translated as "the work of the people." To speak of "the work of the people" assumes a work, an offering, or the human capacity to give something to God that God doesn't have. Translating *leitourgia* as "the work of the people," a distinctly post-Enlightenment translation, inverts the human's relation to the salvific offering of the Son to the Father. That is, this redefining of liturgy elicits a lack in God — the lack of God's own worship. Additionally, liturgy as the "work of the people" separates the liturgical action from the creative agency of the Son and the human's volitive participation in the re-creating of the world, infinitely actualized — *recapitulated* — in Christ.[1] The Transcendent is hereby *absolutely transcendent*; there is no mingling of God and creation.[2] What is important to note at the outset is that to translate or (re)define *leitourgia* as "the work of the people" detracts from the inherent, relational nature of liturgy as that which gathers the people of God into the eternal life of reciprocity that is Holy Trinity.

The first chapter of this essay will explore how the term *leitourgia* is employed throughout the classical world and by the early fathers of the church. This exploration is to lay the foundation for understanding liturgy as the manifestation of divinity in Christ, attested to by the early and medieval church, and as the anagogic relation of participation that is the essence of the church Catholic. Liturgy is hereby to be understood not as "the work of the people" but as "the work of the One for the sake of the many." Christ himself is this "work," this event, who is the Liturgy he enacts — both priest and victim,[3] an offering to the Father *for the life of the world*.[4]

An ontology of participation is of utmost importance in this regard, especially as this ontology relates to human self-knowing as *a* liturgy of

1 It is worth noting that the documents of Vatican II, while stressing the importance and absolute need for greater participation in liturgy by the faithful — the "laity" — do not refer to the liturgy as "the work of the people" or "people's work." This is largely a Protestant construal of the term that, while the Roman Catholic liturgical renewal movements of the twentieth century certainly provide the language and practice for this development, remains imaginable primarily from a post-Enlightenment understanding of an absolute distance between the temporal and the Eternal.

2 More will be said of this in chapter two.

3 Hebrews 10.

4 John 6:51.

Christ *the* Liturgy, which is in keeping with the earliest articulations of *leitourgia* by Saint Paul, Ignatius of Antioch, Irenaeus, et al. The above is in no way to deny the role of the human in the liturgical action, nor is it to denigrate human action in any way; rather, it is to show how the vitality of human action bears no meaning except in a contingent relation of participation to the singular act of Christ who is himself Liturgy par excellence *for the life of the world*. This, it will be argued, is the inescapable logic of the earliest articulations of the human's relational role as a manifesting participant in redemption, whose liturgical involvement is both her participation in Being and her teleological function as one who gathers creation into the eschatological reality of Christ's reconciling the world to himself through recapitulated human nature. While some commentary on *leitourgia* in its historic use has been done,[5] little exploration as to the implications of defining liturgy in this way has been conducted, nor has the importance of sustaining the singular reference of *leitourgia* to Christ as the absolute fusion of offerer, offering, and act of offering been either strong or clear enough, especially in the West.

LEITOURGIA: TRANSLATION IN CONTEXT

The Greek word from which we derive the term *liturgy* is a compound word literally meaning public (*laos*) work (*ergon*). Λειτο is a derivative of λαός ("people"), meaning "public" and ἔργια, from ἔργον ("work"), meaning service/duty/work. In the ancient world this term carried with it different meanings and was employed in a variety of ways, each having to do with the specific office held or action done that involved a sacrifice of one (λειτουργός) for the sake of the many (πολύς). *Leitourgia* hereby carries the broad meaning of "public service."[6] Additionally, this public service engenders that of a sacrificial gift or donation usually in the form of a financial offering or service

5   See Odo Casel, *The Mystery of Christian Worship*, ed. Burkhard Neunheuser (New York: Crossroad Publishing Company, 1999), and Michael Kunzler, *The Church's Liturgy* (London: Continuum, 2001) as helpful starting points.

6   Sviatoslav Dmitriev, *City Government in Hellenistic and Roman Asia Minor* (Oxford: Oxford University Press, 2005), 17–19.

3

rendered without expectation of return payment, e.g., paying for a festival or holding public office. What is important to note is that *leitourgia* in the ancient world does not bear the connotation of "work"; rather, it is more closely akin to something like a "servant-offering," whereby the one who offers *is* her offering.

In the military obligations of the Greco-Roman world is evidenced the sacrificial, as opposed to financial, underpinnings of this word *leitourgia*.[7] Even the obligation of an official to afford the expenditures associated with his office (e.g., the official that managed the road systems would be expected to pay for road repair, etc.) was not the emphasis of his liturgy. The financial aspects of the office could be delegated to another or, as taxable infrastructure developed, covered by taxable income. In fact, Aristotle shows how the sacrificial element of one's *leitourgia* can be abused. A person's ability to afford the expenditure of an office would make him more likely to acquire the post, if he so desired,[8] as there was a certain prestige that accompanied the liturgical office. In the *Politics*, Aristotle gives the following warning against competing oligarchs and aristocrats:

> It is a good thing to prevent the wealthy citizens, even if they are willing, from undertaking expensive and useless public services, such as the giving of choruses, torch-races, and the like.[9]

Leitourgia is hereby the bearing of a communal burden by those who have the means or ability, so to enable everyone to have a common

---

7 See also Frank Tenney, *An Economic Survey of Ancient Rome: Rome and Italy of the Republic*, vol. I (Baltimore: Johns Hopkins Press, 1936): "Crews were supplied by liturgy. In 214 BC, when a fleet had to be equipped quickly for the impending war in Sicily the Senate imposed a 'liturgy' on the propertied classes of the kind well known from Athenian practice and from the last year of the First Punic War. Rowers were to be supplied by private individuals according to wealth. For instance, men rated from 50,000 to 100,000 *asses* must supply and pay the wage of a rower for six months and supply him with food for a month, while senators had to supply eight men for a year. There is no mention of any proposal to repay these outlays" (86).

8 Ibid., 43–45.

9 Aristotle, *Politics*, V.viii, in *The Complete Works of Aristotle: The Revised Oxford Translation*, ed. Jonathan Barnes, vol. II (Princeton: Princeton University Press, 1984).

sense of human flourishing (Aristotle's *eudaimonia*). Because it is a dutiful contribution to society, it is not seen as a charitable act. The gift is almost always compulsory.

In the classical age, *leitourgia* also exacts a desire for the public good. Aristotle, once again, situates *leitourgia* within the context of friendship and concord.[10] And, as aforementioned, he warns against frequent liturgies by individuals, even when they are able. In this regard, Aristotle is not unusual in his employment of *leitourgia*. Though it is the gift of one it is done for the good and concord of the people. It is plainly and simply a matter of good citizenry.[11] Included in this class of liturgists, then, are not simply the wealthy, but also the priests, doctors, military, or those who provide lodging for travelers to the city. *Leitourgia* for the ancient Greeks is, however, primarily adverbial, describing the manner in which an act is done, i.e., sacrificially. The liturgical action so understood bears an implicit logic of a sacrificial giving of oneself for the good of the body polis.[12]

Liturgies in the ancient world are primarily festive.[13] The three liturgies of the *choragus, gymnasiarch*, and *hestiator*, are solely for entertainment.[14] It is *public* entertainment, but entertainment nonetheless. The choragus contributes the monies necessary to provide choruses for dramatic and lyric contests. The gymnasiarch's liturgy is to organize and pay for and maintain the competitors in the torch races.[15] And the hestiator provides food for his tribe's festivals. The choraguses, gymnasiarchs, hestiators, trierarchs, military, doctors, priests, those who open their homes to travelers, and yes "even jugglers," says Plato, are all liturgists, giving their dutiful services for the common good of the people.[16]

---

10   Aristotle, *Nicomachean Ethics*, trans. H. Rackham (Cambridge: Harvard University Press, 1999), IX.vi.3–4.

11   Demosthenes, "Oration 59," *Private Cases in Neaeram*, trans. A. T. Murray, in Loeb Classical Library, vol. 351 (Cambridge, MA: Harvard University Press, 1939).

12   Dmitriev, *City Government*, 39.

13   Peter Wilson, *The Athenian Institution of the Khoregia: The Chorus, the City, and the Stage* (Cambridge: Cambridge University Press, 2000), 25.

14   Ibid., 11–49; see also Ilias Arnaoutoglou, *Ancient Greek Laws: A Sourcebook* (London: Routledge, 1998), 117–23.

15   Arnaoutoglou, *Ancient Greek Laws*, 117–23.

16   Dmitriev, *City Government*, 34–63.

In each employment of *leitourgia*, the word is used to express the gift of one, or at least a minority of persons, regarding an act-office, for the sake of the *demes* or people. There is a recognized social need and *leitourgia* names the satisfaction for this need as the sacrificial act of one, or a specified group of persons, for the sake of the social body.[17]

LOST IN TRANSLATION

During the third and second centuries B C, much of the Hebrew Scriptures are translated into Greek, what we know as the *Septuagint*. The Hellenistic translation of the Hebrew Scriptures becomes very important in understanding the use of *leitourgia* for Christians. In the Hebrew language there are any number of words used to make distinctions in office held or action done, with regard to the priestly services. The words *'eved* and *'aboda* denote servant and service. *Kohen* is a priest, while *tziva* and *mitzvah* bear the meanings *constitute, command, appoint,* and *privilege*. We find these words in Exodus, Numbers, Leviticus and elsewhere, all of which are translated into the Greek using the general term *leitourgia* or its derivations. It is the spread of the *Septuagint* that begins to refine the meaning of *leitourgia* as having specifically to do with a ministry or service that is done for God's honor and glory, as opposed to the more generalized Greek understanding. The ministerial connotations did not do away with *leitourgia* as a general point of reference in Greek society; however, the Hellenistic influence on the Hebrew texts enables the church's employment of this word to relate specifically to the act-office of Christ as High Priest. Just as the Ancient Greek usage of *leitourgia* has a variety of meanings, each use engendering that of a sacrificial action, likewise does *leitourgia* become for the early church the term directly related to the act-office of a priest.

The Apostle Paul is of utmost importance in the formation of a Christian definition of *leitourgia*. Being trained in the most prestigious of Hebrew schools, Paul would have had at his disposal any number of terms to denote the ministry of priests, offerings gathered, or services

17   Ibid.

rendered, but Paul uses *leitourgia,* as he does with reference to Epaphroditus as λειτουργὸν, in direct relation with one who gathers together the offerings of a people to God. The ministerial connotation pervades here, as someone gathering and offering, or providing service on behalf of a people, to God, for the mutual benefit of all involved. This is Epaphroditus's liturgy, done to God, for Paul, on behalf of the Philippians. The use of *leitourgia* in Paul's letter to the Philippians takes as its precedent the understanding of the temple priest's role in the divine drama of sacrificial offering. The Israelites would bring their gifts to the temple, but it was the priest who mediated their offerings to Israel's God. In Philippians 2:17, 2:25, and 2:30, the term is situated in the context of gathering the offerings of a community for the sake of giving glory to God, whether it is Paul being poured out as a libation on behalf of the Philippians,[18] which is his sacrificial service, his λειτουργία, to God for their mutual benefit (θυσια — sacrifice — now linked by Paul with λειτουργία — liturgy) or Epaphroditus's coming to Paul's aid, bearing the gifts and support of the Philippians.[19]

In Paul's letter to the Romans, *leitourgia* is used in the same way as it is in his letter to the Philippians. The *minister*/λειτουργὸν of Christ is the one who gathers the people's — in this case the Gentiles' — offerings together, so that their offering will be acceptable to God by the Holy Spirit, through the apostle of Christ:

> I myself feel confident about you, my brothers and sisters, that you yourselves are full of goodness, filled with all knowledge, and able to instruct one another. Nevertheless, on some points I have written to you rather boldly by way of reminder, because of the grace given me by God to be a *minister* (λειτουργὸν) of Christ Jesus to the Gentiles in the *priestly service* (ιερουργουντα) of the gospel of God, so that the offering of the Gentiles may be acceptable, sanctified by the Holy Spirit.[20]

18 Philippians 2:17.
19 Philippians 2:25, 2:30.
20 Romans 15:14–16.

Paul makes a distinction here between the particular office of *min-ister* and the universal *priestly service* of the Gospel. The common service of all people to the gospel of God (ἱερουργέω) has within it specific roles for those that make up the ἱερουργουντα of all believers, of which Paul's λειτουργία is as an administrator of the world to the Father as one holding the office of apostle. This is also the context of Paul's gathering of the resources from the Macedonians and Achaians,[21] in order to give to the poor in Jerusalem. Paul, as God's λειτουργὸν, gathers the offerings of the many for the sake of Christ and only then extending it to others; this is his liturgical office — who he *is* in the Divine Economy. As in the classical Greek usage of the term, act and office are inextricably linked. Paul *is* the liturgy he enacts — Christ. His liturgical role is to serve as Christ, to gather the offerings of the faithful into the offering Jesus is in himself. Only in this way do the liturgical actions — offerings — of a people become bound to the offering of Jesus to the Father — the one, holy, acceptable offering.

It is this gathering together of gifts that becomes of central impor-tance, especially in the letter to the church in Corinth. In Paul's first letter he addresses their shortcomings in the liturgical economy. "When you come together, it is not really to eat the Lord's Supper. For when the time comes to eat, each of you goes ahead with your own supper, and one goes hungry whilst another becomes drunk."[22] Paul condemns their practice of gathering together in a public space (*ekklesia*) for a shared meal — the Lord's Supper — and yet having complete disregard for one another, not discerning rightly the make-up of the Body they are in Christ. He emphasizes to the Corinthians that every meal is an image of and participation in the Last Supper when Christ broke bread and gave, not to a few, but to all gathered, even giving his body to one who would betray him. Not to gather the gifts as a single offering to God, that is, not to gather together as one body, is to reject *being gathered* into Christ's Body. The gathering of the body through its offering is the realization of the church as sacrament — as God's unifying force in the world, whereby communication with the triune God is made available.

21   Romans 15:27.
22   1 Corinthians 11:21–22.

It is important to note that Paul's criticism of the Corinthian meal is that it has as its paradigm the meals of the idol temples and common meals, whereby social status determines food preference and seating arrangements. The Lord's Supper, however, shifts the paradigm so that all meals, feasts, services of worship, and all bonds of human relations participate in the shared communion of the human with the Father, in Christ, through the Spirit. Not to gather the resources together as shared resources is a refusal to *be* gathered into Christ. Hierarchy of succession, however, is not eliminated with the abolition of a hierarchy of goods. In this light is the bishop best understood as the *primus inter pares* — the first among equals. None are deserving of the benefits of God — none deserve to be gathered into the Godhead — but the same gift is offered to sinner and saint alike, which demands that all goods be shared in common. The corrective for the Corinthians is undergirded by Paul's articulation of giving in his letter to the Philippians, as mentioned above. To give is to give to God, necessitating as a consequence the benefit to one's neighbor, which has the double effect of a mutual binding in Christ.[23]

Clement of Rome, as with Paul and the ancient writers before him, carries forward the union between office and action expressed by the word *leitourgia*. In Clement's *Epistle to the Corinthians*, *leitourgia* is used in reference to the priestly office, specifically bearing the meaning of the temple priest as one who speaks repentance.[24] Clement makes no

23 This could also be seen as a positive carry-over of the negative side found in Psalm 51, "against thee only have I sinned." Sins are committed against God, which, as a consequence, fracture the human relationship. Reading this in conjunction with Matthew 5, where the offerer is called to be reconciled with his brother prior to making his offering, shows not that the brotherly relation establishes the relation to Christ; rather, reconciliation and communion with God demands reconciliation and communion with one another. Reconciliation with your brother or sister presumes a prior participation in the life of God, which is why the reconciliation between brothers and sisters is a necessary consequence of communion with God, though not the establishment of it. Right relation with others, then, is understood as a consequence of right relatedness to God, even though a necessary consequence. This is reinforced also by Christ's radicalization of the first and second commandment — "Thou shalt love the Lord your God with all your heart, soul, mind and strength, *and* your neighbor as yourself."

24 Clement of Rome, "The First Epistle to the Corinthians," VIII, in *The Epistles of St. Clement of Rome and St. Ignatius of Antioch*, trans. James A. Kleist, ed. Johannes Quasten and Joseph C. Plumpe (New York: Newman Press, 1946).

distinction between the office held and the action done. *Leitourgia* also takes on a more generalized definition of a service done in obedience to God, which Clement compares with Noah's obedience in building the ark and gathering the animals,[25] and even the liturgy of the wind as it participates in its proper fashion within the economy of creation.[26] Nevertheless, following his explanation of the wind's liturgy, participating in due fashion within the order of creation, Clement goes on to narrow the use of *leitourgia* as the hierarchical offices of all, each person having his or her role in the liturgy of Jesus through the *liturgies* prescribed to them. Drawing on Hebrews 10, Clement links λειτουργία (liturgy) with θυσία (sacrifice) and προσφέρω (to offer), so that the priest is the one who offers the people's sacrifice. Following the logic found in Hebrews, the people so gathered are "consecrated through the offering of the body of Jesus Christ," enabling Clement to say that every liturgist, each in his/her order, participates in the liturgy Jesus *is*.[27] It is through participation in Jesus's liturgy that the Christian is consecrated to God.[28] It is worthwhile to include the whole passage here.

> Since, therefore, this is evident to all of us, and we have explored the depths of the divine knowledge, we are obliged to carry out in fullest detail what the Master has commanded us to do at stated times. He has ordered the sacrifices to be offered (προσφοράς) and the services to be held (λειτουργίας), and this not in a

25   Ibid., IX.

26   Ibid., XX. We see this also in John Chrysostom, who speaks of the day and the night as *ministers* (λειτουργὸν) who perform their liturgies for the sake of humanity, drawing humanity closer together as a unity. The wild beasts are also liturgists, as they drive men into cities out of fear, forcing humanity to live in solidarity with one another, living peacefully and harmoniously, rather than being eaten alive in the wilderness alone (see Chrysostom, *Homily on the Statutes*, 8.1).

27   Clement does not say explicitly "Jesus *is*" the liturgy; however, his articulation of liturgy as synonymous with *office* makes it possible to equate the act-office of Christ with the liturgy he performs.

28   Clement of Rome, *The First Epistle to the Corinthians*, VIII–XLII, especially XL and XLI. Clement reiterates the argument made in Hebrews 10, where it is Christ who is the sacrifice, the one offering, and it is in his liturgy that Christians participate when they come to offer themselves as a living sacrifice, and it is the bishop who stands as Christ and gathers the people into God's economy.

random and irregular fashion, but at definite times and seasons. He has, moreover, Himself, by His sovereign will determined where and by whom He wants them to be carried out. Thus all things are done religiously, acceptable to His good pleasure, dependent on His will. Those, therefore, that make their offerings at the prescribed times are acceptable and blessed; for, since they comply with the ordinances of the Master, they do not sin. Special functions (λειτουργίαι) are assigned to the high priest; a special office is imposed upon the priests; and special ministrations fall to the Levites. The layman is bound by the rules laid down for the laity. Each of us, brethren, must in his own place endeavor to please God with a good conscience, reverently taking care not to deviate from the established rule of service (λειτουργίας).[29]

The liturgies of the bishop, deacon, and layperson are likened to those of the angels.[30] It is hereby that Clement links the bishop with Christ. Christ's liturgy is now assigned to the bishop to continue, gathering the offerings of the many into one as acceptable and pleasing to God.[31] The offerings of the people are inseparable from the people themselves. When the bishop gathers the gifts of the people, he simultaneously gathers the people, so that what is consecrated and given to God is not merely the people's offering; it is they who are presented *with* the offering.[32] Clement specifically locates the plurality of liturgical activity within the singularity of Christ's liturgical act. As with Ignatius of Antioch, the bishop stands as Christ; it is he who gathers the body, discerning rightly according to each order, making the many offerings of the masses a single, consecrated and blessed offering acceptable to God.

29 Clement of Rome, *The First Epistle to the Corinthians*, XL–XLI.

30 Ibid., XXXVI, again drawing on Hebrews (1:10). See also Leviticus 3:5.

31 Ibid., XL. It is in this passage that Clement makes most explicit the ordering of the liturgical economy by Christ, whose services/liturgies are now assigned to the episcopate, and through him are enjoined the offerings to be presented and the services to be performed to the glory of the Lord. See also XL–XLI, XLIV.

32 There is no distinction to be made here between the signified (bread) and the thing-signified (giver). As will be shown later in chapter four, the bread and its donor are inseparable.

In Ignatius, a bishop is undeniably Christ to the church. "Plainly... one should look upon the bishop as upon the Lord Himself."[33] The bishop is hereby the οἰκονομίαν for the οἰκοδεσπότης — the economist/administrator for the economy/household of the Master.[34] He is the master on behalf of *the* Master, God; he is one who administrates the Lord's economy in the terrestrial realm as analogous to its orchestration in the celestial or heavenly realm, through whom in Christ these realms co-inhere. For Ignatius, then, Christ is the gatherer of the whole world into God, the chief economist if you will, and the bishop — επισκοπος (*episcopos*) — is the gatherer of the people in Christ, literally the over-seer (ἐπί over/above, σκοπος sight/see) of the economy, through whom the peoples' offerings — that is, the people themselves — are assimilated to God.[35]

GIVER AND RECEIVER ARE ONE

The Greek meaning of λειτουργία is both carried forth and given new meaning in Jesus of Nazareth. It maintains its emphasis both as sacrifice and donation; however, the meaning is radicalized in the sense that there is now only *one* who can give the gift, Jesus, and his specific form of self-offering now establishes the very nature of sacrifice and how a liturgical economy is to be enacted. *Leitourgia* is a sacrificial offering to God, which is consequentially beneficial to others.

Very much in the same vein as the Apostle Paul, we find an interesting correlation in *Similitude 5* of the Shepherd of Hermas. Hermas sees in the spiritual discipline of fasting a way for Christians to participate in the self-offering of Christ; however, merely abstaining from food is not the mark of true sacrifice. Fasting, to be a true fast, should benefit others.

> After having done what is prescribed, on the day of your fast do
> not taste anything except bread and water. Compute the total

33 Ignatius, "Epistle to the Ephesians," VI, in *The Epistles of St. Clement of Rome and St. Ignatius of Antioch*, trans. James A. Kleist, ed. Johannes Quasten and Joseph C. Plumpe (New York: Newman Press, 1946).
34 Ibid.
35 Ibid.

expense for the food you would have eaten on the day on which you intended to keep a fast and give it to a widow, an orphan, or someone in need. In this way you will become humble in soul, so that the beneficiary of your humility may fill his soul and pray to the Lord for you. If you perform your fast, then, in the way I have just commanded, your sacrifice (θυσία) will be acceptable in the sight of God and this fast will be entered in the account [in your favor]; a service (λειτουργία) so performed is beautiful, joyous, and acceptable in the sight of the Lord.[36]

If a person fasted and kept the money that would have afforded her meals, says Hermas, there would be a gain involved in the sacrificial act, which would not fully participate in the self-emptying of God on the cross.[37] Fasting—abstaining from eating—does not mean that food is wasted, says Hermas. It means that it is denied by one for the sake of another's enjoyment. In this way fasting participates in Jesus's liturgy, whose offering is always *to* the glory of the Father and *for* the life of the world.

36 Shepherd of Hermas, "Parables," V.iii, in *The Apostolic Fathers*, trans. Francis Xavier Glimm, Joseph Marie Felix Marique, and Gerald Groveland Walsh (Washington: Catholic University of America Press, 1969).

37 It is important to remember that St. Paul's emphasis on the service is not *to* the other, even though it is *for* the other. It is a *necessary consequence* that service to God is for the benefit of others; however, it remains a consequence of the liturgical action, not what determines the liturgical action. Benefitting the other is the natural outcome of spiritual discipline, as we see with the Shepherd of Hermas; one does not seek to do good to the other and thereby praise God. It is the praise and faithfulness to God that benefits those around us, not unlike Bernard of Clairvaux's notion of the Reservoir in *Sermon XVIII* on the *Song of Songs*. This also directly relates to what Jesus says about sheep and goats in Matthew 25. "Then the righteous will answer him, 'Lord, when was it that we saw you hungry and gave you food, or thirsty and gave you something to drink? And when was it that we saw you a stranger and welcomed you, or naked and gave you clothing? And when was it that we saw you sick or in prison and visited you?' And the king will answer them, 'Truly I tell you, just as you did it to one of the least of these who are members of my family, you did it to me'" (Matthew 25:37–40). What it is interesting about the sheep and goats is that neither the righteous nor the unrighteous know that they have just served or denied Christ. Whereas the unrighteous sees only his own need, the righteous sees only the need of the other. The former rejects Christ in the other, the latter receives Christ in the other, which is unbeknownst to each.

A gift given to another does not necessarily mean that it is a mimesis of Jesus's self-offering. In other words, it is *not* the "thought" that counts. How the gift is given and what is actually given determines whether the gift accords with the gift of Christ. An offering to God is to bear witness to the sacrificial self-offering of Christ, while at the same time being of benefit to another or others who are not involved in offering the gift. The spiritual blessing comes when the offering *to* God is marked by self-emptying. The radicalization of *leitourgia* is found in the mimetic offering of *one* as a living sacrifice, whereby God is glorified, the *other* receives the benefit(s), and the offerer is drawn further into communion with God.

When the gifts are gathered as an offering to God, they are then distributed to those in need, be they the poor or an apostle. It is here that λειτουργία comes into direct contact with κοινωνια (*koinonia*—a gift jointly contributed, as exhibiting proof of joint fellowship). Paul describes this fellowship in his letter to the Philippians, where the gifts of the Macedonians and Achaians bind them together in the fellowship of Christ with the Christians in Jerusalem. But such κοινωνια is never unilateral for Paul; it is inherently reciprocal. The ἐκοινώνησεν (*ekoinonāsen/sharing*) is in δόσεως (*doseos/giving*) and λήμψεως (*lāmpseos/receiving*).[38] Nowhere in Paul's letters is this shared liturgy more explicit than in his second letter to the church in Corinth. "Through us," says Paul, the liturgy of the Corinthians will be a "thanksgivings to God,"[39] and it is through their liturgy that *koinonia* with other Christians is possible, which glorifies God.[40] This *koinonia*, however, is a mimesis of the "indescribable gift" of God in Christ—the Holy Spirit—who simultaneously realizes with the Christian community the *koinonia*[41] in God through the same Spirit.[42]

In his marvelous work, *The Gift*, Marcel Mauss shows how giving has historically defined the nature of human relations within a local

38   Philippians 4:15.
39   2 Corinthians 9:11–12.
40   2 Corinthians 13.
41   *Koinonia* here is a distinctly shared life, relative to Paul's description of the body of Christ where each limb is inseparable from the other. None is of greater or lesser importance; each exists for Christ and the benefit of others.
42   2 Corinthians 13:13.

community and between differentiated bodies of people.[43] All giving occurs in and through the fellowship of those who participate in the social body or the fellowship between social bodies. This is due to the nature of a gift. A gift is never to be understood as a thing that bears meaning apart from its giver or recipient. In giving a gift, "one gives away what is in reality a part of one's nature and substance, while to receive something is to receive a part of someone's spiritual essence."[44] The gift creates a shared life between giver and recipient. Fellowship, however, is contingent upon reciprocity—upon the reception of the gift and an anticipated return. The offering is not enough to bind two persons or groups together. The gift must be received.[45] If the gift is denied, it is as though the would-be recipient has declared war on the giver.[46]

This is analogous with the parable of the man who held a banquet for his son[47] where none who were invited came. By not attending the banquet, all those invited were not simply refusing to attend a meal at the home of the one married or his father; each was denying fellowship with the one who extended the invitation to the banquet. The ancient gift-economy illustrated by Mauss is extremely helpful in discerning how fellowship between persons or bodies of people is established and sustained, especially as it relates to the development of liturgy throughout church history. The tangible gifts shared between people are not understood to be inert objects, but as endowed with the spirit of the giver, and by receiving a gift the recipient enters into fellowship with the giver.[48]

43   Marcel Mauss, *The Gift: Forms and Functions of Exchange in Archaic Societies* (New York: Norton, 1967), 2–3.

44   Ibid., 10.

45   To suggest that a gift must be received is to recognize that in order for a gift to be a gift reception is required. There are no unilateral gifts. However, it is to be recognized that the gift of God in Christ does not need to be received by humans for it to be a gift. The gift has already been received in the eternal giving and receiving that is the Holy Trinity. This gift is extended to humanity; however, it remains gift apart from human reception, even if it is not *for us* a gift unless it is received. The gift that God in Christ is is not contingent upon the human's need for the gift; rather, God *is* gift and, as aforesaid, God can only give himself to himself in the communion of Father, Son and Holy Spirit.

46   Mauss, *The Gift*, 11.

47   Matthew 22.

48   Mauss, *The Gift*, 48.

In *Against Heresies*, Irenaeus of Lyons discusses in this regard the widow and her mite. Throwing what she has into the treasury is far more than casting a couple of insignificant copper coins. It is she herself that is "put in."

> The oblation of the Church, therefore, which the Lord gave instructions to be offered throughout all the world, is accounted with God a pure sacrifice, and is acceptable to Him; not that He stands in need of a sacrifice from us, but that *he who offers* is himself glorified in *what he does offer*, if his gift be accepted. For by the gift both honour and affection are shown forth towards the King; and the Lord, wishing us to offer it in all simplicity and innocence, did express Himself thus: "Therefore, when thou offerest thy gift upon the altar, and shalt remember that thy brother hath aught against thee, leave thy gift before the altar, and go thy way; first be reconciled to thy brother, and then return and offer thy gift." We are bound, therefore, to offer to God the first-fruits of His creation, as Moses also says, "Thou shalt not appear in the presence of the Lord thy God empty"; so that man, being accounted as grateful, by those things in which he has shown his gratitude, may receive that honour which flows from Him. And the class of oblations in general has not been set aside; for there were both oblations there [among the Jews], and there are oblations here [among the Christians]. Sacrifices there were among the people; sacrifices there are, too, in the Church: but the species alone has been changed, inasmuch as the offering is now made, not by slaves, but by freemen. For the Lord is [ever] one and the same; but the character of a servile oblation is peculiar [to itself], as is also that of freemen, in order that, by the very oblations, the indication of liberty may be set forth. For with Him there is nothing purposeless, nor without signification, nor without design. And for this reason they (the Jews) had indeed the tithes of their goods consecrated to Him, but those who have received liberty set aside all their possessions for the Lord's purposes, bestowing joyfully and

> freely not the less valuable portions of their property, since they
> have the hope of better things [hereafter]; as that poor widow
> acted who cast all her living into the treasury of God.[49]

The widow, in casting all her living into the treasury, has given also
herself to God, entirely; she is glorified in what she has offered, because
she has received the Gift to now *be* gift. In her poverty she becomes
wealthy, because she has emptied herself to God's glory, and is now the
dwelling place of the Lord. Emptying herself of all she has opens her
to being filled with the fullness of God. This is the way of simplicity
and self-denial, "A condition of complete simplicity / (Costing not less
than everything)."[50]

Koinonia for the Christian community becomes distinct, however,
because of the gathering of many offerings into a unified offering. A
gift cannot be given in isolation or unilaterally. All giving in a Christian community is an extension of divine generosity and a *drawing into*
absolute reciprocity. Christ has given the only gift that can be given.
All other gifts either participate in or deny the kenotic gift of the Son
to the Father. The willed self-emptying and *slavehood* of the Son is
the Gift; it is the action by which the whole of creation is united as
a single offering to the Father. This willed self-emptying is the liturgy
of the Son, and fellowship *in* Christ is inseparable from participation
in the liturgical action *of* Christ. *Koinonia* is hereby exacted by the
liturgical action. The Father gives the Son to the world and the Son
gathers the world into himself as a consecrated — assimilated — offering in his return to the Father. This procession and return is sustained by the shared life of the Spirit now made available through the
church. Through the *mysteries* the human is initiated and gathered
into this procession and return, whereby she becomes a vessel of the
holy,[51] — she becomes *mystery* — being co-opted, as it were, into the
divine drama.

---

49 Irenaeus, *Against Heresies*, IV.xviii.1–2 (ANF).
50 T. S. Eliot, "Little Gidding," in *Four Quartets* (New York: Harcourt Brace & Co.,
1971), 59.
51 Ignatius, *Epistle to the Ephesians*, XII.

Ambrose, perhaps better than any other, draws together the essence of *koinonia* (or in his case *communicatio*) as the manifestation of the liturgy of the Son.

> So the Father gave His Son, and the Son Himself gave Himself. Charity is preserved, and devoutness is not harmed, for there can be no harm to devoutness, where there is no hardship in giving. He gave Him who was willing; He gave Him who offered Himself; surely the Father did not give the Son for punishment but for grace. If you inquire into the merit of the deed question the word "devoutness." The vessel of election clearly shows this unity of divine charity, for both Father gave the Son, and the Son Himself gave Himself. The Father gave, who "spared not even His own Son, but delivered Him up for us all" (Romans 8:32). Of the Son also he says: "Who delivered Himself for me" (Galatians 11:20)... [As] the Father gave the Son, and the Son Himself gave Himself, learn that the Spirit also gave Him. For it is written: "Then Jesus was led by the Spirit into the desert to be tempted by the devil" (Matthew 4:1). So the Spirit, too, loved the Son of God and gave Him... Moreover, it is manifest that there is fellowship with the Father and with the Son, for it is written: "Our fellowship with the Father and with His Son, Jesus Christ"; and elsewhere: "The communication of the Holy Ghost be with you all" (1 John 1:3; 2 Corinthians 13:13)....[52]

Offerer, *offering*, and the *act of offering* converge in the giving of the Son, which is the fullness of the Godhead — God the Father, God the Son, and God the Holy Spirit — who gives himself — the whole of Divinity — establishing *koinonia* with all of humanity through the receiving of *the Gift*, as giver and recipient cohere together in ecstatic, unconfused union of Love.

---

[52] Ambrose, *Theological and Dogmatic Works*, trans. Roy J. Deferrari, The Fathers of the Church, vol. 44 (Washington: Catholic University of America Press, 1963), 82.

Koinonia with Christ, therefore, is the telos — the end or aim — of humanity, which occurs by sharing in Christ's sufferings and death.[53] This can only mean that the gift received through the *mysteries*, which incorporates the human into the Triune Communion, is now her gift to endlessly give. A gift can be given, because *the Gift* has been given. By receiving this gift the human becomes bound to God and, consequentially, to her neighbor, for with the gift comes the fullness of the giver. The human is bound through Christ's liturgy, as he has gathered humanity into himself in obedience to the Father. Being so gathered, the faithful now participate as an assimilated body that labors together, strives in company together, sleeps together, awakens together, as liturgists of God.[54] It is in this shared fellowship with others in Christ that the human exhibits her likeness of the Triune God.

Once again, however, it is the primacy of the bishop that comes to the fore, as it is through his liturgical office as *christotokos* that God deigns to continue the ministry of reconciliation. Nevertheless, as Ignatius and Cyprian remind us, the singular liturgy of the church is a conjoined liturgy of the whole body, whereby the bishop can perform his office as bishop only to the extent that the layperson performs her office as layperson, and vice versa.[55] Office and action, as in the ancient world, are inseparable in Christ. The hierarchical administration of the liturgical economy is a division of labor, not a partitioning of classes. Just as the bishop makes the people available to God, likewise do the people make God available to the bishop. There is a logic of reciprocity embedded in the action. By necessity of her communion with God, the Christian must be in fellowship with Christ's holy church, through its bishops.[56]

---

53 Philippians 3:10.

54 Ignatius, *The Epistle of Ignatius to Polycarp*, VI (ANF).

55 Ignatius, *Epistle to the Ephesians*, I.6; Cyprian, "Letter XVI," in *The Letters of St. Cyprian of Carthage*, trans. G. W. Clarke, vol. I (New York: Newman Press, 1984); see also Gregory Dix, *The Shape of the Liturgy* (London/New York: Continuum, 2005), 117.

56 Cyprian, "Letter LI," in *The Letters of St. Cyprian of Carthage*, trans. G. W. Clarke, vol. II (New York: Newman Press, 1984). It is here that we can reframe, as it were, the Catholic dictum "no salvation outside the Church." It is not the Church by which one gains access to God and his saving grace; rather, the essential and unique relation of each person assimilated in Christ naturally and consequentially binds the human to the

PREFIGURING THE GIFT

The nature of sacrifice in the ancient world and how this is transformed by Christ is of utmost importance for discerning how liturgy is to be understood, especially given the inherent nature of liturgy as a self-emptying of God and assimilation of humanity—the gratuitous refusal of the Creator to live apart from creation. The form is anticipated in Israel, as Hebrew sacrifice is not something that establishes the relation, but presumes an a priori relation to God. God's action is always primary; human action is always a response to divine action.

In the world of ancient Greece, offering sacrifices to the gods is a complex affair bound together with deep-rooted customs and surrounded by prayers that make the reciprocal relation between Greek and god sensible.[57] Among other things, the primary role of sacrifice for the ancient Greek is to remind the god(s) invoked that they are the offerers' god(s). This means that if the god is to expect continual sacrifices from the offerer the god had better ensure the well being of the offerer.[58] If the god does not save the life of the offerer in battle it would effectively put an end to the sacrifices made to the god by that person or people. The god has a dog in the fight, as it were, depending on the pleasure derived from the sacrifice.[59] The expectation, however, was surely that the god would respond in kind to the offerer(s), which was the purpose of the accompanying prayers in the ritual offering.[60]

---

community of those who are likewise uniquely bound to God in Christ. We will explore this in a later section with Maximus Confessor. Suffice it to say for now that the human is a portion of God, and it is as portion of God that union with others is effected. It is not union with others that effects one's relationship with God.

57   Simon Pulleyn, *Prayer in Greek Religion* (Oxford: Clarendon Press, 1997), 1–69; Robert Parker, *On Greek Religion* (Ithaca: Cornell University Press, 2011), 64–102; and Brooke Holmes, *The Symptom and the Subject: The Emergence of the Physical Body in Ancient Greece* (Princeton: Princeton University Press, 2010), 92–95.

58   Pulleyn, *Prayer in Greek Religion*, 13–17.

59   Ibid., 7. As Pulleyn has shown, the relation between the Greek and her god was, while reciprocal, essentially one of give and take. "The feeling that the relationship between men and gods was essentially one of give-and-take through sacrifice and prayer is very clear from the frequent association in our surviving texts of the verbs θυειν ('to sacrifice') and ευχεσθαι ('to pray')."

60   Robert Parker, *On Greek Religion*, x.

Without the accompanying prayer the god would not know exactly what the offerer hoped to receive from the offering.[61] There is no hint, says Simon Pulleyn, that the Greek gods were omniscient.[62] The gods require clear instruction from the offerer as to how they should reciprocate, aside from general mindfulness of the offerers' flourishing.

Robert Parker has shown that the sacrificial engagement between Greeks and gods is integral to the cohesiveness of the social body.[63] Like Greek heroes, the gods are offered sacrifices because of the benefits procured in the present.[64] It also meets a distinctly human need for contact with the invisible world, maintaining confidence in the hidden reality.[65] The primary way the Greeks gained access to this unseen world is through animal sacrifices, which are understood to be "self-offerings" to the god(s) — vicarious offerings.[66] Animal sacrifices also evidence a relationship that is initiated by the offerer, rather than the god.[67] The relation is reciprocal, even if "give-and-take," and while the initial engagement may not be from the human, it remains the sacrifice that sets the stage for the god to return in kind.[68] In Homer's *Iliad*, Chryses recalls to Apollo, after the failed attempt to free his daughter from the hands of Agamemnon, to remember his sacrifices and "in exchange" avenge his daughter.

> Hear me, you of the silver bow, who protect Chryses and holy Cilla and rule with might over Tenedos, if ever I have roofed over for you a pleasing temple or burnt up for you fat thighs of bulls or goats, fulfill for me this wish: may the Danaans pay for my tears by your arrows.[69]

---

61   Pulleyn, *Prayer in Greek Religion*, 14.
62   Ibid.
63   Parker, *On Greek Religion*, 264.
64   Ibid., 224–64.
65   Ibid.
66   Holmes, *The Symptom and the Subject*, 185–93.
67   Jan N. Bremmer and Andrew Erskine, eds., *The Gods of Ancient Greece: Identities and Transformations* (Edinburgh: Edinburgh University Press, 2010), 90.
68   Pulleyn, *Prayer in Greek Religion*, 1–38.
69   Homer, *Iliad*, 1.37ff.

Here Chryses makes a prayer, one that he assimilates with past sacrifices to Apollo in his holy temple. The animal sacrifice hereby serves as a sort of binding contract between god and human. This should not be understood in the typical way one might understand a contract today, however; rather, it is that which binds together the reciprocal relation between the two parties. The offerer obliges herself in the offering and the god returns the obligation by receiving the offering.[70]

This transaction-like reciprocity runs markedly opposed to the form of sacrifice and prayer we find in ancient Israel. As Simon Pulleyn has argued, the crucial difference for the Hebrew is that the covenant relation between human and God is a relation instigated by God.[71] Additionally, whereas χάρις (*karis/grace*) is an obliged return for the Greek god, for YHWH it definitely is not.[72] As for the sacrifice, the offerings and activities of the Hebrews are *responsive* rather than antecedent.[73]

The most notable Hebrew sacrifice that comes to mind is the story of Abraham and Isaac. Abraham is told by God to offer his son, Isaac — his only son — as a burnt-offering.[74] This "test of faith" is often read solely from the vantage point of God demanding the only son of Abraham. What is often overlooked in the assessment is the fact that God first gives Isaac to Abraham. Isaac is the offering that God has given, not the other way around. Abraham has nothing of his own to give to God; he can only offer to God that which God has given him to offer. And when the ram is offered in Isaac's stead, it remains God who has provided the sacrifice.

The burnt-offering in ancient Israel is a thank-offering, whereby the offerer and God are united by the offering. In the case of Abraham, it is presumed that union with God will be made available to Abraham through the sacrifice of Isaac. Other forms of offering within Judaism

---

70 Pulleyn, *Prayer in Greek Religion*, 16–17.

71 Ibid., 18.

72 Ibid., 21. As Pulleyn has shown, there is a world of difference between Hebrew prayer and the prayer of Chryses or any other Homeric hero who expects his god to pay back one good turn with another.

73 Ibid.

74 Genesis 22.

are *peace-offerings, meal offerings,* as well as *sin and guilt offerings.*[75] The *peace-offerings* are offerings of thanksgiving. These offerings are given in response to God's redemption of Israel, and in anticipation of the coming restoration of Israel. *Meal offerings* are sacrifices made from the fruits of the land, which had been given to Israel by God. A *sin offering* is a sacrifice made as reparation for sins committed in ignorance. The *sin offering* acknowledges a failure to properly participate in the life God has given to his people. *Guilt offerings* differ from *sin offerings* to the extent that the sin was committed knowingly and the sacrifice was meant to be expiatory — that is, the animal sacrificed was symbolic of the person offering. Through the animals dies the sinful life of the offerer that he might live holy to God. The sacrifice served to repair the covenantal relation established by God with his people. The sin and guilt offerings are not efforts to gain or regain favor with God; they are meant to mourn the fractured relationship between God and his people who favors the people even when they sin against him. What is important to grasp here is the initiating factor of the covenant. For the Greek, a covenant with a god is established by the sacrifice of a people, whereas for the Hebrews, the covenant is the gift of God who comes before, not after, the human. The sacrificial offerings of the Hebrews are in response to the gifts of YHWH, who creates *ex nihilo.*

Isaac stands as paradigmatic for Jewish understandings of sacrificial offering.[76] God's gift precedes all forms of giving. "All things come from thee, [O Lord,] and of thine own have we given thee."[77] God's giving, however, anticipates a return from the human, even if it does not necessitate a return; it is the return that seals the union with God. In offering Isaac to be sacrificed, Abraham is offering himself, who confesses through knowledge of God's *prevenience* that "God will provide." God has provided Isaac, beyond all biological certainty. By returning Isaac to God, Abraham is drawn into the fullness of the

---

75   See Max Thurian, *The Eucharistic Memorial* (Richmond: John Knox Press, 1960), for a complete discussion on Hebrew sacrifice. See also Jacob Neusner, *The Four Stages of Rabbinic Judaism* (London: Routledge, 1999), 86–91.

76   See Yael S. Feldman, *Glory and Agony: Isaac's Sacrifice and National Narrative* (Stanford: Stanford University Press, 2010).

77   1 Chronicles 29:14.

divine economy—gathering Isaac into this same economy—wherein all necessary means of giving are provided.[78] The test of Abraham is whether or not he trusts that all things truly come from God, as opposed to human ingenuity.[79] God is the sole giver of gifts; and it is only God who can receive God. Abraham's giving and receiving are to be understood, therefore, as a participation in the giving and receiving of God from and to God.

TO RECEIVE IS TO GIVE

Within Judaism sacrifice takes on a true *leitourgia*.[80] Abraham's offering of Isaac is a liturgical act. Abraham informs those who have traveled to the land of Moriah with him to stay behind, that "the boy and I will go over there; we will worship, and then we will come back to you."[81] The procession up the mountaintop by Abraham with Isaac is Abraham's offertory procession with the gift God has given him to give—Isaac. Nevertheless, the gift of Isaac is transformed by God's giving the ram, and Isaac returns to Abraham radiating the glory of the Lord. It is upon this liturgical backdrop that the cross is staged. The notions of sacrifice found in the ancient world of the Greeks is turned on its head, while the Hebrew liturgical offerings find their eternal rest. Christ, in his procession before the world, ushers in a complete transfiguration of the sacrificial offering of a people, locating all sacrifice and offering within his singular liturgy, foreshadowed in the liturgy of Abraham and Isaac.

78   Paul V. M. Flesher and Bruce Chilton, *The Targums: A Critical Introduction* (Waco: Baylor University Press, 2011), 439–73. Flesher and Chilton also explore how the story of Isaac is transformed with Judaism over time, whereby the passive Isaac becomes seen more and more as the willing self-offering.

79   Again, this later becomes for Judaism the test of Isaac as well. In the *Targum Pseudo-Jonathan*, to which Flesher and Chilton draw our attention, it is Isaac who says to Abraham, "Bind me well, so that I do not jerk convulsively from pain of my soul, and I be thrust into the pit of destruction, and there be found a blemish in your offering" (465). The obedience of Isaac, not merely the faithfulness of Abraham, helps to ensure the purity of Abraham's offering. See also Jon Douglas Levenson, *Abraham between Torah and Gospel* (Milwaukee: Marquette University Press, 2011), 56.

80   Wout Jac. van Bekkum, "The Aqedah and its Interpretations in Midrash and Piyyut," in Edward Noort and Eibert J. C. Tigchelaar, eds., *The Sacrifice of Isaac: The Aqedah (Genesis 22) and Its Interpretations* (Leiden: Brill, 2002), 83–95.

81   Genesis 22:5.

When we come to Paul, what we find in his letters is a clear articulation that the sacrificial offerings to God and one another participate in Jesus's liturgy, which is his obedience to the Father. The Son's liturgy is the gathering together of the whole world, sanctifying the whole of creation, which makes the *liturgies* of humans acceptable and pleasing to the Father, who in turn blesses and returns human offerings *for the life of the world*, uniting heaven and earth in the gift of the Holy Spirit, making humankind's continual offering to God possible, and God's continual return available. This *liturgical drama* between God and Creation effectually incorporates God's people into the divine economy through *koinonia* in Christ's self-emptying, sacrificial offering.[82] The Son is the ultimate *Gift* of the Father. In receiving the Son, the human is conjoined to the Second Person of the Holy Trinity. The Father receives the human with the Son and returns to humanity the Holy Spirit, who makes continual fellowship in the love of the Father for the Son and obedience of the Son to the Father possible — a glorious cycle of procession and return of God from and to God. To receive the Son is simultaneously to give oneself to the Father. Receiving a gift, as seen earlier, is to receive the one who gives the gift; it is to bind oneself, through the same reception, to the donor. Christian liturgy is, then, a participation in the faithful obedience of the Son who is Liturgy. Through the Holy Spirit one enters into the mutual, self-emptying reciprocal love that is the Triune Communion.

In the same manner that God has given Isaac to Abraham, so has the Father given the Son to all. Likewise, as Isaac is demanded by God to be offered in return, so is the Son exacted, and God provides. The ram is given for Isaac, as bread and wine are given for the faithful. Having received Christ through the Spirit, the Christian is now bound to the Father. Return to the Father is hereby demanded, and God provides. Because God provides the offering, the continuation of reciprocal love between Creator and creation is made available. In offering bread and wine as symbols of the living sacrifice Christians *are*, God receives the offerings, gathered as they are into and along with Christ,

---

82   Philippians 3:10.

and returns them endowed with the fullness of his power and grace, his body and blood. In consuming the flesh and blood of God, the Christian is consumed — incorporated through the *corpus mysticum*, to become the *corpus verum* — a body that reaches beyond all spatial barriers to unite both seen and unseen. The Body of Christ is then sent out into the world in its many parts; *and it is sent out to return.*

In the *Letter to the Hebrews*, the nature of sacrifice and how it participates in the liturgical drama of God is made quite explicit. "Through him then let us continually offer up a sacrifice of praise to God, that is, the fruit of lips that give glory to his name."[83] The sacrificial offering here not only takes on a "spiritual" connotation — that is, it is a participation in the sacrifice of Jesus, not an animal being slain or the like, but most importantly the author unites sacrifice and offering with the liturgical action of Jesus as High Priest, who gathers creation into himself as a single offering in its return to the Father. Liturgy and sacrifice go hand in hand. The liturgies of a people are analogous to the divine liturgy Jesus *is*, inasmuch as one participates in the singular, self-emptying, and sacrificial offering of the Son to the Father.

The liturgical sacrifice offered by the community to God, because it participates by way of analogy in the liturgy of Jesus, must be a pure offering. This *pure offering* is directly linked to the Eucharist — the spiritual sacrifice. The bread of the Eucharistic offering, however, is inseparable from those making the offering. Both Cyril and Irenaeus are explicit about the offering of the community and the offering of Christ as being indistinguishable, whereby the various liturgies of the people participate in the one true offering.

> After this the bishop says: "Holy things for the holy." The offerings are holy, because they have received the descent of the Holy Spirit, and you are holy too because you have been granted the Holy Spirit; thus the holy things are appropriate for holy people. Then you say: "One is holy, one is Lord, Jesus Christ." For truly there is one who is holy, holy by nature; for though we are

83 Hebrews 13:15.

holy, we are not so by nature, but by participation and discipline and prayer. After this you hear the cantor to a sacred melody encouraging you to receive the holy mysteries. "Taste and see," he sings, "the goodness of the Lord" (Ps 33:9; 34:8). Do not rely on the judgment of your physical throat but on that of unhesitating faith. For what you taste is not bread and wine but Christ's body and blood, which they symbolize. So when you approach do not come with your wrists extended or your fingers parted. Make your left hand a throne for your right, which is about to receive the King, and receive Christ's body in the hollow of your hand, replying "Amen." Before you consume it, carefully bless your eyes with the touch of the holy body, watching not to lose any part of it; for if you do lose any of it, *it is as if it were part of your own body that is being lost.*[84]

As for Irenaeus, what Christians offer is the "beginning of the new creation's harvest—the humanity of Christ, in which the deification of human nature is perfected and offered to us."[85] To participate, therefore, as mentioned above in the gift of the widow's mite, is to be gathered into the *kenotic* love of God. It is a love that humans are incapable of enacting on their own. The human cannot, as it were, love God. All love is a participation in triune reciprocity—humanity's share in God's fullness. The Spirit, as Cyril articulates, enables one to participate in the offering, Christ, in the self-emptying of God on the cross. Sacrifice, hereby understood, cannot be made by humanity. Only God can sacrifice. Only God can suffer. Only God can drink the cup. All sacrificial action, then, is participatory. Indeed, all action in the proper sense is Christ.[86]

Furthermore, as we see in the early writings of the *Didache*, following Jesus's teaching on bringing gifts to the altar,[87] the established relationship of God with humanity requires right-relatedness within

---

84   Edward Yarnold, trans., *Cyril of Jerusalem* (London: Routledge, 2000), 186.
85   Rowan Williams, *Eucharistic Sacrifice: The Roots of a Metaphor* (Nottinghamshire: Grove Books, 1982), 10.
86   Dietrich Bonhoeffer, *Ethics* (New York: Macmillan, 1955), 43–48.
87   Matthew 5.

the community in order to participate in the life-giving sacrifice of the Eucharist. The sacrifice is profaned if there is division involved in the one offering her gift.[88] Into the latter part of the first and the early second century, there is a clear continuation and linkage between the sacrificial offering, the gift, and the liturgy itself that is identified with the offerer. The *Didache* not only locates sacrificial offering in the liturgical action, but also connects it with the breaking of bread that occurs when the community is gathered. The breaking of bread is how God makes himself available to his people, but reconciliation, which is revealed through the incarnation, death, and resurrection of Jesus, is not somehow confected by divine fiat; rather, reconciliation is the order of the table. Communion with God requires reconciliation with neighbor as a necessary consequence for being assimilated to the eternal Son. All of this finds itself once again in the midst of the hierarchical liturgy of the people. For all the reasons above, the *Didache* enjoins the Christian community to "appoint, then, for yourselves, bishop and deacons worthy of the Lord, gentle and not money-loving and truthful and tested; for to you they likewise serve (unpaid) the λειτουργγουσι (*leitourgousi/the unpaid public service*) of the prophet-teachers."[89] In the *Didache* hierarchy is brought to the fore. It is necessary to have faithful leaders who stand as representatives of and to God, those who will gather the gifts of a people together as a single offering, so that a people do in fact participate in the fullness of divine power and love. The office of the bishop is clearly addressed:

> You, therefore, O bishops, are to your people priests and Levites, ministering (λειτουργησαντας) to the holy tabernacle, the holy Catholic Church; who stand at the altar of the Lord your God, and *offer to Him reasonable and unbloody sacrifices through Jesus the great High Priest.* You are to the laity prophets, rulers, governors, and kings; the mediators between God

---

88 *The Didache: Text, Translation, Analysis, and Commentary*, trans. Aaron Milavec (Collegeville: Liturgical Press, 2004), XIV.ii.

89 Ibid., XV.i.

and His faithful people, who receive and declare His word, well acquainted with the Scriptures. Ye are the voice of God, and witnesses of His will, who bear the sins of all, and intercede for all.... For you imitate Christ the Lord; and as He "bare the sins of us all upon the tree" at His crucifixion, the innocent for those who deserved punishment, so also you ought to make the sins of the people your own.... As you are patterns for others, so have you Christ for your pattern.[90]

The bishop, as Christ to the church, gathers together the living sacrifices (the people), conjoining through the power of the Holy Spirit the body to its head (Christ), as a single, pure and acceptable offering to the Father. The bishop stands as chief liturgist, analogous to Christ the one true liturgist, with whom the many liturgies of the people — the many living sacrifices — converge into one polyphonic unity in God.

The harmonious participation in the cruciform liturgy of the gathered community enables the human to realize her nature as created in the divine image. It is the Word — the flesh of God speaking — that brings before the whole world the truth of its created-ness.

And then, again, this Word was manifested when the Word of God was made man, assimilating Himself to man, and man to Himself, so that by means of his resemblance to the Son, man might become precious to the Father. For in times long past, it was *said* that man was created after the image of God, but it was not [actually] *shown*; for the Word was as yet invisible, after whose image man was created, wherefore also he did easily lose the similitude. When, however, the Word of God became flesh, He confirmed both of these: for He both showed forth the image truly, since He became Himself what was His image; and He re-established the similitude after a sure manner, by assimilating man to the invisible Father through means of the visible Word.[91]

90 *Constitution of the Holy Apostles*, XXV (ANF).
91 Irenaeus, *Against Heresies*, V.xvi (ANF).

29

It is humankind's resemblance to the Son, through participation in the liturgy Jesus is — the convergence of office and action, that is, the union of God and creation[92]— that assimilates humanity to the Divine. This assimilation is a continuation of the sacrificial system of the Hebrews, for the point of departure from Hebraic understandings of sacrifice in the early church does not contradict the *prevenient grace* of God. It completes the sacrificial law because the sacrificial offering not only comes from God but *is* God Incarnate. The suffering and death of God on the cross makes participation in resurrection available to humanity. By bearing in her body the sufferings and death of the spoken Word of the Father the human is resurrected with the Son to become Son. Sacrifice as spiritually abstract is made unintelligible. Sacrificial action is a person, and his name is Jesus. To participate, then, is to *become*.

THE LITURGICAL ECONOMY

It is important now to back up and discern the overarching context of Paul's employment of *leitourgia* as evoking one who gathers the offering of the people, mediating *koinonia* in the Spirit. It is Paul's testimony that he is an icon of Christ, seeking *koinonia* in, by, and through Christ's suffering and death, that he might have *koinonia* with Christ in his resurrection.[93] God has hereby made him an οικονομους (*oikonomous/administrator*) of the μυστήριον (*mysterion/sacraments*) of God.[94] It is Paul's arbitration of God's *economy*, made intelligible by his enslavement to Christ, that incorporates others into the *divine economy*. Though free from all, with Christ, Paul makes himself a slave to all, as this is the fabric of God's οικονομια (*oikonomia/economy*).[95] *Leitourgia*, the apostolic office and action of gathering together the people as an offering to God, is what makes humankind's entrance into

92 This is later expressed by Maximus in *The Church's Mystagogy*, I, solidly keeping with Irenaeus: "[Holy] Church bears the imprint and image of God since it has the same *activity* as he does by imitation and in figure." See George C. Berthold, trans., *Maximus Confessor: Selected Writings* (New York: Paulist Press, 1985), 186.

93 Philippians 3.

94 1 Corinthians 4.

95 1 Corinthians 9.

the Triune economy possible, participation in the self-emptying of God in Christ made available through the *mysteries/the sacraments*, whereby one, as offering, is assimilated to grace. Paul's liturgy is his apostolic office of mediating *the economy* of God.

Christ, according to Paul, is both *oikonomia* (economy) and *oikonomous* (economic administrator). He is economy par excellence, the administrator of the economy he himself is. Paul uses *oikonomia* in his letter to the Ephesians to describe the totality of the plan of salvation made-manifest in Jesus of Nazareth. Being gathered into this economy removes all divisions between giver and recipient. It is the conflation of giving poles into one that Christ's mediation through the sacraments makes possible. The Giver is the Gift, and the recipient comes to bear the Spirit of the Giver through this self-same Gift, hereby becoming gift.

The whole of the economy—the plan of salvation who is Christ—is the *gathering* of persons who, being assimilated as *gift* to *the* Gift, Christ, bear in their bodies the self-dispossession of God, which is their participation in liturgy, the fullness of God's power and life. Liturgy, hereby understood, is its own end. It is the procession and return of God from and to himself, made-manifest in Jesus of Nazareth.

For Paul, *oikonomia* bespeaks the totality of the divine plan of salvation through the incarnate Word. In Paul, as aforesaid, Christ is both *oikonomia* and *oikonomous*, because Christ is salvation qua salvation and the unfolding thereof through incarnation, death, and resurrection. As Paul writes in his letter to the Ephesians:

> In him we have redemption through his blood, the forgiveness of our trespasses, according to the riches of his grace that he lavished on us. With all wisdom and insight he has made known to us the mystery of his will, according to his good pleasure that he set forth in Christ, as *the economy* for the fullness of time, to *gather up* all things in him, things in heaven and things on earth.[96]

---

96 Ephesians 1:7–10.

Paul pulls together the radical, participatory nature of the divine economy.

> So then you are no longer strangers and aliens, but you are citizens with the saints and also members of the household (οἰκεος) of God, built upon the foundation of the apostles and prophets, with Christ Jesus himself as the cornerstone. In him the whole structure is joined together and grows into a holy temple in the Lord; in whom you also are built together spiritually into a dwelling place (κατοικητηριον) for God. This is the reason that I, Paul, am a prisoner for Christ Jesus for the sake of you Gentiles — for surely you have already heard of the *economy* of God's grace that was given me for you....[97]

It follows then that the divine economy is the body of Christ and the *building up* (οἰκοδομήν) of this body on earth. This household is, however, all-encompassing, such that even the earthly authorities are *liturgists* of God.[98] Nothing is outside the divine economy, and all, in its own way, participates in the administration of this economy, whether positively or negatively.[99]

It is to this liturgical economy that Paul refers throughout his writings, illustrated most clearly in his letter to the Galatians where he says, "I have been crucified *with* Christ; it is no longer I who live, but Christ who lives in me...."[100] The force of this claim comes from the logic of the liturgical action of Jesus, who, by his incarnation, death, and resurrection, identifies the nature of the divine economy. The new nature the human *puts on* in her baptism is the death and resurrection of Jesus, which brings about, through the one Spirit, the new life of participation in the economy of God.[101]

Irenaeus likewise presses the reciprocal nature of this economy exemplified in Christ. Giving is not an exchange of goods with the

97   Ephesians 2:19–3.2.
98   Romans 13:6.
99   This understanding of "all things" in their participatory relation, either positively or negatively, will be teased out further in chapter two with Maximus Confessor.
100   Galatians 2:19–20.
101   Ephesians 4.

divine, as if humankind had something God lacked; rather, it is the action through which one enters into the reciprocal love God *is*. Through human reception of the heavenly reality—the Good—earth and heaven touch, to the glory of God *for the life of the world*.

> For we offer to Him His own, announcing consistently the fellowship and union of the flesh and Spirit. For as the bread, which is produced from the earth, when it receives the invocation of God, is no longer common bread, but the Eucharist, consisting of two realities, earthly and heavenly; so also our bodies, when they receive the Eucharist, are no longer corruptible, having the hope of the resurrection to eternity. Now we make offering to Him, not as though He stood in need of it, but rendering thanks for His gift, and thus sanctifying what has been created... As, therefore, He does not stand in need of these [liturgies], yet does desire that we should render them for our own benefit, lest we be unfruitful; so did the Word give to the people that very precept as to the making of oblations, although He stood in no need of them, that they might learn to serve God: thus is it, therefore, also His will that we, too, should offer a gift at the altar, frequently and without intermission. The altar, then, is in heaven (for towards that place are our prayers and oblations directed); the temple likewise [is there], as John says in the Apocalypse, "And the temple of God was opened:" the tabernacle also: "For, behold," He says, "the tabernacle of God, in which He will dwell with men."[102]

There is no distinction made between the church's offering and Christ's offering in the Eucharist. In receiving *the* Gift, Christ, Christians become gift, adding nothing to God, yet becoming gods through the Spirit. Christians come to possess the fullness of God's power and life

---

102 Irenaeus, *Against Heresies*, IV.xviii.5–6 (ANF). Note in Irenaeus the distinct nature of human action in Christ as a similitude of divine action. That is, God acts according to God's nature, which benefits humanity. The human acts in accordance with the divine action, which benefits humanity in the process.

through their very self-dispossession, having emptied themselves with Christ, to become, in the words of Chrysostom, "little christs."

God, in trinity of Persons and unity of Substance, is the model for every economy, and the Son is the eternal event of this economy, who assimilates time — human action — to himself through his liturgy. Though *free from all*, God in Jesus of Nazareth binds himself *to* all, extending the invitation for humanity to be equally bound. In receiving the self-offering of Christ, the human obliges herself to *be* a self-offering to God *for* others. Here is realized the radical, participatory nature of the liturgical economy, whereby all sacrifice and suffering, all gifts and offering, and all human fellowship between persons, creation, and God exists within the eternal Liturgy God is — the Divine Economy.

ONLY GOD CAN SUFFER

The commonplace (mis)translation of *leitourgia* as "the work of the people"[103] describes a chasm between what Christians do when they gather to worship and who the God they confess to worship is. The modern translation of this term dislocates the human from the action of Christ, thereby suspending the gift from the recipient — giver and receiver remain separate. In a falsely humanistic attempt to emphasize the work of humans in liturgy, "the work of the people" actually narrates a deistic understanding of the human as completely separate from God, or univocally maintains a sameness between God and humanity in "Being."[104]

103 Frank C. Senn, *New Creation: A Liturgical Worldview* (Minneapolis: Fortress Press, 2000), 17–29. Senn presses toward a deeper sense of participation in the liturgical action; however, his analysis falls short because he does not trace the etymology of *leitourgia* back to its true participatory articulation as the work of One. Senn evidences the common mistake made by many liturgical scholars who endeavor to "renew" liturgy but cannot match speech with act due to this mistranslation.

104 John Duns Scotus, "Ordinatio," I.3, in *Philosophical Writings: A Selection*, trans. Allan Bernard Wolter (Indianapolis: Hackett Publishing, 1987), 4–8. By suggesting that "being" is predicated univocally, Scotus suggests that God and humans have a univocal share in Being with God, rendering the relationship between God and humans at once unnecessary yet substantially the same. There is no *analogia entis*, as we find in Aquinas, whereby God and creatures are related through divine, creative activity, enabling humans to perceive God — even manifest God — through participation in a creation that pulses with divine energy. For Scotus, knowledge of God is one of degree. I am imperfect;

To become one with Christ is hereby a daily coming to bear Christ in one's body. This is what Paul is getting at when he writes to the Corinthians that he carries the death of Jesus in his body.

> We are afflicted in every way, but not crushed; perplexed, but not driven to despair; persecuted, but not forsaken; struck down, but not destroyed; always carrying in the body the death of Jesus, so that the life of Jesus may also be made visible in our bodies. For while we live, we are always being given up to death for Jesus' sake, so that the life of Jesus may be made visible in our mortal flesh. So death is at work in us, but life in you.[105]

Paul's sufferings are the sufferings of Christ, born in his body, for the sake of the church.[106] It is the cross that is paradigmatic for participating in divine action — in the Liturgy-Christ. The cross is also that which makes all suffering intelligible and meaningful. The oft-repeated notion that Christ suffers when we suffer is yet another aggrandizing of the human in relation to her sufferings. We must not invert the relation between the suffering of Jesus and the sufferings of humanity. Again, while it may at first seem to elevate the suffering of humans to say that God suffers with us, it has the adverse effect of flattening human suffering as something that in no way transcends the present sensation of pain.

---

therefore, God must be perfect, for God is "the first being" ("Ordinatio," I.5). Further, if there is a natural knowledge of God it can only be because being is natural to both created and uncreated ("Ordinatio," I.3). It would seem that univocity offers a closer relationship between God and humans; however, as Catherine Pickstock has shown, this notion of Being creates an "unmediable" gap between finite and infinite, making God altogether unknowable. The point, here, is to emphasize the participatory nature of liturgical action as a divine movement that humans are caught up into with Christ, whereby the human is known in her being-known by God through divine liturgy. See further discussion below in chapter 2. See Wolter, n. 2, 165. See also Catherine Pickstock, *After Writing: On the Liturgical Consummation of Philosophy* (Oxford: Blackwell Publishers, 1998), 122–66.

105 2 Corinthians 4:8–12.

106 This is the meaning we must be careful not to misunderstand in Paul's Letter to the Colossians. See Colossians 1, especially 1:24.

What makes human suffering meaningful is that it participates in the bodily suffering of God on the cross. This brings to the fore the dialogue of Jesus with the sons of Zebedee when they ask if they can sit on the right and left side of Jesus in his kingdom, to which he responds "Can you drink of this cup?" But Jesus goes on to say that they will drink of *his* cup; they will become inebriated with *his* passion. It is this bodily bearing of Christ's passion that Ignatius uses in his argument against the Gnostics.

> Stop your ears therefore when anyone speaks to you that stands apart from Jesus Christ, from David's scion and Mary's Son, who was really born and ate and drank, really persecuted by Pontius Pilate, really crucified and died while heaven and earth and the underworld looked on; who also really rose from the dead, since His Father raised Him up — His Father, who will likewise raise us also who believe in Him through Jesus Christ, apart from whom we have no real life. But if, as some atheists, that is, unbelievers, say, His suffering was but a make-believe — when, in reality, they themselves are make-believers — then why am I in chains? Why do I even pray that I may fight wild beasts? In vain, then, do I die! My testimony is, after all, but a lie about the Lord![107]

This is a continuation of Paul who states that, "if Christ has not been raised then our proclamation is in vain and our faith is in vain."[108] Ignatius, however, turns the notch a bit further, making it undeniably clear that the death of Jesus is, in fact, the death and passion of God,[109] and it is the very passion and death of God that informs the human condition.[110]

The logic of participation found in the early fathers refutes the modern notion that "Christ is with us in our suffering," as though he

---

107 Ignatius, *Epistle to the Trallians*, IX–XX.
108 1 Corinthians 15:14.
109 Ignatius, *Epistle to the Romans*, VI.
110 Ignatius, *Epistle to the Smyrneans*, I.

is sitting in the car with the victim as it sinks to the bottom of the lake, dying all over again with her. This is the disembodied *logos* of the Gnostics, not the fleshy Jesus who actually suffered, died, and was resurrected. While this may sound pastorally sensitive and therapeutically beneficial, it ironically denigrates human suffering. What Paul, Ignatius and the early fathers with them understood, is that in them only one has suffered — only one can suffer, and any suffering that may come upon the Christian is a participation in the *singular suffering* of God in Christ. This in no way makes suffering on earth inconsequential; rather, the pain and suffering in this life, because of Christ and only because of his passion, death, resurrection, and ascension, has meaning. God is not an empathizing therapist in the sky. God is the suffering Lord. By bearing the sufferings of Christ in one's body, the human is gathered into the offering of the Son to the Father, and with Christ, by the power of the Spirit, the human is received by the Father. *God with us*, then, is not a moral or sentimental imperative, but *with us* in the sense that the active receiving of Christ's passion is to be received into the Godhead. No one has the ability to suffer.[111] It is Christ who grants such ability, for whose sake suffering is endured that one might find fellowship in him.[112] The offering and sacrifice of praise and thanksgiving, i.e., liturgy, is a person; it is Jesus the Christ of God.

The identity that is given to the church is not a system of obligations or ritual expressions, as important as these things may be. The identity found in *leitourgia* as the singular Gift of God in Christ, which is the working out of the Divine Economy in creation, is marked by the ecstatic love exemplified in the incarnation, death, resurrection, and ascension of Jesus, whereby multiplicity is gathered into unity as a single offering and sacrifice of praise and thanksgiving that is the fellowship of the Triune God. It is this identity — the liturgy Jesus is — that exacts a mimetic form of expression through ritual action. For this reason is the Eucharistic gathering properly called "liturgy," not because it is the work of a people, but because it is a people's participation in the mighty act of God in Christ. Participation in the liturgical action of

111 Ibid., IV.
112 Ibid. See also chapter three of Paul's letter to the Ephesians.

the church is the habituation of the human, body, mind and soul, and it is in giving herself to this action that the human is assimilated to God in Christ, which is her "natural nature."[113] The church's liturgy, then, is the ritual expression of who God is, though not merely expressive. In its Eucharistic feast the poles of heaven and earth are folded into one and the body of persons is gathered into God through the mystical feast, binding them together in actuality as the body of Christ.

Liturgy, therefore, is its own end, because it is the procession and return of God from and to himself made-manifest in Jesus of Nazareth. Jesus as the economy he himself administrates is humankind's entrance into the reciprocal love that is the Triune God, as the human receives the Gift and thereby becomes gift, which is her offering and sacrifice *with* the Son, through the Spirit, to the Father—Doxology.

CONCLUSION

We have seen how liturgy as "the people's work" locates a person's identity in her own hands—the human nature entirely separable from divinity—a liturgical nominalism, as it were. Naming, as it does, the service of worship of the church, liturgy has been mistaken to be humanistic in the worst sense of the term. It has been wrongly understood as an isolated act in time, either performed by a professional class of persons (clergy) for an audience (laity) or enacted collectively as a body of people (priesthood of all believers), which can only be assented to by faith, not participated in through *the reason of the body*. In each instance the understanding is the same: God has given salvation to those who follow Christ; Christians, therefore, perform liturgies to offer thanks and praise for the gift of salvation. The assumption here is that the baptized have a gift to offer unto Almighty God, i.e., their selves. To say that the human has something she can give—even herself—to God, is to suggest that a person possesses within her being the capacity to initiate contact with God, thereby inverting the Creator-created relation. It is at once a rejection of human contingency

---

113 This "natural nature" will be explored in greater detail when we deal with Maximus Confessor later. However, it is immediately to suggest that what is natural to human nature is the divinity of Christ. Christ is the true human.

and a denial of God as his own absolute contingency. God becomes somehow dependent on creation. This "self-possession" is the ultimate affront by the created to her Creator; it is the sin of all sins — it is Adam and Eve.

Leitourgia as illuminated throughout the writings of the early fathers refuses both the Gnostic rejection of matter and the humanist departure from metaphysics. The modern mistranslation is more than a matter of semantics; it is an ontological chasm. This redefining of the term, however, is not the direct result of a new system of ideas or revelation in understanding. It is, rather, the result of an evolution of rituals and practices throughout history that have served to dislocate the human from her participation in the singular, liturgical action that Christ is as Second Person of the Triune God, whose liturgy is the ontological union of *God with us*.

Throughout the rest of this essay, we will explore that nature of liturgical action as made-manifest in the human's participation in Christ, whose Liturgy, coalescing with the church's participation in divine liturgy, reveals the truth of human nature as a portion of God — a liturgy of the Liturgy. As a participation in Christ's Liturgy, a participation in the Triune Economy, the church's liturgy is the manner by which a person comes to understand the truth of her humanity, whereby Christ is made-manifest in her body.

2

Apprehending God

By the grace of God I am what I am....

St. Paul

We do not see things as they are, we see them as we are.

Anais Nin

We get into the habit of living before we acquire the habit of thinking.

Albert Camus

INTRODUCTION

When I was a junior in college, nineteen years old, I found myself one day in the Episcopal Cathedral in Nashville, Tennessee. Christ's Cathedral is a breathtaking Victorian Gothic structure, not busy or fussy, timelessly crafted with its granite columns, dark wood, and rich stained glass. I had driven by the church numerous times, but seeing that the doors were open I decided to wander in. I parked along the side street and entered the large wooden doors. The lights were out, except for the small chapel off to the side, and no one was in sight. I gazed upon the windows and was struck by the brilliance of their colors, especially one window of a young boy, situated in the north vault of the ceiling, which was dark and rich, except for the lantern in the boy's hand that seemed to catch all available exterior light, causing the interior of the church to glow with the light of God. For this country boy from South Carolina, it was quite a sight. The only stained glass I had ever seen before going off to college was the stuff you see in old Baptist churches that looks like a three-year-old threw some paint on a sheet of glass and baked it in an oven. I was captivated to say the least.

As I explored the building, I found myself wandering into the chapel, which was small, yet beautiful in its simplicity of stone and wood. As I sat taking in my new environment, people started coming into the chapel and sitting down. I found myself caught up in what swiftly had become a geriatric ward. As I planned my getaway, an elderly priest walked in, closed the door, and said, "Blessed be God, Father, Son, and Holy Spirit."

I soon realized that I was stuck in a midday worship service with no hope of getting out until it was all over. When you're from South Carolina, you are raised to mind your manners and not to make a scene. So I stayed. I had never been to a service of Holy Eucharist. I had only recently learned what "Eucharist" means. Where I'm from, communion wine comes in a shot glass—and it's not wine, it's grape juice, very disappointing, along with an oyster cracker, which often seems like an upgrade from the Styrofoam wafer. If you think believing that a communion wafer is the body of Christ is hard, try swallowing an oyster cracker with a half-ounce of grape juice—very challenging to believe God is nearby. This, I am convinced, is why Protestants don't believe in transubstantiation, and perhaps why the Orthodox find it so much easier than the rest, with their sweet, transmutating loaf.

Everyone responded to the priest: "And blessed be his Kingdom, now and forever. Amen." He prayed a prayer, and then everyone joined in what I would eventually learn was the *Gloria*; he prayed another prayer, and as everyone sat down I followed suit. As I endured my first lesson in Episcopal calisthenics, the little old lady sitting next to me in the chapel realized I was out of sorts. She pulled out a little red book from the pew rack, opened it to the appropriate page, and handed me a *Book of Common Prayer*. I followed along as best I could, trying not to look too out of place.

After *the Peace*, the priest rehearsed the story of salvation, and the way he held the bread and the cup of wine, his mannerisms and gestures, all focused our attention on the fact that the bread and wine were becoming more than they are, or perhaps what they were always intended to be. I followed everyone to the altar rail—again trying not to appear disoriented, extended my arms, opened my hands, and when he placed that tiny little wafer in my hands, he calmly, but carefully said, "The body of our Lord Jesus Christ, which was given for thee, preserve thy body and soul unto everlasting life." I paused for what seemed to me like several minutes as I gazed at that life-changing wafer, which still tasted like packaging peanuts, pondering those words, "The body of our Lord Jesus Christ, which was given for thee...." After receiving the body and blood of Christ, I returned to my seat. Eventually, everyone left the chapel, but I remained in my chair for at least an hour or so, trying to wrap my head around what had just happened. Gregory of Nyssa refers to such encounters as "sliding into God,"[1] or what we might call *drifting into God*. The emphasis here being the near accidental nature of how a person encounters God, for happening upon God is always simultaneously a bumping into our true selves.[2]

In the first chapter I discussed the use of *leitourgia* in the classical world, in scripture, and in the early church, offering a more faithful rendering of the term as "the work of the one for the sake of the many." The singular nature of liturgy is the action of Christ, who is himself Liturgy. Accordingly, as will be discussed in this chapter, the Liturgy who is Christ is also the revelation of the Triune God as Liturgy. God is his own procession and return, the Gift-Giving-Giver—his own absolute contingency. As I will show later in chapter four, liturgical action is not the action of the worshipping participants who fill the pews on Sunday; rather, it is the singular action of God in Christ—*the work of the One*—in which the worshipper is intimately and volitionally involved—*for the sake of the many*. This act of worship, while its origin precedes the worshipper, nonetheless remains part and parcel of who the worshipper is. It is also to suggest that at the core of human nature recapitulated in Christ *is* offering, the gratuitous gift of God himself. In other words, human nature is inherently divine. Even so, our *natural nature*,[3] as Maximus Confessor puts it, is hidden to us apart from our participation in the liturgical action of the church. Accordingly, it is by contact with God in Christ through sacramental mediation that a person recognizes what it means to be human. Liturgy, then, is the

---

1 Gregory of Nyssa, *The Life of Moses*, trans. Everett Ferguson and Abraham Malherbe (New York: Paulist Press, 1978), 69.

2 An interesting analysis of this can been seen in Sebastian Moore, *The Crucified Jesus Is No Stranger* (New York: Paulist Press, 1977).

3 Maximus Confessor, *Ambiguum 7*, 1084B–C, in *On Difficulties in the Church Fathers: The Ambigua*, vol. 1, trans. Nicholas Constas (Cambridge: Harvard University Press, 2014).

re-assimilation of the human to the action of Christ — her *being recapit-ulated* in Christ — and in proportion to the worshipper's willed partici-pation in the apostles' teaching and fellowship, in the breaking of bread and in the prayers, is her *natural nature* made-manifest in her body, enabling the worshipper to recognize *being* recapitulated in Christ.

THE SECRET DISPOSITION

The way the fathers of the church speak of this christic manifesting in the body is by distinguishing between two aspects of created human nature: *image* and *likeness*. "Then God said, 'Let us make humankind in our *image*, according to our *likeness*.'"[4] The distinction between *image* and *likeness* in the early church is important for recognizing at once what it means for divinity to be bound up with humanity in Christ and how the human comes to recognize the principle of her nature as a portion of God. The *image* is that in which humankind is created. The *likeness*, as Maximus Confessor articulates, is acquired by the human's volitive habituation in the life of virtue — the life of faith.

> To the inherent goodness of the image is added the likeness acquired by the practice of virtue and exercise of the will. The inclination to ascend to see one's proper beginning was implanted in man by nature.[5]

Accordingly, human nature is naturally good, naturally inclined to or endowed with the "*logos* of wisdom."[6] Indeed, says Maximus, the human is a "portion of God."[7] This *logos* or image is the secret dispo-sition of the soul, which lays hidden, unless it is raised to the surface through the embodiment of virtuous activity by a "tenacious habit of contemplation."[8] This secret disposition of the soul, the truth of what it means to be human, remains in some sense dormant, hidden in

4 Genesis 1:26a.

5 Maximus Confessor, *Ambiguum 7*, 1084B–C.

6 Maximus, *Letter 2*, 408B, in Andrew Louth, *Maximus the Confessor* (New York: Routledge, 1996).

7 Maximus, *Ambiguum 7*, 1081C.

8 Maximus, *Chapters on Love*, III.69; see also *Letter 2*, 408 in Louth.

the recesses of the soul until a person begins to engage in the bodily practice of the virtues. Likeness, hereby, is the virtuous ordering of human perception.[9] Likeness equals virtue; image equals a kind of divine endowment, sustained by the gratuitous generosity of God. The human moves from grace (*image*) to virtue (*likeness*), from virtue to knowledge (awareness of the image), from knowledge to contemplation (increase in likeness), and from contemplation back to the grace operative in her at the outset—a procession and return from and to the image of God in which the human is created, the awareness and fullness thereof continually being completed and made-manifest in proportion to the human's likeness through the practice of the virtues. Reason and the ascetic struggle are hereby inextricably linked, which provide the "background" for contemplation.[10] The Word is operative in the soul. Nevertheless, divine action refuses coercion. Volitive participation is essential, whereby likeness to one's image is attained, yet always given. Just as a person cannot understand what it means to give birth to a child without experiencing the growth of that child and rupture into the world through her body, likewise is the experience of knowing the truth of one's self unavailable apart from giving birth to that portion of God within the human that is the essence of humanity. To be human is to give birth to God. Mary is an archetype of faith.[11]

To summarize, we might think of likeness as compost. Good compost requires some attention, the mixing together of leaves, food, grass, worms, and so on. The gardener turns or rotates the compost, which enables the ingredients to mingle together and the enzymes to do their work. After some time, the gardener stops putting new food and yard waste in the bin and allows the compost to mature and come together

9 Again, perception here is not an abstract "thinking" of the world but a particular bodily comportment that conditions the field of knowledge of the human. Perceiving is imbedded in the movements of each person that limit or extend the range of human knowing.

10 Maximus, *Difficulty 10*, 1108A.

11 In addition to Mary the *theotokos*, who gives birth to God, as well as Ignatius' call for humans to be *christotokos*, bearers of the world to Christ, the importance of womanhood, with regard to the human's relationship with God as expectancy and anticipation through silence and contemplation, is wonderfully highlighted in *Meditations on the Tarot: A Journey into Christian Hermeticism* (Brooklyn, NY: Angelico Press, 2020), esp. 29–49.

as soil, renewed by the turning and rotating. After several weeks, the saturation and maturation that occur gives way to a life source exceeding anything synthetic the gardener might buy in the store. Even so, the gardener must place seeds in the soil for it to bear fruit (unless seeds linger from the composting process). Rotating and turning the compost is necessary, but the seeds come from outside. In the same manner, grace—the image in which we are created, the compost bin, as it were—meets us in our likeness—our practice of the virtues, the continual adding of vegetation, turning, rotating and so on, which grace then deigns to seed. We then water the seed—likeness. But the seed, the water, and the sun that give life are gifts of grace. It is the tending to which our lives must be devoted. The analogy above is to suggest that there is an eternal, liturgical procession and return of God from and to himself, in which participants in the church's liturgy are gathered, in proportion to their willed participation. The human is *homo liturgicus*, a liturgical animal; Christ the Liturgy is the image in which humans are created. Likeness to this image through human action—a kind of *active-passivity*[12]—is met by the non-compulsory compulsion of grace completing human nature, in proportion to willed participation.

> Heaven did not become the image of God, nor the moon, nor the sun, nor the beautiful stars—nor a single other one of the things that appear in the created order. Only you came into existence as a copy of the Nature that transcends every intellect, a likeness of the incorruptible Beauty, as impress of the true Deity—a model of that true Light in the contemplation of which you become what it is, imitating that which shines within you by the ray that shines forth in response from your purity. None of the things that exist is so great as to be compared to your greatness.[13]

12 For an interesting analogous discussion on being "actively passive," see Enzo Bianchi, *God Where Are You?* (Brewster, MA: Paraclete Press, 2014), 40. We will explore this relation between active and passive in chapter four when we deal with the middle voice.

13 Gregory of Nyssa, *Homilies on the Song of Songs*, trans. Richard Norris (Atlanta: Society of Biblical Literature, 2012), Homily 2, p. 75.

Gregory of Nyssa offers one of the clearest articulations of knowing the image within through embodied likeness to Christ without. For Gregory, to "look up" to Christ is a matter turning one's gaze toward Christ through bodily habituation in the life of virtue. This is how the human reconnects herself to the secret disposition of the soul.

Building on Gregory of Nyssa, Maximus Confessor will later articulate that humans are created for incarnation. "The word of God and God wills always and in all things to accomplish the mystery of his embodiment."[14] Accordingly, the incarnation of the Son is a *natural event* of God's eternal creative action, which the human receives — becomes — by participation.[15]

> When we learn the essential nature of living things, in what respect, how, and out of what they exist, we will not be driven by desire to know more. For if we know God our knowledge of each and every thing will be brought to perfection, and, insofar as humanly possible, the infinite, divine and ineffable dwelling place will be ours to enjoy. For this is what our sainted teacher said in his philosophical aphorism: "For we shall know as we are known," when we mingle our god-formed mind and divine reason to what is properly its own and the image returns to the archetype for which it now longs.[16]

This mingling of the god-formed mind and divine reason hereby *depends* on the human's volitive nature. Again, as Augustine makes clear, "God who created us without us will not save us without us." While the human is naturally disposed to virtue, as a *logos* of the *Logos*, the human has unnaturally fallen.[17] For Maximus, and most of the early fathers with him, sinful nature is inbred, not innate.[18] There is no room for human depravity in a liturgical anthropology.[19] The human

---

14 Maximus, *Ambiguum 7*, 1084D.
15 Ibid., 1084A.
16 Ibid., 1077A–B.
17 Maximus, *Ambiguum 42*, 1321B.
18 Maximus, *Ambiguum 8*, 1104D.
19 Maximus, *Chapters on Love*, IV.14: "Evil is not to be regarded as in the substance of creatures but in its mistaken and irrational movement."

is separated from herself by her actions, not by nature, as an alcoholic is separated from his true self in the overconsumption of alcohol. Sin divides body (likeness) and soul (image), which God's becoming Human has restored, recapitulating all things in the eternal *Logos*.[20] Body and soul are inseparable; image exacts likeness; likeness manifests the image within.[21] Through this manifest likeness, the human comes to know her *natural nature*, the principle of her being (*logoi*) as a portion of God.

Briefly, when *leitourgia* is defined as the "work of the people," not only does it assume that humans have something to offer God that he does not have, it also suggests that God is not the principle of one's being. In other words, if liturgy is not a participation in the singular action of God in Christ but a work done by humans for the sake of God or because of Christ, what God has done is reduced to the level of bare human action. Jesus becomes exemplary, but not fully divine. Why? Because if human action is not animated by divine action in the soul, then what is natural to humanity is not the *imago Dei* but at best a created nature that seems to have risen high on the evolutionary food chain. Or, the result of human sin in the fall not only distorts the likeness of the human's disposition toward grace but also distorts or even vanquishes the image in which the human is created. Liturgy as "the work of the people" is a definition that can only have arisen in a post-Reformation, post-Enlightenment and deistic world where God's creative act is but a momentary event, or an occasional event, rather than an eternal action, whereby the human and all of creation are continually being created.

This will become more clear when we discuss the middle-voice in chapter four. For now, let us turn our attention toward the liturgical nature of God and how our participation in the life of virtues through sacramental habituation in the church makes-manifest who we are and thereby provides a window into who God is.

---

20 Maximus, *Ambiguum 7*, 1080B.
21 Ibid., 1100C.

GO TOWARD YOURSELF

It is after Abraham's father dies in the land of Haran that God calls out to him. In so doing, "The Lord said to Abram, *lekh lekha*...." In calling Abraham forth into the "land that I will show you,"[22] God says to Abram, "lekh lekha," which means "to go toward yourself." As Enzo Bianchi notes, the Hebrew *lekh lekha* corresponds to the Greek γνῶθι σεαυτόν — *know yourself*.[23] The Socratic "know yourself" is naturally picked up by the early fathers, perhaps most notably Gregory of Nyssa, which is due to the recognition that God's nature is unknowable; however, the energy of God active in creation, especially within the human person, reveals what can be perceived of God if the human is attentive. To know oneself, then, remains for Christians our best hope for knowing the God who has united human nature and divine nature in Christ.

There is a clear sense throughout the early church that the human knows God in proportion to the extent that she gives herself to being-known through a participation in the liturgical actions of the church, actions by which God makes himself knowable.[24] A person likewise knows who he or she is in being-known by God through active participation in erotic-knowing.[25] Liturgy names this inter-Trinitarian

22 Genesis 12:1.
23 Enzo Bianchi, *God Where are You?*, 20.
24 Gregory of Nyssa, *The Life of Moses*, II.163–83.
25 Erotic-knowing here describes the mingled subjectivity of knowing, where subject and object coalesce in the activity of making known, being-known, and being-made-known. Desire and understanding are hereby inseparable. To know erotically, therefore, is to know within the act of being-known-by that which one desires to know and thereby knows oneself as a participant in this contingent being-known-by a knower. Erotic-knowing refuses unilateral understanding; it is a knowing that is inherently reciprocal, a mutual giving and receiving that infinitely expands by the desire to know as known-by. See Hans Urs Von Balthasar, *The Glory of the Lord*, vol. 2: *Studies in Theological Style: Clerical Styles*, ed. John Kenneth Riches, trans. Andrew Louth, Francis McDonagh, and Brian McNeil, C.R.V. (San Francisco: Ignatius Press, 1984), 95–106. See especially Maurice Merleau-Ponty, *Phenomenology of Perception*, trans. Colin Smith (London: Routledge, 2002), 178–201. For Merleau-Ponty, "Erotic perception is not a *cogitation* which aims at a *cogitatum*; through one body it aims at another body, and takes place in the world, not in a consciousness (note that Merleau-Ponty offers both an intellective consciousness and a body consciousness). A sight has a sexual significance for me, not when I consider, even confusedly, its possible relationship to the sexual organs or to pleasurable states, but when it exists for my body, for that power always available for bringing together into an erotic

relation that has been made known to humanity through the mighty act of God in Christ — Grace — that makes available the entrance of humanity into the reciprocal, eternal relation God is. Gathered into the self-offering of the Son[26] to the Father through the Spirit, the human takes from God's own store to offer herself as an offering with the Son qua *Offering* — whose self-offering is eternally present to the Father for the life of the world. The human's self-offering or living sacrifice is not to be understood, then, as an entering into a subject-object relation with God. Rather, it is to become lost in erotic-knowing, having been adopted into the interpenetration of the Triune God by the Son's assimilating of human nature to the divine nature. This *being lost*, however, is the ultimate receiving of one's identity — the being-known of God. Grace moves humanity beyond its natural divisiveness,[27] gathered into Reciprocity by assimilation, without negating difference. No longer can the human know herself as human — cannot know the limitations and possibilities of her nature — apart from her assimilation to Divinity. The human's being is eternally located in divine action — *esse actus purus*.

God creates humanity to redeem humanity — to deify humanity to become God. Created life, then, is good by nature,[28] but as created it is continually *being created*. When the human willfully[29] ascends through liturgical participation to the location of her identity in this erotic-knowing of the Holy Trinity, she realizes her personhood to be sustained in, by, and through the shared life that is Father, Son, Spirit — *Thought, Word, Deed*.[30] That is, she loses herself, and in this

---

situation the stimuli applied, and adapting sexual conduct to it. There is an erotic 'comprehension' not of the order of understanding, since understanding subsumes an experience, once perceived, under some idea, while desire comprehends blindly by linking body to body" (181). This "comprehending blindly" is to suggest embodied habits that link bodies together, whereby human understanding is first and foremost intuited by sense perception and only secondarily intellective, even though intellection is vital to the relation.

26 Hebrews 10.

27 Maximus, "Chapters on Knowledge," II.21, in George C. Berthold, trans., *Maximus Confessor: Selected Writings* (New York: Paulist Press, 1985).

28 John Meyendorff, *Christ in Eastern Christian Thought* (Washington: Corpus Books, 1969), 149.

29 Ibid., 145–51.

30 This is in no way to introduce any hint of modalism; rather, it is to draw together

losing is the ultimate receiving of her identity in the being-known of God. The human becomes known *with* the Son *through* the Spirit *by* the Father, and thereby knows herself as the Father's own, eternally identified with the Son.

Gregory of Nyssa speaks of knowledge as available only to one who participates in the severe and rigorous way of Christ. To those who are incontinent, knowledge is inaccessible. The incontinent are like thieves who try to steal the fruit of the pomegranate tree and are cut and pricked by the thorns that guard its fruit. The incontinent do not realize that the pleasure and joy of the pomegranate is available only to those who are disciplined by faith, bearing the yoke of Christ. For the continent person *formed in the way*, the thorns yield, permitting full access to the fruit. The continent is one who has not grown soft by the luxuries and pleasures of the present life and is truly able to taste the fruit of the tree. Disciplined by the sacramental life of the church, the continent one progresses further and further in the grove of faith.

> For the limit that the virtuous life approaches is likeness to the Divine, and for the sake of this goal both the soul's purity and its separation from any passionate disposition are in virtuous persons carefully realized, so that a certain impress of the transcendent Nature comes to them also, on account of the nobler quality of their life.[31]

When purity is cultivated in a person, she is able to see and to "know herself," for the glory of the Lord that lies within will have been made known to her. Gregory elaborates this point in terms of the beauty of the invisible made visible by the mirror of human nature. First, however, it must be understood what Gregory means by mirror.

---

the implications of liturgy as the coming together for the human of thought, word, and deed, which is her being gathered into the Liturgy that is the perichoretic union of the Holy Trinity, the God who *is* the Thought he thinks, the Word he speaks, and the Deed he does, known as none other than Father, Son, and Holy Spirit.

31 Gregory of Nyssa, *Homilies on the Song of Songs*, Homily 9, p. 287. See also *The Life of Moses*, II.157.

In the modern age it is standard to understand the mirror in terms of its reflective use. Accordingly, a mirror is a reflecting tool that is wholly external to the image it reflects. There is no engagement or interaction that occurs between the mirror and the image reflected. The two are fixed, isolated entities. The modern mirror as a reflecting tool reduces the image to the image in-itself, something re-presented back to the subject whose image is reflected.

The modern Venetian mirror of the fourteenth century introduces the first clear image, a looking glass without stains or bubbles, enabling persons to see for the first time not in a glass darkly or dimly but clearly and perfectly. One could now see the unclouded image of God. This *pure* reflection of the image alters the whole meaning of what a mirror is and does. The new looking-glass provides a release from the reciprocal essence of human nature, imposing an unilateral logic upon its viewer. This modernized tool of reflection bears the logic of the self-knowing self—a person who can be seen through her own eyes, perfectly reflected.

Prior to the clarified mirror, self-knowledge is acquired only through a reciprocal engagement with people, places, and things in a mingling of lights. In the ancient world, the mirror is understood in very different terms. Following a Platonic logic of the mirror as described in the *Timaeus*, what takes place when a person stands in front of the mirror is that the light of the eyes mingle (coalesce) with the light on the surface of the mirror, the two lights forming the image on the mirror.[32] There are at least two lights involved in the forming of the image, made present to the eye of the beholder. The image is real; it is *there* on the surface of the mirror. Here the mirror can be anything. The light of the human eye is not a kind of filter by which it sees the object before the person simply as something consumed by the eye. Rather, the thing looks back at her with its own light. The two lights come together to form the image that is thereby known by the human. The two lights permeate one another, mingle together to form an image. It is in this sense that beauty lies in the eye of the beholder. The co-mingling of

32 Plato, *Timaeus*, trans. Robert Gregg Bury (Cambridge: Harvard University Press, 1981), 46.A–C.

lights creates an image that is received as beautiful based on the form made-manifest by the co-mingling of lights. Beauty does not simply reside in the object of the human's gaze (Hume), nor does beauty lie purely in the abstracted, rationally trained eye (Kant). Rather, the quality of light produced by the object and likewise the subject mingle together to form an image, thereby construed as beautiful or hideous on the basis of the compatibility of lights.

There is evidence of this *mingling* in the words of Jesus in the Gospels of Matthew and Luke, where Jesus speaks of the lamp of the body.[33] The language is primarily located in what is gazed upon by the human; however, it is clear in the gospels that objects emit their own light, be it darkened or dazzling.

> Your eye is the lamp of the body. If your eye is healthy, your whole body is full of light; but if your eye is not healthy, your whole body is full of darkness. Therefore, consider whether the light in you is not darkness. If then your whole body is full of light, with no part of it in darkness, it will be as full of light as when a lamp gives you light with its rays.[34]

In Luke's gospel, this discussion of light is preceded by a reference to the story of Jonah's relation to Nineveh as a sign of God's Kingdom—the light of Christ. Jonah is the mirror by which the light of God emanates to reconcile the people of Nineveh. Jonah, the reluctant missionary, was no less a vehicle of light. Reading the story of Jonah in light of Luke's gospel, Jonah is as Peter, who walked out upon the sea gazing upon the Lord and lost sight of the light because of the tumultuous winds and waves. Jonah saw only the darkness of Nineveh. The light emitted from the Ninevites was a darkened light; but gazing only upon their darkness Jonah is himself filled with darkness and moved to anger, even after Nineveh turns from its wickedness to serve "the God of heaven, who made the sea and the dry land."[35]

33 Matthew 6:22–23; Luke 11:34–36.
34 Luke 11:34–36.
35 Jonah 1:9.

Jesus goes further and says, "No one after lighting a lamp puts it in a cellar, but on a lamp stand so that those who enter may see the light."[36] Jonah, however, as we see evidenced in the two passages, had tried to do just that, place the light of God in a cellar, which is the same behavior for which Jesus condemns the Pharisees,[37] reminiscent of the dialogue between God and Jonah under the bush outside of Nineveh.[38] The Pharisees offered a simulation of divine light, while consumed by darkness within.[39] Jesus goes on to say that the Ninevites received the sign, Jonah, though he was but a mirror reflecting God's light, but this generation of Israel would be condemned by the Ninevites because, making a subtle reference to the light he is, "something greater than Jonah is here!"[40]

We find here in Luke's gospel a continuation of the Song of Simeon: "For my eyes have seen your salvation, which you have prepared in the presence of all peoples, a light for revelation to the Gentiles and for glory to your people Israel."[41] Simeon addresses Mary and Joseph after his blessing, saying that Jesus would reveal the inner thoughts of humans.[42] Not only does the light of Christ expose the darkness covering the world; the gaze of God in Christ also exposes the divine light within all created life. Christ is the gaze of God upon all creation. He is the light that permeates the light inherent in creation as created, opening the human to her contingent lucidity in the co-mingling of divine and created lights.

Accordingly, the healthy body is made healthy by its gaze upon the light, Christ. This is brought into full view in Matthew's account, whereby the preceding passage regards storing up treasures on earth[43] and the following passage concerns serving two masters.[44] "Where your treasure is, there also is your heart,"[45] is likewise a casting of one's gaze.

36 Luke 11:33.
37 Luke 11:37–41.
38 Jonah 4:6–11.
39 Luke 11:39.
40 Luke 11:32.
41 Luke 2:30–32.
42 Luke 2:35.
43 Matthew 6:19–21.
44 Matthew 6:24.
45 Matthew 6:21.

That upon which one's gaze is cast is that which fills the body. This casting of gaze, however, is no mere looking at objects; rather, it involves a master-slave relation. The human's gaze—her seeing and knowledge of all things—is located in her obedience to and being disciplined by the object of her gaze. To gaze upon the light of God (Christ) is to be permeated by divinity, whereby the created light of the human mingles with the divine light (Christ), so that the human sees all things with a double-light, an unconfused light, that reveals the object of gaze to the human in its own manner of participation in divine contingency.

For Plato, the light of the form is the light that goes forth from the object of gaze. The object participates in its eternal form by its likeness to the form. The light of the object is not a light particular to itself but receives its light from the idea/form. Christ, however, introduces himself as the primordial Form, i.e., Light, who has given the created a light "of its own." This light remains contingent upon *the* Light, Christ, yet the light of the created exists as an endowment. It is *there*, embedded in the person, place or thing. The all-permeating light, Christ, does not simply shine through the empty vessel; rather, the Light permeates the created light whereby the two lights—Creator and created—mingle together to show forth the truth of the created's nature with implications for knowing the Creator. This third light—the Light, Christ—mingles with both created lights of subject and object, forming an image that is made visible in its contingent relation to the illuminating God, strengthening the distinction of subject and object while simultaneously removing the apparent division between the two. Christ is the unconfused union of all things.

THE SENSE-ABLE GOD

How the human knows herself and the world around her is, for Gregory of Nyssa, the difference between the two trees in the Garden of Eden. The contrast between the tree of life and the tree of the knowledge of good and evil is nearly identical in the accounts of Athanasius, Gregory of Nyssa, Gregory of Nazianzen, Basil, and John of Damascus. The tree of life is the tree of obedience—Christ's cross. The tree of the knowledge of good and evil is disobedience, whereby the human understands his or her relation to creation only in terms of his or her aligned or misaligned passions and desires. To eat the fruit of the tree of knowledge is to phenomenologize the world, a kind of Kantian, reasoned tastefulness.[46] That is, to notice the other as naked is to see only the body—to see only matter,[47] which is not to truly see the body in its relation to the soul and its co-mingling with divine light. It is to construe the object of one's gaze in a kind of radical subjectivity, permitting no reciprocal identification, only projection.

There are, then, two faculties of vision, "there is one operation by which it sees the truth, and another that is led astray by attending to things that amount to nothing."[48] The tree of life does not see through the bodily passions where all objects are objects of desire. The tree of death—the tree of knowledge of good and evil—is the tree of non-being or privation of good.[49] The two trees are two distinct forms of perceiving. The first is through active participation in the good, the co-mingling of lights; the second denies the penetrating light of divinity, which is the result of an absence of virtue in action—privation of good.[50]

As seen with Aristotle, it is not that human action necessarily or causally gives way to knowledge, any more than knowledge necessarily produces action. Nevertheless, a person's activities construe how one understands and what is intelligible to a person. For instance, to continue the analogy of the mirror, the modern mirror conditions how the human sees herself, by construing *how* she sees. The human becomes an object of her own gaze, conflating the subjectivity and objectivity of the self into a *self-objectified-subjectivity*.

This construal of the ancient mirror logic promotes a self that knows only by its own unilateral light, projected upon all objects, which, as

46   Hans-Georg Gadamer, *Truth and Method*, trans. Joel Weinsheimer (London: Continuum, 2006), 37–39.

47   Conor Cunningham, "Suspending the Natural Attitude," in *Transcendence and Phenomenology*, ed. Peter M. Candler and Conor Cunningham (London: SCM Press, 2007), 260–87.

48   Gregory of Nyssa, *Homilies on the Song of Songs,* Homily 8, p. 271.

49   Ibid., Homily 12.

50   Ibid.

it were, have no light to reciprocate. The un-mirrored self stands in a quite different relation to her object of gaze. One knows an object to have a "life of its own," which enables the self-subject to enter into a knowing relationship *with* the object. The human looks upon, for instance, a beautiful daisy. The daisy (object) is a real flower. It does not exist in the eye of its beholder, even though the beholder uniquely sees the daisy. One's perceiving of the daisy in no way alters the truth of the daisy. It is there, whether it is admired for its beauty or not seen at all. The subject-object relation of a person to a daisy is not, therefore, unilateral. The human is not the only one involved in the knowing that occurs between the person and a daisy. The daisy does have something to say, namely that the human is not a daisy, which it says quite loudly. It is as in the film *The Seventh Seal*,[51] where a medieval squire stops to ask a dead man sitting on a rock for directions. He returns to his knight saying, "Eloquent." To which the Knight responds, "What did he say?" "Too dark to repeat," says the squire. There is a reciprocity of knowing between the human and a daisy, even the dead, and such reciprocal knowing is vital for human self-knowledge. This is necessary whether the subject-object relation occurs between a flower, a rock, or another person. Self-knowledge occurs when one becomes open to the knowledge of oneself from that which is not oneself—when an awareness of the created light is visible in all things. The modern mirror deconstructs this field of knowledge. Its very existence imposes a logic of individuation that is not easily avoided. To gaze into a mirror is to enter into a unilateral, subject-object relation with oneself, whereby the subject (self) is the object (self) and the object (self) is the subject (self)—tautology.[52] Self-knowledge is available to the self-subject by the self-object, and the human knows herself in this falsely reciprocal, unilateral and virtual relation.

One thinks here of Johannes Gumpp's *Self-Portrait* (1646).[53] The painting is that of one in the act of painting his own image via his

51   *The Seventh Seal*, dir. Ingmar Bergman (Stockholm, Sweden: Svensk Filmindustri, 1957).

52   Sabine Melchior-Bonnet, *The Mirror: A History* (New York: Routledge, 2001), 168.

53   Ibid., 166–68.

reflected image. The artist's back is the portrayed "self," who is reflected in the mirror image to his left, with the canvas receiving the artist's reflected image being painted on the right. The artist bears witness of himself to himself; all is conjecture and subjectivity.[54] The individual portrait, which arises when the human comes to understand herself as a human subject, capable of objectivity, comes about on the heels of the perfected glass mirror. It would be impossible to construe this argument causally, i.e., chicken or egg, yet it should not be dismissed that the logic of the mirror is evidenced in the rise of the self-portrait in the 15th century—the self-subject self. Without the mirror, the self as subject may never have been thought. This cannot be more than conjectured; however, the self as knowing itself by being known by itself—the self as "self-revelatory"—*is* known with the mirror. The mirror, like the photograph, assures the viewer that she is. Following a sort of Cartesian logic, one could say with the modern mirror that "I reflect; therefore, I am." It should come as no surprise, here, that during the Enlightenment the reflected image becomes proof of one's being. The living-dead, the vampire, has no reflection. He is dead. Therefore, only the self can bear witness, via the reflecting-tool—the mirror—to itself that it is alive.[55] Gumpp's *Self-Portrait* is important, not because he used a mirror to paint his own face; it is important because he painted himself bearing witness to himself that he is, revealing the unilateral self-knowledge that the mirror guises as reciprocal knowing.[56] The modern Venetian mirror does not simply provide a perfected reflection to its image; it (mis)construes its viewer and her being-in-the-world. The clarified mirror is itself a *Weltanschauung*. The world-view created by the mirror, however, does exactly what it

---

54 Ibid., 168.

55 One could also argue here that the vampire is the truly alive, for he only knows of his existence in his relation to the living. He cannot "know himself" as himself, but only knows himself in his relation to others; literally feeding on the lives of others.

56 See Melchior-Bonnet, *The Mirror*, 101–32. Melchior-Bonnet traces the development of the modern mirror, harkening back to the early medieval understanding of creation as the mirror of God, a mirror that bears a distinctly participatory relation to its creator. However, with a looking glass that returns a perfect image of its viewer, that relation is rent asunder.

cannot do, which is to provide an exact image of its viewer. The mirror only deconstructs its viewer to what the mirror can reflect, which is only the material object in view, absent of mind and soul. With Gregory, however, to know oneself is not to see by way of the reflected re-presentation. Gregory's call to *know yourself* is a call to know the Good and know human nature only in its relation to the Light of God. Indeed, "our greatest safeguard," says Gregory, is self knowledge.[57] To do so, however, humans must rightly appraise themselves. For those who do not, see in themselves

> strength or beauty or glory or power or abundance or riches or pride or dignity or bodily size or good looks or some other such thing, and they take it for themselves. For this reason they are unreliable keepers of themselves. With their interest fixed on what is alien, they allow what is their own to go unprotected. For how shall anyone guard what he has no knowledge of? So the most secure watch over the good things within us is not to be ignorant of ourselves and for each to know what he is and to distinguish clearly between himself and the things around his edges, so that he may not end up keeping guard over what is alien rather than over himself.[58]

The human, for Gregory, is at her core a participant in the divine life. Only humans "come into existence as a copy of the Nature that transcends every intellect, a likeness of the incorruptible Beauty, an impress of the true Deity...

> ...and fixing your gaze in all circumstances on the immaterial good, you will be watchful concerning the error of the ways of this life... [so that] you will hear the sweet voice that say to the wool-bearing and tame sheep, "Come, O blessed of my Father,

---

57 Gregory of Nyssa, *Homilies on the Song of Songs*, Homily 2, p. 71. As Richard Norris notes in his translation, Gregory clearly has in mind the classical maxim "know thyself" with regard to this increased spiritual know-how. See p. 71, n. 32.

58 Ibid.

and inherit the kingdom prepared for you from the foundation of the cosmos" — of which we may be found worthy in Christ Jesus our Lord, to whom be glory to the ages. Amen.[59]

To *know yourself*, then, is to know oneself as the mirror upon which the Light — Christ, the Image-Light of God — is cast and re-cast. Such knowledge is made present to the human through the gaze of virtue, a continual becoming in likeness to the Image through participation in the tree of life — the taking up of one's cross, the fruit showing forth the true nature of a tree,[60] the brilliance of light showing the quality of the lamp. Full illumination, deification, is the end of virtue. The mutual gaze of God upon the human and the human upon God is made known in the willed and active gathering of created lights into this reciprocal co-mingling in virtue.

It is the human's participation in virtuous action that transforms her and makes known to her the nature of her humanity as a vessel for this double mingling of lights.

> The only way for the soul to be attached to the incorruptible God is for it to make itself as pure as it can. In this way, reflecting *as the mirror does*, when it submits itself to the purity of God, it will be formed according to its participation in and reflection of the prototypal beauty.[61]

The logic, here, is that the divine light that shines upon the human, who has placed herself before God, supplies the image. The mingling of lights on the surface of the mirror that is the object — in this case the Light of Christ and the light of the human — is, for Gregory, an active and mutual penetration of the two natures, divine and human, inasmuch as the human's gaze is locked on Christ. The human has "her own beauty," but it is not Beauty; rather, it is the truth of her

---

59 Ibid., 75–77.

60 Ibid., Homily 12.

61 Gregory of Nyssa, "On Virginity," XI, in *Saint Gregory of Nyssa: Ascetical Works*, trans. Virginia Woods Callahan (Washington: Catholic University of America Press, 1967).

createdness. The human is made into the likeness, according to Gregory, of the image — the beauty on which her gaze is cast. This works positively and negatively. To gaze upon evil forms an image of the beholder as depraved and capable only of sinful actions. Casting one's gaze upon God, however, makes manifest the human's true nature — the divine image, a participant in divine goodness.

One need not take such elaborate examples to understand what Gregory is getting at here. If a person is continually watching the exemplar of faith in the manner of her actions and does so long enough, a person will, in all likelihood, be moved to so act. It is in this way that husbands and wives grow closer together and further apart. If the two who are bound together as one in holy matrimony are continually present with each other, they will begin to share many of the same characteristics in behavior and understanding. This is certainly true for children, the most observant of humans walking the earth, who see (or do not see) their parents day in and day out. Children become near carbon copies of their parents' character, some spending many years in therapy for it. Gregory's observation here is quite elemental: you become the image formed by the co-mingling of lights, those of the human and her object of gaze.

> In days of old the human race grew cold with the chill of idolatry, and man's changeable nature was transformed into the nature of the immobile objects which he worshipped... For those who look toward the true God receive within themselves the characteristics of the divine nature; so too, those who turn their minds to the vanity of idols are transformed into the objects which they look at, and become stones instead of men.[62]

Subject and object are hereby indivisible. The two mutually *know* one another. And the extent to which the human's gaze is cast upon her object is the degree to which she locates her identity in the object of her gaze. The two are folded into one, making the human subject into the

---

62 Gregory of Nyssa, *Commentary on Ecclesiastes*, Sermon V.

likeness of the object — more specifically the object of worship, which, if the object of gaze is not God, is a forsaking of her true image — she is as all who gazed into the eyes of Medusa and are turned to stone.

This form of knowledge is clearly participatory. Like Aristotle, Gregory makes the point clear that the ability to receive and process knowledge is contingent upon the human having been formed by the virtues — the sacramental life of the church.[63]

> How after all is it possible for a beautiful image to appear in a mirror unless the mirror has received the impression of a lovely form? Hence the mirror that is human nature *does not become beautiful until it has drawn close to the Beautiful and been formed by the image of the divine Beauty.* For just as human nature took the form of the serpent as long as it lay prostrate upon the earth and directed its gaze on him, in the same way, when it has risen up and shown itself to be face to face with the Good by turning its back upon evil, it is shaped in accordance with that which it looks upon — and what it looks upon is the archetypal Beauty. When, therefore, it has drawn close to the Light, it becomes light, and in this light the beautiful form of the dove is imaged — and the dove I am talking about is the one whose form makes known the presence of the Holy Spirit.[64]

The mirror of human nature shows forth the beauty of the image to the extent that the lights of the human and God mingle together on the mirror of the soul[65] to show forth their union in glory by a likeness in participation and mutual penetration[66] — human nature having been pre-penetrated by divine *esse* at creation,[67] fully held together in Christ. To say that the human is a mirror, then, is to say that she

---

63 Gregory of Nyssa, *On Virginity*, XII.
64 Gregory of Nyssa, *Commentary on the Song of Songs*, Homily 5, p. 163, italics mine.
65 Ibid., Sermon X.
66 Gregory of Nyssa, *The Life of Moses*, II.167–69.
67 Gregory of Nyssa, *Commentary on the Song of Songs*, Homily 8.

is the mirror *for* (not of) the *imago Dei*. The mingling of lights is an active participation that realigns the human gaze. Human action limits or expands the field of knowledge.[68] In order for the human to know Beauty she must become beautiful; she must be impressed with Beauty's form. Only when the human has been rightly formed through participation can she truly know; for the vision of the Good is made possible by a uniformity of life to virtue.[69] This is the reason why the virtuous take great pains to cultivate purity of soul and freedom from the passions, so that the form, as it were, of transcendent Being might be revealed in them because of their more perfect life.[70]

Self-knowledge is made available by a mystical seeing of the image of God revealed to the human through the cultivation of virtue. Virtuous activity opens the human to self-knowledge, and, therefore, knowledge of God. This knowledge, as we said before, is not causal. It is as a farm field. God creates the human — the soil; the human tills — disciplines — the body, which opens the human to the seed — Christ — of life, to be continually nurtured by the mingling of lights — divine and human — upon the mirror of the soul. Gregory makes it clear that it is the mysteries of the church that discipline the human to receive knowledge of the Good and know herself as a participant in the Good. Virtue — the clothing of the soul — is none other than the actions of the body, which give way to knowledge of the self. The body is the perfect image of the soul. Gregory here foreshadows Wittgenstein.[71] In his interpretation of the liturgical vestments of the priest, Gregory claims that these are no less than the actions that adorn the soul, "woven by the exercise of the virtues."[72]

The garments of faith, then, are the actions of the baptized that participate in the sacrificial action of Christ on the cross. This, says

---

68   Ibid., Homily 4.

69   Ibid., Homily 8.

70   Ibid., Homily 9.

71   In the *Philosophical Investigations*, Wittgenstein comments that, "The human body is the best picture of the human soul," drawing attention to the reality that humans manifest in their bodies an intellectual disposition inseparable from their embodiment. See Ludwig Wittgenstein, *Philosophical Investigations*, trans. G. E. M. Anscombe (Oxford: Basil Blackwell, 1958), II.4.

72   Gregory of Nyssa, *The Life of Moses*, II.191.

Gregory, is what Paul means by living sacrifice. The garment of faith is a participation in the actions that are the eating of the fruit that comes from the tree of life. To put on the garment of sensuous life—the tree of the knowledge of good and evil—is to weigh down the soul with that which is thick and heavy, not allowing the human to ascend toward the holy.[73] One must be careful to understand the nuances that Gregory makes when he speaks of the sensuous life, however, as he has a great tendency to speak of sensation both positively and negatively, and often does so in the same sections of his writings.

Sarah Coakley has shown how important Gregory of Nyssa is to gaining a cohesive understanding of embodied perceiving.[74] Directing our attention to Gregory's important and often overlooked *De anima et resurrectione*, Coakley shows how Gregory's robust understanding of knowledge and its acquisition—following the apostle Paul, especially 1 Corinthians 15—occurs through a systematic increase in understanding by a series of sensual purgations.[75] Coakley's essay deals largely with Jean Daniélou's description of Gregory's "doctrine" of the spiritual senses in his influential work, *Platonisme et théologie mystique*.[76] Coakley argues that Daniélou does not therein adequately address the nature of the spiritual senses in relation to epistemology in Gregory, faulting him for his lack of attention to *De anima*. It must be noted that Coakley's accusation against Daniélou's treatment is focused on his earlier work in *Platonisme et théologie mystique*, where he outlines this "doctrine." Coakley does point this out, although not until the final paragraph of the essay, which is a bit misleading. Daniélou does, however, account for this graded elevation of spiritual sense in the introduction to his selected texts from Gregory's writings, *From Glory to Glory*.[77]

73   Ibid.

74   Sarah Coakley, "Gregory of Nyssa on the Spiritual Senses: A Reconsideration," in *The Spiritual Senses: Perceiving God in Western Christianity*, eds. Paul L. Gavrilyuk and Sarah Coakley (Cambridge: Cambridge University Press), 36–55.

75   Ibid.

76   Coakley, *Gregory of Nyssa on the Spiritual Senses*, 36–55. Coakley sets out to challenge Daniélou's notion of "doctrine" with regard to the spiritual senses.

77   Daniélou, *From Glory to Glory*, 3–78. Coakley implies that Daniélou's selection and translation of Nyssen's texts in *From Glory to Glory* follow a disjunction of spiritual sense from physical sense; however, given Daniélou's account to the contrary in the

Whether Daniélou adequately addresses Gregory's progression of spiritual sensing in his *Platonisme et théologie mystique* is debatable; however, he does address this elsewhere[78] and succinctly in his introduction to *From Glory to Glory*, which Coakley curiously does not mention.[79]

Coakley's reemphasizing of *De anima* is important, as it shows in Gregory an important account of physiological sensation as participating

---

introduction, coupled with the selection of the texts that outline this progressive movement in Gregory from sense perception toward spiritual sensibility, I find Coakley's argument unfounded (see especially Daniélou, introduction, 46–56). Perhaps Coakley is correct to point out that Gregory does not have a "doctrine" of spiritual sense; nevertheless, this does not negate Daniélou's otherwise sound treatment of Gregory on sense perception.

78 See Jean Daniélou, *God and the Ways of Knowing* (San Francisco: Ignatius Press, 2003), 187–210, and idem, *The Bible and the Liturgy* (Notre Dame: University of Notre Dame Press, 2005), esp. 19–53, 124–26.

79 Daniélou appears to anticipate and respond directly to Coakley's accusation (2012) in his introduction to *From Glory to Glory* (1961). "Indeed Daniélou avers [in *Platonisme et théologie mystique*] that Gregory does not significantly advance on the position of Origen, despite a few characteristic phrases in his *Commentary on the Song* which are novel and distinctive," see Coakley, *Gregory of Nyssa on the Spiritual Senses*, 39; *Platonisme et théologie mystique*, 238–41. However, "responds" Daniélou, while Gregory's doctrine of the spiritual senses is "inherited from Origen [it is] developed quite extensively." See Daniélou, introduction to *From Glory to Glory*, 25. Again, while this may not be explicit in Daniélou's *Platonisme et théologie mystique*, he is otherwise well aware of Gregory's novelty and the importance of the *De anima*. Again, Coakley claims that Daniélou "does not spell out how sensation in the ordinary, physiological sense can *become* 'spiritual sensation,'" stating that this implies a disjunction in Gregory's own understanding of the mystical experience; however, we find a very telling passage in the *De anima* that may shed more light on this so-called disjunction. "Since, then, the soul becomes godlike when it has put off all the varied impulses of its nature, and when it has passed beyond desire it has entered into that towards which it was previously being raised by desire, *it no longer gives any place in itself either to hope or to memory* (italics mine). It has what it was hoping for, and it drives out memory from its mind in its occupation with the enjoyment of good things. Thus it imitates the superior life, being conformed to the properties of the divine Nature, so that nothing else is left to it but the disposition of love, as it becomes attached in its nature to the beautiful" (*De anima*, 79–80). This is likely where Maximus derives his claim that "authentic knowledge [is] gained only by actual experience," whereby a "direct perception" supplants "relative knowledge based on reason and ideas." See Maximus, *Ambiguum 60*, in *On the Cosmic Mystery of Jesus Christ: Selected Writings from St. Maximus the Confessor*, trans. Paul M. Blowers and Robert Louis Wilken (Crestwood: St. Vladimir's Seminary Press, 2003). There is no disjunction, here, as Coakley rightly points out, but neither is there in Daniélou's account of Gregory. Rather, it is the paradoxical illumination by darkness and the true vision of not seeing that Gregory expresses. See Gregory of Nyssa, *The Life of Moses*, II.162–64, to which Daniélou directs our attention.

in true wisdom and understanding.[80] Again, Daniélou does emphasize Gregory's understanding of progressive change as essential to human nature, regarding perfection as a "perpetual progress,"[81] an "infinite growth,"[82] a "constant becoming."[83] This is the purpose of the *garment of skin*, says Daniélou.[84] Gregory's understanding of the body, as Daniélou underscores, is a corrective to Origen's speculation that the body is a punishment for sin.[85] Gregory's notion of the *garment of skin*, however, is for the soul's remedy (both following and moving beyond Origen), not its punishment.[86] What Gregory outlines in *De anima* is a spiritual ascent of descent, a luminous darkness, an entering into knowing by way of unknowing, all of which for Gregory is a sort of embodied disembodiment.[87] As Coakley has shown, Gregory's position here involves delving eternally into darkness through the continuous purifying of human sensibility, whereby the prisoner and the free man, while "very much alike in body during their lives [come to] differ greatly from each other in their experience of pleasure or

80 Gregory of Nyssa, *On the Soul and the Resurrection*, trans. Catherine Roth (New York: St. Vladimir's Seminary Press, 2002), 34.

81 Daniélou, *From Glory to Glory*, 47.

82 Ibid., 46.

83 Ibid., 54. See also *The Life of Moses*, II.219–55.

84 Ibid., 11.

85 Ibid., 12.

86 Ibid.

87 Gregory of Nyssa, *On the Soul and the Resurrection*, 97–101. As Catherine Roth notes, Macrina denies in this section the "materiality of matter" (99 n.4). See also Vladimir Lossky, *In the Image and Likeness of God* (New York: St. Vladimir's Seminary Press, 1974), 31–43. Lossky shows how distinct Gregory's understanding of gnosis truly is, differing greatly from Origen (and Evagrius). He also remarks how well aware of this Fr. Daniélou is, describing Gregory to be "passing beyond" Origen in Daniélou's book on Origen. This "luminous darkness" is perhaps nowhere more clear in Gregory than in the *Life of Moses*. By the disciplining of sense perception the human opens the intellective part of her soul to deeper and deeper contemplation of the incomprehensible and thereby sees God in not seeing. On this point, see Gregory of Nyssa, *The Life of Moses*, II.163; see also Rowan Williams, *The Wound of Knowledge* (Eugene, OR: Wipf and Stock, 1998), 62–67, where Williams notes that Daniélou presents Gregory's understanding of the relation between the soul and the senses as "revolutionary," although Williams does appear to be working on a problematic understanding of Platonism — separating sensibility from the soul's "celestial journey," a reading of Plato that Coakley rightly reminds us is not Platonic.

pain."[88] This difference is the difference between one disciplined by virtue and another disciplined by the senses.

> Some people ascribe to the good part whatever seems pleasant
> to sense-perception, while others believe that only what appears
> to the mind both is good and should be so called. Those who
> have not trained their reasoning and have not examined what
> is better spend gluttonously in the fleshly life the share of good
> which is owed to their nature, saving up nothing for the life
> hereafter. But those who manage their life with critical reasoning
> and self-control, although in this short life they are distressed by
> those misfortunes which trouble the senses, yet store up good
> for the subsequent age, so that the better portion is extended for
> them throughout their eternal life.[89]

This is the gulf, says Macrina, that is made by "the decisions of human lives divided towards opposite choices."[90] The senses, while they are part of this purifying journey of the soul, are nevertheless to

88 Gregory of Nyssa, *On the Soul and the Resurrection*, 120. For Gregory, this growth is eternal. At no point is the darkness surpassed; rather, each natural growth of the human in Christ is a growth that continually reveals the absolute transcendence of the God who is at once fully present to the human but so vast that all one can hope for is a deeper awareness that knowledge of God can never be exhausted or fully acquired; see Gregory of Nyssa, *On the Soul and the Resurrection*, 87; *The Life of Moses*, II.162–69.

89 Gregory of Nyssa, *On the Soul and the Resurrection*, 71. See also Gregory of Nyssa, *The Life of Moses*, II.157. In *The Life of Moses*, Gregory makes the more clear distinction between rational and irrational animals, whereby the irrational animals are those governed solely by sense perception, divorced from rationality. Following Gregory, we might say that understanding is gained through rational appropriation of the senses, which leads to spiritual sense, but apart from the intellective faculty the spirited and appetitive leave the soul to be trampled upon by insatiable passions (II.94–96, 154–58).

90 Gregory of Nyssa, *On the Soul and the Resurrection*, 71. This understanding of decision or choice is, again, found throughout Gregory's *The Life of Moses*; see especially II.70–88. "We have in ourselves, in our own nature and by our own choice, the causes of light and darkness, since we place ourselves in whichever sphere we wish to be" (II.80). Gregory makes a distinction throughout *The Life of Moses* regarding what is "within" human nature and what comes to it from the outside. The cause of light or virtue is within, part of the fabric of human nature, while the cause of darkness or vice comes from the outside, although through an exercise of free will, which is within.

be on the *passive* side of the soul's activity. This "passivity" is clearer in *The Life of Moses*, wherein Gregory continuously emphasizes the role of free will in the human's elevation to virtue or descent to vice. It is the activity of the human's free will that conditions her toward a sensitivity or insensitivity to virtue.[91] Gregory here refers to the hardening of Pharaoh's heart by God. Pharaoh's resistance to the divine will, says Gregory, is not caused by God; rather, Pharaoh resists God because he has inclined his sensibilities to evil and is thereby hardened to the "word that softens resistance."[92]

It is here that Coakley's (re)assessment is of utmost importance. Her concern is that any disjunction between epistemology and spirituality in Gregory of Nyssa is a failure to see "an emerging and developing sense of the significance of bodily life for 'spiritual sensation.'"[93] This union is perhaps clearer, however, in Gregory's discussion of the soul in *The Life of Moses*. Gregory follows an Aristotelian classification of the tripartite soul (vegetative, sensitive, and rational).[94] For Gregory, the soul is as the doorpost of the Hebrew in Egypt, which received the blood of the lamb to protect the virtue within.[95] The upper doorpost is the rational part; the side posts of the entrance are the vegetative and sensitive ("appetitive" and "spirited").[96] The rational part keeps the side posts from evil thoughts, while the appetitive and spirited free the upper doorpost more and more to greater illumination. There is a strong sense of reciprocity in Gregory's understanding of the relation between each part of the soul, whereby each in its own way protects the others, all for the sake of participating in the divine life. This is also in keeping with Gregory's strong sense that Divinity is made-manifest to the degree that the human is capable of receiving.[97] What is most

---

91   Gregory of Nyssa, *The Life of Moses*, II.86–87.

92   Ibid., II.76. Gregory's point here is that God cannot be the cause of any evil or the source of evil. Rather, nothing evil exists apart from human generation by an act of the will (II.88).

93   Coakley, "Gregory of Nyssa on the Spiritual Senses," 52.

94   Gregory of Nyssa, *The Life of Moses*, II.96, 169 n.116.

95   Ibid., II.89–101.

96   Ibid., II.96.

97   Ibid., II.119.

telling, however, with regard to Gregory's understanding of the senses in their participation in the human's ever progressing spiritual sensibility, is how he describes what is most natural to human desire with regard to physiological sensation, most notably in his description of the "stomach's nature."

> Even if much more were prepared than is needed, it is not in the stomach's nature to exceed its proper measure or to be stretched by the insatiate desire for what is prepared.[98]

What is natural to human nature, even to the stomach, is to have what is needed; it is not to be filled through insatiable greed, moving human nature toward what is unnatural, for excess and hoarding lead only to covetousness.[99] This continual progress in virtue — the disciplining of the side posts of the soul — is the realignment of the senses to the spiritual sensation of the rational faculty, which leads to that eternal Sabbath. There is surely no division between epistemology and spirituality to be found in Gregory; rather, it is the epistemological alignment with spiritual sense that leads the human toward her true nature, whereby the soul by virtuous activity reweaves the body to suit its true nature.[100]

The difficulty with Gregory is the lack of specificity with regard to spiritual sense, coupled with his continued back and forth use of "flesh," "garment," and "sense," as there is no uniform employment of these terms. If only he were as clear as John of Damascus who, perhaps clarifying Gregory on the matter of spiritual sense, is more to the point. The Damascene discusses the goal of persons bringing their minds to see the beatific vision,

> which means to be guided by their sense perceptions up to that which is beyond all sense perception and comprehension, which is He who is the Author and Maker and Creator of all.

98   Ibid., II.142.
99   Ibid., II.143.
100   Ibid., II.191.

"For by the beauty of his own creatures the creator is by analogy discovered," and "the invisible things of him from the creation of the world are clearly seen, being understood by the things that are made."[101]

This is Gregory's point as well, which is again clearer in *The Life of Moses*, that the spiritual senses are not separable from the physical; rather, spiritual sense is the transcendental nature of the physical sense, the garment God provides for the attainment of beatific vision, which is one's stepping into the dark cloud in order to comprehend the incomprehensible by realizing the insurmountability of God. For Gregory, as with John of Damascus, one who attends to the spiritual life is borne by sense perception to the Good.[102] Gregory's deepest concern is to secure a right apprehension of Being.[103] God has given the human the garment of skin so that she might put on the garment of obedience and thereby rightly apprehend Being, which is true knowledge.[104] This occurs through sense perception, for it is only through the senses that the human is capable of perception;[105] however, once the human recognizes the truth of her subsistent relation to God it is then, through sense perception, that the spiritual senses are activated, as it were, to know God alone as existence himself—beyond sense perception. This "flight" from the senses does not leave sense perception behind; rather, the human knows herself as contingent when she has become aware

101   John of Damascus, "Philosophical Chapters," I, in Frederic Hathaway Chase, Jr., trans., *Saint John of Damascus: Writings* (New York: Fathers of the Church, 1958).

102   Gregory of Nyssa, *The Life of Moses*, II.6–8. Gregory describes the waters that carry Moses down the Nile, which toss him to and fro; however, because of "education" Moses is "naturally" thrust onto firm ground. What is natural is transformed by human education or discipline to the Good, re-creating (with God) the natural to divine purposes. For Gregory, the human is her own mid-wife, giving birth to her true self through the disciplining of sense perception that raises the human, not beyond herself, per se, but toward herself.

103   Ibid., II.23.

104   Ibid. Again, Gregory teeters back and forth here with "garment." The garment of skin is at once the "garment of disobedience" and God's gift to the human to attain the garment of obedience. The discipline of virtue is the garment of obedience, which is acquired by the human through the active manifesting of the truth of Being in one's body.

105   Ibid., II.25.

of her perception as physiologically conditioned and thereby attends to the One whose perceiving is self-contingent, unchanged by nothing external — God. (Ironically for Gregory, attending to the passions of the body is more akin to a flight from sense perception, as the senses are given that the human might realize her contingent relation to God — her *natural nature*.[106] The senses are given as a bride-companion for the human's ascending of the mountain.[107])

CAN GOD HAVE FRIENDS?

The understanding of spiritual sensibility outlined above is an awareness of human perception conditioned and informed by one's participation in the life of God in the world. Aligning human perception to spiritual sensibility entails, as aforesaid, a becoming in likeness to what the human is as created in the image of God. It should come as no surprise, then, that the fathers of the church, evidenced most notably with Gregory of Nyssa, understood this virtuous ascent to be a continuous revealing of who God is and how God relates to creation. How the human relates to God and all others is to be analogous to the inter-relatedness of the Persons of the Holy Trinity.

What it means for God to be God, following the early fathers of the church, is to exist as a mutual adoration and service of inter-Trinitarian self-offering. That is, the Son is the eternal worship of the Father and the Father of the Son, and both of the Spirit and the Spirit of Father and Son.[108] The Persons of the Trinity relate one to another in mutual obedience and penetration of love in the giving of the Son to the Father and the Father to the Son, which is the reciprocal giving and receiving in and of the self-same Spirit. God hereby lacks nothing, not even his own worship.[109] The mutually submissive Persons of the One Substance

---

106 Maximus, *Ambiguum 7*, 1084D.
107 Gregory of Nyssa, *The Life of Moses*, II.157.
108 Irenaeus, *Against Heresies*, IV.vii.3.
109 Pierre de Bérulle is known as having stated that God lacks only his own worship. However, as Irenaeus reminds us, even this is complete and not lacking in the Godhead. See note above. See also John Milbank, "Sophiology and Theurgy: The New Theological Horizon," in Pabst and Schneider, *Encounters Between Eastern Orthodoxy and Radical Orthodoxy* (New York: Routledge, 2009), 80.

offer to one another their distinctive selfhoods. The Father's giving of himself to the Son and the Son's receiving of the Father is the shared gift that is the Spirit. Reciprocal love and mutual submission occurs in the Son's return to the Father and the Father's reception of the Son, which is the gift-giving, active-being that is the same Spirit.[110] The eternal Person of the Spirit names the endless procession of the giving and receiving of God from and through himself in the Personhoods of Father and Son.

The subsisting persons of the Trinity give to each their own property, receiving from the other the same. Each Person of the Trinity, then, knows itself only in light of its being-known by each subsisting Person. The Father knows himself as Father only to the extent that the Son knows the Father as *his* Father. Likewise, the Son knows himself as Son only to the extent that the Father knows the Son as *his* Son. This knowing is made possible by the Spirit who, following Augustine, separates the Father to know the Son as Son and for the Son to know the Father as Father. One receives Personhood — identity — in being-known by the other subsisting Persons.

With Maximus Confessor, the elevation of grace over nature discloses how it is that this knowledge is made available to humanity. It is through grace that the human comes to know her true nature,[111] as one cannot arrive at this knowledge by any other way save the divine illumination of the Spirit.[112] For the human to know herself as human she must, through grace, come to know her nature in being-known by the eternal Son.[113]

> The one who knows the meaning of the mystery and who is so incessantly lifted up both in work and in word through all things until he acquires what is sent down to him is likewise a messenger of the great plan of God... [Christ] underwent in

110 The active-being here described is not unlike the account of Divine Sophia expounded in Michael Martin, *The Submerged Reality: Sophiology and the Turn to a Poetic Metaphysics* (Brooklyn: Angelico Press, 2015).

111 Maximus, *Chapters on Knowledge*, II.21.

112 Ibid., II.24.

113 Ibid., II.60.

himself through the incarnation as man our future destiny. Let the one who is moved by a love of knowledge mystically rejoice in learning of the great destiny he has promised to those who love the Lord.[114]

The human's identity rests in its being-known by Mind,[115] thereby learning of her subsistent nature, having been moved *beyond* her own nature by grace. Grace transforms human nature, not into something unnatural, but into what is at once so deeply and thoroughly human that it is more than human because it engages all of nature with the same gracious reciprocity by which God the Son has adopted human nature. The worshipper realizes herself as a participant in the grace that gathers her into the being-known of God, whereby the subject-object relation coalesces in divine unity. The Father is not the subject whose object is the Son, nor is the Son a subject whose object is the Father, and neither is the Spirit to Father or Son. Subject-object relations qualify the temporal *exchanges* between created beings.[116] Humans are divisible, whereas God is complete oneness.[117] The Persons of the Holy Trinity do not name divisibility within the Godhead, but rather bespeak the mysterious nature of eternal erotic-knowing. As will be explored further in chapter four, there is no objectivity in God or between God and creation; rather, as *actus purus* God's act of knowing gathers the known into the triune being-known, whereby the human who is known is known as part of God's own self-knowing. God deigns to involve

114   Ibid., II.23–24.
115   Ibid., II.22.
116   This, it must be remembered, is a recent development in human history, articulated in the late 14th century when the human becomes a "subject" whose experiences are subjective rather than collective. The field of knowledge is altered forever. Such knowing is made possible only by way of creating an ontological division between corporeal and incorporeal realms. Eric Voegelin argues that this begins to happen ideologically with the shift from pantheism to Christian monotheism during the reign of Theodosius in the late 4th and early 5th centuries. He remarks that Celsus criticized Christianity, stating that it brought with it a "de-divinization" of the world. By destroying the local divinities of each culture Christianity destroyed national and local culture. See Eric Voegelin, *The New Science of Politics, an Introduction* (Chicago: University of Chicago Press, 1952), Chapter 3.
117   Maximus, *Ambiguum 7*, in *On the Cosmic Mystery of Jesus Christ*, 7.4.

the human in his own agency and action. The human is hereby not an object of divine love or knowing; rather, the human, whose personhood remains intact — the human is not absorbed into divinity but is, analogous to Christ, unconfusedly united — stands within the action of God, an action that is also the internal principle (*logos*) of human nature.

The human gains such knowledge through the Son's descent. But to know the Son, the human must first know this eternal Person as flesh. In knowing the Word made flesh, the human comes to know the eternal nature of God the Son. This knowing, however, first comes through the human's being-known as flesh[118] by the all-knowing eternal One. Knowledge — God — makes *himself* knowable through his being-known to *himself* as both human and divine. God hereby knows *himself* as God by nature, fully and eternally complete, yet by grace knows *himself* in being-known to himself as divine-human permeation. Human nature is adopted into the divine self-knowing through Christ's Incarnation — the gracious condescension of mutually permeating natures, divine and human, in God. For the human not to know herself in light of God's own self-knowing, then, is to know neither God nor oneself. *Created in the image of God* is revealed only in *the* Image — Christ, the *mutual communication* that God makes available by *his* being-known. God is his own being-known, as it were, who receives his identity from *himself* through *his* own love and offering of *himself* to *himself*. God knows *himself* only as *he* is known by *himself*.[119]

The life of God is not that which unfolds in time; rather, the life of God gathers time into God's own being-known. Love is not deposited into humanity or creation. These and all things are gathered into Love and only in this sense can there be love. Accordingly, created love is always in some sense passive. Only God is active Love, for God *is* Love. Love does demand willed participation of the created in uncreated Love.[120] Only in this sense can human action be understood. Human

---

118   PG 44.804A–808B.

119   Irenaeus, *Against Heresies*, iv.6.3–6.7 (ANF).

120   "Demand," here, is to be understood as a sort of non-compulsory compulsion, whereby love is absolutely free in its giving but receiving the free Love God *is* requires a return — a non-identical reciprocal engagement.

activity can be both willed and unwilled; it can be for good or evil; and it can rejoice in Christ who makes all action intelligible or it can negate the truth of Christ.

Situating this dialogue of love in the context of friendship with God also clarifies Aristotle's rejection of the human capacity for friendship with God. Aristotle is precisely correct: friendship with God is impossible.[121] Only God can love and know God. "Depart from me for I never knew you"[122] could be read as Jesus's declaration of this reality. What does not participate in the love of God in Christ is not assimilated to Christ, and, therefore, is *unknown* to God. God cannot love what is not united — assimilated — to the Son.

God in Christ assimilates human nature to himself that the human might participate in the love of God, in the eternal friendship God is. It is here that Aquinas both rightly and wrongly employs Aristotle's *Metaphysics*. For Aristotle, God is absolutely transcendent, and because friendship requires community such a bond is impossible between what is unchangeable and what is changeable. God himself is subsistent thought; God cannot think outside of God. That is, God cannot think not-God, which is why creation is to be understood as always existing as a portion of God and within God, such that the changeable — created life — is eternally being-changed into God. The changeable enters into subsistence with the unchanging at creation. This inherent lovability of God's portion within human nature is the dignity of humanity.

It is with John of Damascus that this subsistent knowing gains full force. Drawing on Gregory of Nazianzen, Gregory of Nyssa, Basil the Great, Denys the Areopagite, Maximus, and others, the Damascene weaves together the finest of thread from each of the great theologians. For the Damascene, when the Father, who is the primal cause of all things, speaks, his spoken Word subsists with him.

---

121 Aristotle, *Nicomachean Ethics*, VIII.7, in Barnes, ed., *Complete Works of Aristotle*, vol. II.
122 Matthew 7:23.

Because our nature is mortal and subject to dissolution, for this reason our speech is non-subsistent. But, since God is existing always and is perfect, His Word must be always existing, living, perfect, distinctly subsistent, and having all things that His Begetter has. Now, our speech in proceeding from our mind is not entirely distinct from it. For, in so far as it comes from the mind, it is something distinct from it; whereas, in so far as it reveals the mind itself, it is not entirely distinct from it. Actually, it is identical with it in nature while distinct from it in its subject. Similarly, the Word of God, in so far as He subsists in Himself, is distinct from Him from whom He has His subsistence. But, since He exhibits in Himself those same things which are discerned in God, then in His nature He is identical with God. For, just as perfection in all things is to be found in the Father, so is it also to be found in the Word begotten of Him.[123]

Unlike created persons, whose words dissolve in their speaking, the Person of the Son subsists and is differentiated from him from whom he derives subsistence. The Son is begotten by the Father through the procession of the Spirit. It is the Spirit that resides "between the unbegotten and begotten, and [is] united to the Father through the Son."[124] The Spirit hereby subsists eternally with both Father and Son,

a substantial power found in its own individuating personality, proceeding from the Father, coming to rest in the Word and declaring Him, not separated from God in essence or from the Word with whom it is associated, having might, not dissipated away into non-existence, but distinctly subsistent like the Word—living, endowed with will, self-moving, active, at all times willing good, exercising His power for the prosecution of every design in accordance with His will, without beginning and without end. For the Word fell short of the

123 John of Damascus, *Orthodox Faith*, i.6.
124 Ibid., i.13.

Father in nothing, and the Spirit did not fall short of the Word in anything.[125]

The Spirit is the eternal differentiating bond with whom the Father and Son subsist and *are* Reciprocity—eternal, erotic being-known.

In speaking, the Father gives the Son his Sonship. This giving is the Spirit, who receives its Spiritship in the procession from the Father through the Word's return to its cause—the Father. It is in this begetting and proceeding that the Father knows himself as Father. The Son's receiving of Sonship from the Father and the Son's return to the Father makes known to the Spirit the Spirit's own identity as gift-giving-giver—as the procession from the Father to the Son and through the Son as return to the Father. This eternal knowing of the subsisting Persons of the Godhead in no way alters or surprises either Person. Reciprocal knowing is who God is.

It is this knowing that occurs in the incarnate relation of the two natures of Christ. The Son, in uniting divinity and humanity in Jesus through the Spirit, permeates human nature with divinity. This permeation of the human nature *causes* Jesus to know himself only as subsisting in the eternal relation that is Father, Spirit, Son. Christ's human nature in turn permeates divinity by God the Son's entering into relation with human nature.[126] And, just as Jesus hereby knows himself by divine permeation, so also does the Son know himself in relation to the subsisting human nature of Jesus. This is a mutual communication, says John of Damascus: "each nature communicates its own properties to the other through the identity of their person and their *mutual immanence.*"[127] It is the "mutual immanence" of the Son of God (divinity) and the Son of Man (humanity) that names the entrance of the human into the eternal knowing of each Person of the Triune God with the other two subsisting, eternal Persons. God graciously refuses to know

125 Ibid., i.7. See also Maximus, *Chapters on Knowledge*, II.20–25, from which it appears that John of Damascus draws.

126 This language is following John of Damascus, Son of God as Divinity qua Divinity, Son of Man as Human Nature qua Human Nature.

127 John of Damascus, *Orthodox Faith*, iii.4, italics mine.

himself apart from his being-known by the human nature of Christ. That is, God refuses to know *himself* as Trinity apart from the incorporation of humanity into subsistent, eternal interpenetration, for though the divine action and permeation precedes human permeation of the divine, it permeates divinity nonetheless, and both without confusion.

Christ, the union of the Word of God and human flesh, is the revelation of both the equality of the Divine Persons of the Trinity and the drawing of humanity into erotic-knowing. John of Damascus tirelessly makes this point throughout his *De Fide Orthodoxa*. He examines the union and distinction of the two natures within the one person, Jesus. The flesh of Christ is permeated by divinity, which enables his human nature to permeate divinity as well.

> Because of the hypostatic union the flesh is said to have been deified, to have become God and of the same divinity with the Word; at the same time God the Word is said to have been made flesh, to have become man, to be declared a creature and called last. This is not because the two natures were transformed into one compound nature — it is impossible for contradictory natural qualities to exist together in one nature — but because they were hypostatically united and indwell mutually one in the other without confusion or transformation. The mutual indwelling, however, did not come from the flesh, but from the divinity, because it is inconceivable that the flesh should indwell the divinity — rather, at once the divine nature indwelt the flesh, it gave the flesh this same ineffable mutual indwelling, which, indeed, we call union.[128]

However, humanity, unlike the subsisting persons of the Trinity, though marked by divinity with the *imago Dei* (internal), nevertheless receives this permeating capacity from the Creator (external); the permeability of the created is not generative but derivative.[129] Human nature

---

128   John of Damascus, *Orthodox Faith*, 4.18.

129   Ibid. John continues to delicately walk this tightrope as to how God is penetrated by creation, making the clear point that it is God who initiates contact. Because it is God

must receive the deifying grace of the Holy Spirit, that which substantiates the union of the unconfused natures of Christ. It is hereby that God can be both eternally impassible and yet procure salvation through a passible body.[130] This mutual permeation does not, however, elicit change in the Godhead. The begetting of the Son does not come as a surprise to the Father; rather, the erotic knowing as known by the second hypostasis is *an eternal event* in God. Permeation as well is not to be understood as a new occurrence but rather names the very state of creation in its continually being-created. Human nature is gathered into triune reciprocity through the cross on that eternal day of creation. Humankind is by nature, then, a participant in erotic knowing, which is the *created in the image of God*. The human is designed for the mutual permeation essential to its nature. The realization of this endowment of grace as *created in the image of God*, however, occurs through a willed becoming in likeness by the non-compulsory participation in compulsory grace.

Humanity comes to understand this, says John of Damascus, through Christ's full embrace of human nature. Though the sayings and actions of Jesus seem to confuse the shared life of the Son with the Father, one is made to understand that the seemingly contradictory words of Jesus, most notably the cry from the cross, are solely for the efficacy of human understanding.[131] They are not, as the Damascene makes clear, to be understood as revealing some kind of hidden knowledge the Father has to which the Son is not privy, nor as an accusation by the Son against the Father. God's forsaking of God on the cross reveals the eternal constituting of humanity in kenotic reciprocity. God empties himself to assimilate divinity to humanity, which establishes humanity in divinity. This is the wisdom of Athanasius: "God became what we were so we might become what he is."

---

who initiates the relation it is God who permeates God from creation, which enables creation to enjoy the mutual permeation of the divine life through volitive participation, but such participation is always secondary to God's own self-relating to which creation is assimilated by Christ. "The mutual indwelling," he says, "did not come from the flesh, but from the divinity," for when "the divine nature indwelt the flesh, it gave the flesh this same ineffable mutual indwelling, which, indeed, we call union."

130   Ibid.
131   Ibid.

This knowledge, or more appropriately *way of knowing*, is not to be reduced to a perspectival understanding whereby liturgy is a didactic, habit-forming ritual that grants the human a new way of seeing the tree in the forest. Rather, it is an ontological transelementing of human nature that opens the knower to an engagement with all things in the same manner that God in Christ has opened himself to the vulnerability of divine-human permeation.[132] It is *knowledge by contact*, by participation in the being-known of God. As God in Christ refuses to know *himself* as Trinity apart from the Son's assimilation to human nature, likewise through liturgy is the human made to reject any form of existence that relieves her from the mutual binding of the whole of humanity in Christ. It is true that even trees will look different according to this *way of knowing*, as every tree becomes for the Christian that which points beyond itself to the tree of life once stained by the blood of God. The cross grants to trees their transformed nature as something that extends human life, and inasmuch as it does extend human life it is a type. To the extent that a tree is not used *for the life of the world*, it ceases to abide analogously. Any element of creation that is used against its transelementation in Christ — used not to extend life to creation — is sin.[133] This *way of knowing* is the human's participation in becoming what God is, made possible, as Athanasius taught, by virtue of God's becoming what the human is.

In Christ, the Spirit fuses together humanity and divinity in subsistent, eternal reciprocity of permeating knowledge, whereby each is known only in its being-known in the Spirit by the other subsisting Persons. The entrance of human nature into subsistent relation does not, however, establish a kind of demigod or fourth hypostasis of the

132 Cyril of Alexandria, "Commentary on John," 96b–97b, in Norman Russell, trans., *Cyril of Alexandria* (London: Routledge, 2000).

133 I will not get into theodicy here and describe what this might mean for tsunamis, earthquakes, or other natural disasters; it is only to say that all of creation has been transformed by the cross of Christ, which exacts a particular form of human engagement with the whole of creation. A base example of this would be to say that any arrow made from the wood of a tree, if it is used to pierce the body of a man, does not participate in the *way of knowing* into which Christ has incorporated the world. If a tree is cut down to provide wood for the fire upon which meat will be cooked and prepared for a family, the tree is participating in its truth (though the vegan might disagree).

Trinity. Human nature enters into subsistence with the Second Hypostasis of the Trinity—assimilation. Following, as each Person of the triune God subsists in the other, and as the action of one is ascribed to all,[134] humanity subsists in the Father and Spirit, assimilated, as it is, to the Son. The Father, then, does not simply know himself as Father of the eternal Son with whom he subsists, but knows himself as Father in relation to the assimilated natures of Christ, both human and divine. Through the eternal Son, the Father is united with humanity, and likewise the Spirit,[135] as the subsisting Persons remain one divinity, assimilated without confusion to human nature.

This ontological identity of humanity as expressed by the fathers of the church is made available in and sustained by liturgical action. Liturgy creates and sustains humanity—the human as a participant in the being-known of God through Christ the Liturgy. Its particular form breeds a particular people. Liturgy is theology, and theology is liturgy. That is, *lex orandi, lex credendi, est lex credendi, lex orandi.*[136] However, this claim is only to be understood in the specific sense that the liturgical action is that which constitutes theology—the conditions for doing theology, as it were. Likewise, credo or theological articulation of the faith is incapable of abstraction from liturgical action. Theological articulation always arises out of the particular *body schema* of the church. No prayer, no theology.

To believe is to know through action. Action precedes thought. Action makes thought possible. As Aquinas says regarding faith and action, "Just as man assents to first principles, by the natural light of his intellect, so does a virtuous man, by the habit of virtue, judge aright of things concerning that virtue."[137] As created, humankind is

---

134 Cyril of Alexandria, *Commentary on John*, 97c–e.

135 Ibid., 96d–e.

136 This will be explored further in chapter three regarding liturgy as theology and theology as liturgy. In each instance, whether it is the rule of prayer and faith or liturgical action and theological articulation, each is capable of being differentiated but must always be understood as an inseparable part of a whole way of being and becoming. See Alexander Schmemann, *Introduction to a Liturgical Theology* (Crestwood: St Vladimir's Seminary Press, 2003).

137 Aquinas, *Summa Theologiae*, II-II.2.4.

endowed with a natural light, an innate ability to think and reflect on that which crosses one's path. Nevertheless, to judge aright is to participate in that which is judged. With regard to knowing the truth of faith, this is acquired only through a supernatural participation in divine goodness.[138] Within the liturgical economy knowing does not occur abstractly. Knowledge is not ethereal but occurs through material engagement with the God who transubstantiates himself in bread and wine and transelements human nature through assimilating human nature to *himself*.[139] This is the knowledge Paul refers to that occurs through participation in the sufferings of Christ and being made like him in his death.[140] Character and cognition go hand in hand.

This is most explicit in the Letter to the Hebrews, where the writer states clearly that it is the disciplined child of God, the one who pursues peace with everyone, the one who lives the life of holiness, who "will see the Lord."[141] To see God is to see the Lord made manifest in the actions of holy disciplines. It is a knowledge that inebriates the senses with the passion of Christ, participation in which brings the human to know her true self—her natural nature—as Christ's christ.[142]

CONCLUSION

Knowledge of one's natural nature as *imago Dei* is a knowledge by contact, a knowing whereby knower and known become increasingly one in a likeness of activity—one in the act of knowing, of being-known. With great clarity, the earliest Christians articulate that knowing who God is first requires apprehending oneself in Christ through willed participation in God's assimilating human nature to divinity. It is a matter of proximity, as well as an awareness of one's being incorporated into divine action. The double meaning is implied and must become explicit in the modern world: the human is continually *being incorporated* into

---

138   Ibid.
139   Cyril of Alexandria, *Commentary on John*, 96b–97b.
140   Philippians 3.
141   Hebrews 12:14.
142   Casel, *The Mystery of Christian Worship*, 14.

Christ the Liturgy by the grace of God and by her willed participation in it; accordingly, the human's *being* is incorporated into what it means for God to be God. The unconfused union within God the Son hereby extends to human nature in general.

Students of scholasticism are to understand that this is in no way to suggest, as does John Duns Scotus, that God and humans both participate in Being, a shared substance of the two — univocity of Being. Briefly, in the late thirteenth century, John Duns Scotus introduces the notion of a univocity of being, whereby God and humanity are subject to the "metaphysical priority of Being."[143] Scotus stresses a radical distance of the human from God that introduces, says Catherine Pickstock, an abandonment of participatory relating.[144] God and humanity relate to one another not through manifesting encounters of the material world but by a contractual relation of divine and human willing or sovereign voluntarism.[145] Pickstock shows how Scotus relativizes the material, creating a sharp division between matter and form, and divorces form from any necessary attachments at all. Objects for Scotus become independent of their material, which means that an object can be known whether or not it actually exists.[146] Perhaps the most pressing consequence of Scotus's severing of form and content is the consequential elimination of telos. By prioritizing intellection and sovereign will, governed by the forces of contractual obligation, Scotus asserts that the creative will of God is independent from the telos of the material world.[147] In other words, creation is in no way

143 Pickstock, *After Writing*, 121–66. See also Conor Cunningham, *Genealogy of Nihilism: Philosophies of Nothing and the Difference of Theology* (London: Routledge, 2002), 28–56.

144 See p. 34, note 104.

145 Pickstock, *After Writing*, 122–66.

146 Duns Scotus, *Ordinatio*, I.5. Scotus sections off physics from metaphysics, noting the absurdity of physics as the beginning of metaphysics. However, Scotus fails to acknowledge that "physics as the beginning point of metaphysics" is the human condition. This denial of human understanding as first sensible, as is shown above in Gregory of Nyssa, transgresses the progression of knowledge in the created order and stifles Scotus's ability to connect the two, which renders his account of Being implausible.

147 Mary Beth Ingham and Mechthild Dreyer, *The Philosophical Vision of John Duns Scotus: An Introduction* (Washington: Catholic University of America Press, 2004), 38–51.

contingent upon God; rather, the only relationship between the two exists as momentary events through which God intervenes in creation, what Pickstock calls the "fiat of divine volition." By displacing the contingent relation of creation to its Creator, Scotus also displaces act and being within God, such that God's actions, God's essence, and the material relating by God to creation are now arbitrary, which also means that we cannot infer one movement to the next—each action is connected only by divine, sovereign choice.[148] While the early fathers of the church always confessed an inability to know the essence of God, there was also a clear recognition that humans can know God by his energies, by the ways God makes himself manifest in creation. By these energies, we are able to infer certain things about God, as well as acknowledge patterns of behavior with God. "God's property is always to have mercy," for instance, is an inference from Rite I of the *Book of Common Prayer*. It is derived from scripture and attested to by the love of God experienced by Christians over the centuries. It is a reminder that God, who is full and complete in himself, has no need for retribution or compensation when humans screw up—satisfaction theories of atonement are hereby dismissed. While Christians apophatically confess that we cannot know God's properties, we kataphatically confess by the nature of God's revelation in Christ and through God's interconnectedness to the world that God is Love.[149]

The problem with the deistic God of Duns Scotus and others who would follow after is that, in theory, God could just as well relate to humanity in the flesh of Christ as he could in the metal of a modern dinner table. The form no longer bears an inner logic nor does the content have an essential form. Scotus's claim, as Pickstock shows, is that the material "thing" is inconsequential to human knowing. Even if we are conditioned by the tangible, it is not the tangible that is proper to our intellection.[150]

---

148 Pickstock, *After Writing*, 137. This is also the claim of Apocalyptic Theology, whereby God "erupts" in time, but each eruption is arbitrary and bears no essential relation to any event before or after the current.

149 1 John 4:8.

150 Ingham and Dreyer, *The Philosophical Vision of John Duns Scotus*, 38–51.

As I have suggested above, following a renewed understanding of the participatory nature of liturgical action, the unconfused union of natures in Christ is an extension of God's eternal act of creating—the Eternal Liturgy. As Creator, God is actively involved and intimately connected to creation. Creation is not random; rather, all of creation, as a portion of God, manifests to varying degrees the God who is. The human, intimately united to the Second Person of the Trinity and a portion of divinity, is caught up into the erotic-knowing of God, a gratuitous participant in Love and Grace. In proportion to her likeness to Christ the human is re-assimilated to the image and purpose for which she is created.

3

The Architecture of Faith

No one thinks he has to learn how to see.

Edward T. Hall

I cannot imagine any pattern of events without imagining a place where it is happening.

Christopher Alexander

INTRODUCTION

In *A Timeless Way of Building*, Christopher Alexander describes the porous relation between humans and the architectural structures we humans inhabit. We are not affected, says Alexander, merely by each other and the numerous activities surrounding us or in which we engage each day. As embodied creatures we exist within a complex web of relations and events, both human and non-human, which affects the character of a place and, accordingly, the character of its inhabitants.

> The sunshine shining on the windowsill, the wind blowing in the grass are events too — they affect us just as much as social events. Any combination of events, which has a bearing on our lives — an actual physical effect on us — affects our lives.[1]

When that first glimmer of spring descends upon the faces of northern bodies bludgeoned by the cold of winter, a transformation occurs. A new disposition is acquired. The snow begins to be perceived differently and the longer days stir life up again, and no matter how many times this cycle repeats itself it is ever new and always transformative. It is this spatial event that Alexander evokes; it is the recognition that everything we understand to be objectively occurring in our minds is

1 Christopher Alexander, *The Timeless Way of Building* (New York: Oxford University Press, 1979), 64.

actually contingent, richly attached to the world we inhabit, a world as simple and complex as the spaces and people in which and with whom we move. If we desire to understand the life that occurs in a building or town, "we must therefore try to understand the structure of the space itself."[2] We are affected and affecting, and recognizing our affective nature is the first step toward understanding.

But what has any of this to do with Liturgy? The first task of any exploration in liturgical studies, historical or theological, is to make explicit what should be understood as axiomatic, and that is this: the *structure of life is life*. This is to suggest that the spatial structures we inhabit and the practices by which we inhabit them, as well as those with whom we relate in our environments, are modalities of contingency that incline us to perceive, and thereby understand, what it means to be (alive). We are *involved*, to greater and lesser degrees, with each person, place, or thing. This is what it means to be human. It is to be vulnerable. It is, as Charles Taylor has reminded us, poignantly reiterated by James K. A. Smith, to be "*open* to an outside,"[3] open to a shared agency, an agency shared by the plethora of people, places, and things we find ourselves with or in on any given day.

This openness of human nature is a porous relationality with the world—with that which is "external" to the human. We always precede ourselves, as it were.[4] We are pre-disposed to the numerous encounters we face each moment of the day. The emotional register a person has to another's comment or action is not a simple, momentary reaction to a specific statement or activity. Rather, our response is always *from* somewhere; it is constructed.[5] We might think of the following analogy:

---

2   Ibid., 74.

3   James K. A. Smith, *How (Not) To Be Secular* (Grand Rapids: Wm. B. Eerdmans Publishing Co., 2014), 29.

4   See Giorgio Agamben, "Vocation and Voice," in *Qui Parle*, vol. 10, no. 2 (Durham: Duke University Press, Spring/Summer 1997), 89–100.

5   Sarah Feldman Barrett, *How Emotions Are Made* (New York: Houghton Mifflin Harcourt Publishing, 2017), 84–111.

A family's dog was killed by a car in front of their house. They had heard that dog meat was delicious, so they cut up the dog's body and cooked it and ate it for dinner.[6]

Chances are you just grimaced and experienced at least a little disgust at the thought of eating your family pet, especially if you are a happy dog owner. Nevertheless, your repulsion is not merely because you do not enjoy the taste of dog—certainly we all do; rather, your aversion to eating the flesh of a dog, as opposed to a cow, pig, chicken, lamb, or fish, has everything to do with the understood relationship a person has with his or her domesticated animal. This relationship is inscribed on us as persons involved in the wider social body, which rests upon us whether we are pet owners or not. This is what some philosophers have called our "thrownness." It is what we take as a given that we may not even know that we take as given. The emotional register, then, manifests our *thrownness*—our pre-disposition; it manifests what we understand in our bodies before we become aware of it in thought. The knee-jerk reaction that we experience in relation to eating the family pet, riding a rollercoaster, the homeless person we see lying on the sidewalk, or greeting the person who stabbed us in the back last week, is always processed through a perceptive filter—our background or horizon of experience—of which we are never completely aware, and of which we cannot be fully aware in the instance of a particular encounter.

It is in this way that cultural norms are inscribed on us, and are so to such a degree that we cannot help but take them for granted—without knowing, even, that we have taken them for granted. Every encounter, then, is conditioned by how we have come to inhabit the world—by how our world inhabits us—by the totality of our experience up to the point of this or that present encounter, which is inseparable from the spaces in which we live and move on a daily basis. Every person is affected by the space he or she inhabits, conditioning us to inhabit a space according to its structure.

6   Jonathan Haidt, *The Righteous Mind* (New York: Random House, Inc., 2012), 26.

For example, our family's kitchen is situated some distance from the living room, connected by a long hallway, and between them sits a large dining room accessible through an old butler pantry and foyer, with each hallway and room capable of being closed off from the other by sets of doors. This layout suggests that the original family (1907) occupying the home had someone outside the home, or someone other than its primary inhabitants, preparing the meals. The swinging door of the butler pantry, original to the home, also assumes that someone came in and out of the pantry to serve those who sat in the dining room. This spatial arrangement works against the atmosphere we now attempt to create as dwellers in the home. By placing a dinner table in our kitchen, however, we have been able to re-narrate the space of the house according to the movement of our family. Our full-size table in the kitchen restructures the space itself, without which we could not faithfully inhabit the space. Even so, the distance between the stove of the kitchen and the hearth of the living room — the modern space for conversation or, more often than not, entertainment — remains a difficult boundary to transgress. Were these rooms connected in the manner of an open-concept home or in the manner of the older home where the hearth was at the center, the flow of life would come more naturally for our family, as opposed to being border walls we are continually negotiating.

The description above is to show, in the specific example of our home, how space determines the conditions of possibility for how our family inhabits this particular house as home. It delimits movement based on its walls, doorways, size of the rooms, etc. It also opens up certain possibilities that, should we give ourselves to them fully, may form us in unanticipated and, perhaps, fruitful ways. Admittedly, this is always happening under the radar, as it were, and it is impossible to account for every influence of a structure on its inhabitants. What is crucial to note, as we will discuss further below, is how the particularity of the space a person inhabits inclines her to think and move along certain lines, even determining the pace of our stride or uprightness of our posture, along with corresponding emotional state.

THE POROSITY OF SPACE

Researchers have only recently begun to explore the impact of architecture on the human psyche. What is interesting, however, is that without digging too far beneath the surface to understand the long-term effects of space on human cognition, we know that people's behavior changes in relation to the space they inhabit. For instance, Jan Gehl has observed that people walk more quickly in front of buildings with blank façades.[7] James Danckert and Colleen Merrifield have found in their work on cognitive neuroscience that people who visually take in a "boring" environment, for instance the plain frontage of a Wal-Mart store or the shadowy glass exterior of a Whole Foods, develop increased levels of cortisol, the stress hormone related to heart disease and diabetes.[8] Not only this, but Canadian psychologist Donald Hebb has discovered that rats living in enriched environments are markedly more intelligent than those that live in more "Spartan" environs.[9]

If architecture affects our hormones and intellect, how might it affect belief? This is not just to ask what a building tells us about a community's beliefs about God. We know that the clear window panes of a Presbyterian or Congregationalist Church evoke the direct revelation of the Light who has come into the world, whereas the stained glass windows in an Anglican/Episcopal or Roman Catholic Church remind churchgoers of the inability to see God directly, that life with God is a mystery. Erwin Panofksy argued long ago that a church building is itself a theological argument. The question that concerns us here, however, is not so much the messages intended by the interior trappings of a church, but the sensorial effect of one window versus another, wooden pews versus moveable chairs, an east-facing altar versus a west-facing one, and so on, and how these affect a worshipper's understanding of her relationship with God and other—that is, how spaces of worship condition a person's understanding of her relatedness to God. It is not simply to ask what is the theological witness of the space, as important as this may be, but to ask, how does the space "work on" the

7   Collin Ellard, *Places of the Heart* (New York: Bellevue Literary Press, 2015), 109.
8   Ibid., 107–24.
9   Ibid.

worshipper, even, or especially, under the radar of human awareness? And, how might the space affect human sensibility in the absence of liturgical action? That is, how does a space affect our understanding of worship when the liturgical action is not actively underway as a person walks through the building?

To get at these and other questions, let us take a somewhat unexpected detour within architecture and design and explore the modern showroom and office space, which are increasingly redesigned and restructured based on *psychogeographic studies*.[10] A good deal of research and study has been conducted to understand the nature of human consumption and productivity. What are the factors involved in an executive buying this office furniture as opposed to that? What kind of workplace environment lends itself to more creative and productive employees? In a market driven by consumption, productivity and adaptability are among the chiefest of virtues.

The HNI design group, which works with a variety of furniture manufacturers, sells much more than furniture, design concepts, or coordinated office space. They sell "wellbeing." In HNI's promotion booklet, in the "Common Room" section, which features high-end furniture from Gunlocke, HBF, and more, HNI urges companies to "create a climate of wellbeing by encouraging individuals to step away, whether it's to see a friendly face or steal a quiet moment." The move toward "wellbeing" in the modern workplace endeavors to transform workers into "knowledge workers."[11] Knowledge workers are defined as "people who are paid to think." Leaders, designers, researchers, architects, software designers, engineers, writers, film producers, and others like them fall into this category. Every job involves knowledge and thinking, but the knowledge worker is someone whose productivity is defined as "less tangible" than, say, a construction worker or seamstress in a factory.[12] It is not in the scope of this essay to deal with the problems of such

---

10   *Psychogeographic* is an area of research that focuses on how an environment affects an individual's emotions and behavior. Guy Debord coined the term in 1955.

11   Andrew Mawson, *The Six Factors of Knowledge Worker Productivity* (Muscateen, IA: Allsteel).

12   Ibid.

distinctions between "knowledge workers" and other workers. Here we limit ourselves to the spatial configuration that is developed to incite or even elicit creative thinking.

Andrew Mawson, the Founding Director of Advanced Workplace Associates (AWA) in London, has labored to apply academic research to the modern workplace, showing how social cohesion in the workplace translates directly into commercial value.[13] In an attempt to pinpoint "knowledge work productivity," AWA reviewed over 800 research studies related to "knowledge worker productivity and the elements which could affect it."[14] In so doing, AWA identified six factors that increase "knowledge work productivity": Social Cohesion, Perceived Supervisory Support, Information Sharing and the Transactive Memory System, Vision and Goal Clarity, External Communication, and Trust. Together the six factors serve to describe what Mawson calls a "social infrastructure."[15]

Briefly, Social Cohesion refers to the fusion of each individual's knowledge, experiences, and relationships with others in an organization. It seeks to address the interrelatedness of co-workers. Perceived Supervisory Support is the employees' felt sense that they matter and that they can rely on their supervisors for support and encouragement. This occurs when supervisors proactively develop relationships with those in their charge, using positive rather than fear-based management. Information Sharing and the Transactive Memory System is about "short-circuiting" between individuals and teams to utilize each person's skills and knowledge, as opposed to constantly reinventing the wheel. It is a matter of feeling free to share information across organizational lines without fear of judgment or fear of how it may affect an employee's future with the organization. Vision and Goal Clarity has to do with the common understanding of an organization's objectives, so that workers can be "emotionally engaged" in their work.[16] Exter-

---

13 Ibid., 19.
14 Ibid., 37.
15 Ibid., 44.
16 Ibid., 29. "Emotional engagement" is an interesting phrase, as it suggests an attachment to one's work as familial. There is an expressed desire to treat the office space as a home away from home, and many office cafés and break-rooms are beginning to look more and more like a kitchen you might find in today's modern homes.

nal Communication has to do with exposure to others and the ideas of others who are not associated with their team or organization. It is a matter of being exposed to the outside, so that employees do not become stuck in the tiny world of their individual projects, but learn to adapt and learn from unexpected connections. Trust, perhaps the most difficult, is the recognition that "people need to feel that those around them will act in their interest."[17] It is a matter of trusting in another's ability and reliability and how they will use a co-worker's ideas.

The six factors noted above can be gleaned from all manner of organizational models for increased worker productivity, perhaps with even more and alternatively named factors. For our purposes, it is important to note the relationship between the six factors and the particular spatial dynamic of a work place environment identified by AWA.

For instance, if people in an organization sit next to the same people all day every day, they are going to become more cohesive, especially if some effort is made to become so. However, if this cohesion is limited to a small group's desk alignment, the cohesion can become detrimental to the overall organization's productivity. Enabling or even compelling people to sit in different places from time to time, developing new friendships, sharing ideas, and more can promote greater *social cohesion* throughout the whole of the organization. Some executives have even organized "desk bingo" to ensure that this happens. From a design perspective, Mawson shows how simple things can be done to encourage cohesion: creating shared spaces on each floor of a building, designing cafés that encourage lingering and conversation, and using round tables in meeting rooms and social spaces, which aid eye contact and promote involvement in the conversation. Workplaces should also be designed, says Mawson, so that leaders can sit with different members of the team every day, allowing support and coaching and for a team to get to know its supervisor better. Each contributes to a worker's *perception of supervisory support*. For *information sharing and transactive memory* it is important that colleagues have spaces of collective experience: providing teams with their own wall or writing

---

17   Ibid., 35.

board, or having differing meeting spaces across a building with unique names — Facebook's New York office, for instance, has labels such as *Snuggie, Shake Weight,* and *Thigh Master.* Names contribute to our memory of a place, connecting discussions, ideas, and our relationships with others to a shared space. As to *vision and goal clarity,* Mawson describes how enclosed offices, especially within a department or team, work against the common objectives of an organization, keeping people and their ideas secure behind closed doors. It is also important, related to *external communication,* that members from different teams work in different parts of the building or amidst other teams, both to learn and to share what they have learned, increasing each group's and each individual's knowledge and, therefore, productivity. Lastly, Mawson argues that the workplace must be a place of trust. "Having only enclosed spaces with opaque walls so that people can't see what's going on inside isn't going to support trust."[18] Mawson recognizes that private space is always necessary in an office environment, especially for dealing with sensitive personnel matters. However, he shows that there must be a balance between spaces of confidentiality and spaces that create and nurture an open and transparent environment.

AWA's interests lie in assisting organizations with maximizing their commercial value. Nevertheless, the recognized way to do so is by designing and organizing a workplace environment that encourages rather than stifles communication and *casual interaction.* Space matters. There are numerous factors that contribute to such an environment. Lighting, fabrics, room colors, various furniture materials, space configuration, all make certain cultural norms within an environment possible. Materials affect how people feel about a space, which bears upon how they relate to others who inhabit that space with them. Granted, it matters what people do inside the space. If you put a bull in a china shop, the end result will still be broken glass. Nevertheless, if you have ordinary people who are simply finding it difficult to connect and communicate, space configuration can have a tremendous effect on workplace dynamics.

18   Ibid., 46.

One of the shifts in office furniture in recent years has been the shift away from plastic, metal, or laminate desks, tables, and chairs. It was typical that low-level employees or middle management received the functional furniture that, while it may at first be visually appealing, was cold to the touch. Executives, to validate their worth to the company, were the only ones who had the large windows, leather chairs, and solid wood desks in their offices. The message being delivered here is one of status. However, in discussing this shift from furniture that lacks warmth to more natural materials, one former Gunlocke executive said that "the older furniture did not feel touchable."[19] Ms. Hamilton explains that while the more organic furniture may cost an organization more, it helps to create an atmosphere where each employee is valued. "The real wood is no longer just for the executive," she says. It is the whole of the environment that is to be considered. "There is a direct connection," says Hamilton, "between the touch of the chair and the relationships between employees." The porosity of the desk chair and the penetrability of human lives in the workplace go hand in hand. "The itchy, wool and metal office chair in a dark green and brown office space does not lend itself to lingering or conversation. Such materials," Hamilton goes on to explain, "contribute to discomfort and poor communication around the office." However, bright accent colors, comfortable leather chairs in an office with natural lighting, and living plants offer a sense of calm and incite conversation, creativity, and life in the workplace.

The evolution in workplace design, where "innovation, collaboration and wellness take center stage," while relatively new, follows the trend in nearly every industry toward comfort and quality over against cost and utility. Airbnb, the app that connects individuals seeking an alternative to the overpriced hotel, offers travelers the opportunity to be a house guest in every city, or to be at home away from home, giving the traveler a sense of being part of the local culture of a place, even while visiting. Lyft and Uber, apps that provide an alternative to the overpriced taxi-ride in the city, give passengers a sense of being picked up by a friend you haven't seen in years, who chats you up on your way to

19 Diane Hamilton (former Gunlocke employee), interviewed by William Daniel in Geneseo, New York, August, 2017.

the house, pub, or airport. "How long have you been driving for Lyft/ Uber?" is a typical question of every passenger, which begins a conversation between two unsuspecting persons who would otherwise never have crossed paths. These apps and others like them intend to make connections between strangers that are mutually beneficial and feel less like a transaction and more like a casual, blind date. No one asks the taxi-driver how long he's been driving for Yellow Cab. Why? Because nobody cares, and because it's not the driver's back seat you're sliding across on sharp turns; it's a company car. Similar to the natural wood or leather chair of well-designed office space, the personal vehicles of Uber and Lyft drivers offer a porosity that the faux, slippery leather seats of the taxicab do not, which, met with the sliding glass between the front and rear, delimits conversation between driver and passenger to simply providing an address, as the passenger anxiously watches her money vanish on the taximeter. The vehicle itself creates a buffer between the two persons, whereas the Uber driver's Prius with its soft, even if synthetic, leather seats and open air between the front and back of the car, as well as already being on a first name basis with the driver and having his/her picture in hand, creates a porosity between the driver and passenger that begins a conversation well before coming face to face.

Whether it's an office, home, car, or what have you, each space inclines a person toward certain patterns of behavior, patterns that are implicit in its design and use, even if not always noticeable. What is crucial, as Christopher Alexander has noted in his seminal work on architecture, is the need to make explicit how environments condition behavior.

> In a period when languages are no longer widely shared, when people have been robbed of their intuitions by specialists, when they no longer even know the simplest patterns that were once implicit in their habits, it becomes necessary to make patterns explicit, precisely and scientifically, so that they can be shared in a new way—explicitly, instead of implicitly—and discussed in public.[20]

20 Alexander, *The Timeless Way of Building*, 246.

The connection between our habits and the habits of the spaces within which we dwell and how these affect our perception of the world are in need of being made explicit perhaps now more than ever. Space conditions movement. The texture of a space, whether it is warm and inviting or cold to the touch, inclines us to relate to the space and others in it accordingly. While our individual personalities and habits may work with or fight against such spatial configurations, it is inevitable that the places we inhabit will over time affect our patterns of life, thereby conditioning us to perceive the world and others in relation to their warmth or coldness.

It is for this reason that parents disciplining their children should always sit on a cushioned surface. Parents who sit on a rigid surface when dealing with a child's misbehavior are more rigid on their children, whereas parents sitting on a soft couch are more forgiving and empathetic to their child's development and mistaken behavior — more apt to remember that they too were children who made mistakes.[21] My physical discomfort compromises my ability to deal with an uncomfortable situation. Whether it's the weather, the hardness of the chair, my achy back from a poor night's rest, or the headache I have from missing my morning coffee, all are factors that complicate my emotional sense, inclining me to be short with a colleague, irritable with my wife, angry with my son or daughter, or just downright grouchy amidst an already stressful day. A warm, soothing space, or a walk in a quiet park, can alter my disposition to become more receptive toward others. As space compels me toward certain feelings, I am opened or closed to engaging others in peaceful or competitive ways.

We now turn our attention to the space of liturgy. The goal here is to discern how the space of a church building may affect how the worshipper perceives her self, her relation to others, and her relation to God. What is important to recognize is that no space is absent of a theology, nor, therefore, absent of theological affectivity. It is the purpose in what follows to expose how certain church structures influence perception, which may or may not run counter to a Christian way of life. For

---

21   Bruce Feiler, *The Secrets of Happy Families* (New York: William Morrow, 2013), 213.

instance, what are the conditions of possibility imaginable in the very structure of ecclesial space? In other words, how is my perception as a worshipper conditioned, limited or opened, by the very architecture of a space? Is my relationship with God different if there are pews or removable chairs, prayer books and hymnals or projector screens on the wall, an organ and chancel choir or a four-piece band? Is there a difference between a church built in the shape of a cross versus one in a rectangular or circular form? Is a church with a narthex more or less welcoming than one without? Does the location of the baptismal font, or the church with a moveable font, alter my understanding of baptism? We have no need here to ask whether one of these is better than the other. What is important at this juncture is to understand how each space bears upon the spiritual sensibilities of its inhabitants. How does liturgical space affect the imagination of its worshippers?

LITURGICAL HABITATION

When you enter the Chapel of Saint Mary the Virgin at Nashotah House Theological Seminary in Nashotah, Wisconsin, the smell of prayer is palpable. Nashotah House is an Anglo-Catholic Seminary of the Episcopal Church. In Anglican circles it is considered "high church," which means chanting, bells, three sacred ministers at the altar, and incense (and lots of it). Eucharist is celebrated daily, along with Morning Prayer and Evensong, with Matins on Thursday mornings and High Mass on Thursday evenings. The smoke that has filled the air each week for over a hundred and fifty years has left a fragrant residue that is unmistakable. It is a well-worn space with a High Altar and three side chapels. As a seminary chapel it is designed like many cathedral chancels, with choir stalls facing each other for antiphonal chanting. Founded in 1842, in the wake of the Oxford Movement, Nashotah House is unmistakably the Catholic wing of Episcopal seminaries — Benedictine through and through, instilling in its students and faculty a robust rhythm of prayer that transcends the boundaries of the temporal sphere through a rich embodiment in the faith.

The deep conviction of Anglo-Catholicism is a liturgical habituation that bespeaks Incarnation. That is, it is a form of prayer and worship that engages the full spectrum of human sensibilities. Basins of water hang from both sides of each entryway, so that those who enter the Chapel may dip their fingers in the holy water and make the sign of the cross upon their bodies, a visceral reminder that the worshipper has been baptized into the way of the cross, to be taken up daily. Prayer books and hymnals are available for visitors, filled with the prayers and hymns of the saints, rich in scripture and theology that can be touched and perused, yet another reminder of the tangibility of worship. The creaking, wooden floor, the heating pipes that clang throughout winter, the dark wooden stalls, statues, rood screen, and reredos urge those who enter to still their pace and attend to the mysteries carved in wood, the covenants inscribed on parchments along the back wall, and to gaze upon the contours of faith that is St. Mary's Chapel.

As seminarians walk past the Chapel of the Virgin in the nave, they reverence the altar by stopping and bowing their head as they turn to enter the chancel. Crossing through the rood screen, along which are situated the faculty stalls with a large, dark wood carving of Jesus on the cross, with John and the Marys by his side, seminarians reverence the high altar with a somewhat more deliberate pause and bow. Those of "high devotion" often go before the Corpus Christi Chapel in the north transept where the sacrament is reserved, veiled in a monstrance. After they genuflect before Christ, who is ever present in body through the sacrament, they continue to their stall where they may pray or read before services of prayer or Eucharist. It is also customary for seminarians to enter the Chapel in their cassock; indeed, if seminarians do not wear their cassock they are not permitted to sit in their stalls and must remain in the nave. The rule of thumb, however, is that the cassock must be donned anytime one enters the Chapel.

What is important to note is that this habit of entering the Chapel—walking in slowly and quietly in black cassock, crossing oneself with holy water, bowing, genuflecting before the sacred, soaking in the divine presence woven into the earthen materials of the space, inhaling the prayers of those who have gone before, ready to touch and taste God in the sacrament of Holy Eucharist—is a daily occurrence that compels seminarians, faculty, and visitors alike to dwell in the presence of God that is the Chapel. Let us linger with this for a moment. No one is equating God with the Chapel. God cannot be contained, yet God is also not other than the Chapel.

In Heidegger's essay "Building Dwelling Thinking," he argues that *to build* (*bauen*) is coterminous with *to dwell*. The semantic connection Heidegger makes is derived from Nachgebauer, "the near-dweller,"[22] which, he surmises, "tells us that *bauen*, to build, is really to dwell."[23] Heidegger further explains that this is directly related to cultivating the land. The reason this is not at first apparent, says Heidegger, is because it gets concealed as language moves us away from the root meaning or connection shared by *bauen*.[24] *Bauen*, says Heidegger,

> originally means to dwell. Where the word *bauen* still speaks in its original sense it also says *how far* the nature of dwelling reaches. That is, *bauen, buan, bhu, beo*, are our word *bin* in the versions: *ich bin*, I am, *du bist*, you are, the imperative for *bis*, be. What then does *ich bin* mean? The old word for *bauen*, to which the *bin* belongs, answers: *ich bin, du bist* mean I dwell, you dwell. The way in which you are and I am, the manner in which we humans *are* on the earth, is *Buan*, dwelling. To be a human being means to be on the earth as a mortal. It means to dwell.[25]

However, this connection with building and dwelling recedes into the background as cultivation and construction come to the foreground, as "the real sense of *bauen*, namely dwelling, falls into oblivion."[26] This, as Heidegger goes on to describe, is how the human becomes linguistically separable from his habitat, and thereby able to imagine herself as separable from her dwelling. The act of building, the habits of the habitat a person inhabits, come into the foreground of the human imagination as

22 Heidegger, *Poetry, Language, Thought* (New York: Harper Collins Publishers, Inc., 1971), 146–47.
23 Ibid., 147.
24 Ibid., 145–51.
25 Ibid., 147.
26 Ibid., 148.

their connectedness recedes into the background, and as they are lost in the shuffle of language they become lost to the human experience and relatedness of the human with the space of her dwelling.

How might this resonate with the felt experience of modern worshippers today? "Church" enters the English vocabulary through the Old Saxon *kirika*, and Old English as *circe*, meaning "gathering." The term often used to denote a Christian gathering comes from the Greek *ekklesia*, which remains connected. However, the German *kirche* is most likely from the Greek *kyrios*, "ruler, Lord," as in *kyriake oikia*, "the house of the Lord." While *ekklesia* and *basilike* (basilica, from *basileia*) are more common, *kyriake oikia* bears the implication of "the economy of the Lord." After the Reformation, this connectedness of the economy of God with the liturgical activity of Christ's body is severed, and as "church" enters the foreground of much of the Christian world, the house of the Lord as a political-economy under the reign of Christ the King becomes difficult to imagine. Difficult because the meaning that undergirds the active polity of God's Kingdom (*oikonomia*) and the physical structure of the *kyriake oikia* renders the *ekklesia* — the gathered body — separable from divine action. As shown in the first chapter, what enabled theologians in the 19th century to (mis)translate *leitourgia* as "the work of the people" was a mistaken reduction of human worship as separable from, or even possible apart from, the eternal liturgy of the Triune God. One might speculate that this arises from an over-specified vocabulary, which, as Heidegger has shown, causes the plentitude of meanings to recede into the background, lost to all who wittingly or unwittingly remain ignorant of their rootedness in a history of meaning.

David Jones turns the notch even further in his essay *Art and Sacrament*. In a similar manner to Heidegger, Jones deals with the etymology of the term *religio* as that which is implicated by *ars* (art *qua* art).[27] Jones seeks to show that "man" is "man-the-artist."[28] In so doing, Jones

---

27   David Jones, *Epoch and Artist* (London: Faber and Faber Ltd, 1959), 143–79.

28   I use "man" in this section in keeping with David Jones's treatment, in which he uses "man" for "human." Following G. K. Chesterton, "Men are men, but Man is a woman." The poetic usage of "man" is not lost on Jones, and beyond the period in which Jones

reminds the reader of the connectedness between *religio* and *obligatio* as rooted in *ligare* — to bind, as in the word "ligament." Religion, then, is a binding; a repeated obligation that connects the religious to the one to whom she is obliged — God. Obligation, however, strikes the modern reader as limiting, a constraint on human freedom. These notions of "religion" and "obligation" are possible, says Jones, because *ligare* has receded into the background and is no longer "operating in the new forms and attitudes of thought which the civilizational change [has] brought about."[29] However, recognizing that *ligare* implies a binding that supports an organ, assuring its freedom as part of the body, we can begin to see in *religio* and *obligatio* not actions that limit but actions that are free, securing a freedom *to* function. "Cut the ligament and there is atrophy — *corpse* rather than *corpus*."[30] Freedom and *religio* hereby go hand in hand. Indeed, says Jones, to see *religio* as limiting is to misunderstand the very meaning of the word.

Returning now to the Chapel of St. Mary the Virgin, an outsider might see in the movements conditioned by the texture and structure of the Chapel a place that is restrictive and limiting, rather than freeing and transcendent. Those who inhabit the space as the dwelling place of God, where a person can see, hear, touch, taste, and smell God, experience the connective tissue of the wood, incense, bread, wine, water, chanting, stained glass and much more as a space of freedom, where scales fall from the eyes, burdens fall from the shoulders, and peace is made manifest, not as restrictive but restorative, transformative, extending one's very body beyond itself as worshippers stand amidst the great cloud of witnesses whose prayers are still savored today.

Not every liturgical space provides access to this divine, connective tissue. And while I in no way intend to limit the *kyriake oikia* to the physical structure itself, which too would betray the making involved in the Lord's house, I seek to wonder here for a moment whether the

---

writes (mid-20th-century England), his writing seeks to convey in every way possible that "man" is a creator of art, involved in an action beyond the artist's own hands: *Ambabus manibus accepit calicem*, "with both hands he took the cup" (Mass rubric cited by Jones, *Epoch and Artist*, 177).

29 Ibid., 144.
30 Ibid., 158.

empty space of the warehouse or strip mall church can be said to be a dwelling place for God, in the sense of *ligare* noted by David Jones. That is, is cylinder block or drywall conducive to liturgy? Does the warehouse afford the worshipper an attachment to the space of liturgy beyond the scheduled act of worship? If a person walked into the room would it be clear what the space is for, or are such spaces an inadvertent cutting of the ligament that binds the human physically to the celestial, giving way to a kind of spiritual atrophy?

Walking into the Mars Hill Bible Church (MHBC) in Grand Rapids, Michigan, I experience an environment very different from the one noted above with the Chapel of the Virgin in Nashotah. The people of MHBC gather in what was formerly the "anchor store of an old mall," as their website describes,[31] what they have appropriately renamed the *Shed*. The *Shed* is certainly a more fitting name for the space than is "church," given that it is an open space with wall-to-wall carpet, devoid of any religious symbolism. As you enter the *Shed*, there is no signage, save a logo above two sets of double doors where the preexisting store would have had its logo. There is a large foyer at the entry, lined with coffee carafes, so that parishioners may enjoy a cup of Joe during the service.

The atmosphere is intentionally casual; the preacher and most of the band wear jeans and T-shirts. Encircled about the stage are soft, removable chairs in a climate-controlled space. At the center is a stage for the band and preacher, above which hangs a large screen — much like you would see at a basketball game — for projecting choruses, verses of scripture, and bullet points for the sermon. The space is designed for a particular form of worship in which congregants mostly sit relaxed in their chairs while those on stage do the singing and talking, not unlike a band performance or comedy show. This structuring, of course, is quite intentional — neither the church's leaders nor the parishioners would argue otherwise. The ordering is intended to focus everyone's attention on what is taking place at the center, which the space does quite well. There are no ornaments on the walls, not even windows. There is nothing to take away the focus from what happens center

---

31   Mars Hill Bible Church. "Visiting." https://marshill.org/visiting (accessed February 25, 2018).

stage. The minimalist design of the space communicates to the worshipper that while worship does occur inside it remains detached from the building itself. In other words, the space is not a space meant to be inhabited; it is not a place of dwelling. If a person were to walk into the *Shed* at any other time, there would be no visible markers or signs that allow one to recognize it as a place where worship occurs. It is bare, somewhat dismal, lacking anything that might be said to be alive or invoke life, and the only smells are what may linger from having brewed coffee or leftover doughnuts lying around.

The contrast between the Chapel of St. Mary the Virgin and the *Shed* are profound. The former is a space designed to be inhabited by both worshipper and worship, a building that is itself involved in the liturgical action. The latter is transitory by design, which houses a temporary action separable from the space and, perhaps, the worshipper herself. The difference is between *inhabiting* a space and enacting something *within* a space. What is missing from the warehouse church is a deep connection with what the Christian worshipper believes and thinks — the tangibility of faith. The visceral sense of the space is impermanent. Its homogenous character neither requires anything from nor offers anything to its occupants. It is telling that many who worship in these spaces refuse to be married in them. When couples desire a "church wedding," more often than not they inquire at another local church that "looks like a church," or they have their wedding outdoors. Why? Because marriage, something intended for a lifetime, needs a permanent space for vows to feel permanent. The temporary space of the abandoned store signals to young couples that their marriage may not last. The expressed desires are "good wedding pictures," "memories in a holy place," and "for it to feel like a church wedding." The message hidden from a couples' immediate awareness is the need to feel like God is present for their wedding and that their covenant will last. To be and to dwell, as Heidegger notes, are inseparable.[32]

What is problematic, liturgically speaking, with the *Shed* and other spaces like it, is how they separate the act of worship from the space

---

32 Heidegger, *Poetry, Language, Thought*, 147.

of worship. "Church" here denotes the people involved in an act of prayer and praise, which happens to occur in the *Shed*, a space that purposefully does not bear the name "church." Churches that have historic buildings, however, are not immune from the linguistic severing of people and building either. There is a commonly told anecdote that goes something like this: a visitor enters the church office asking to see the church and the priest replies, "I'd love to show you, but they're all at work right now. They will be here on Sunday." Meant to highlight that the church is the people, it succeeds in severing the people from the fullness of what it means to be the church, the *Corpus Christi*. Christ's body is an active presence, a presence that penetrates and permeates the material.

The major difference between the two spaces of worship noted above is that one, the Chapel at Nashotah, is incorporated daily in the making of Holy Eucharist, while I cannot say if this ever occurs at Mars Hill. The irony is that the name Mars Hill invokes a somewhat sacred site, where the Apostle Paul preaches before an altar dedicated to "the Unknown God." One might speculate that Mars Hill in Grand Rapids bears the marks of an Unknown God, given its lack of symbolism or anything that might disclose the space as Christian. Perhaps the name is deliberate to invoke Paul's mission to speak amidst the false god of consumer capitalism, witnessed by the abandoned storefront. Nevertheless, the Eucharist — the sacramental action whereby God creates the church — is that which makes any space a space of dwelling. For this reason it is easy to recognize a space that has been designed by and for Eucharistic action. These are not temporary structures separable from the liturgy, even if they lend themselves to more than just prayer and the breaking of bread. Rather, these are eternal structures created by and for an eternal action, an action that remains present even when the building is empty of its people, because it is separable neither from the people who worship there, nor the God whose action the building and people inhabit.

We use the two more extreme examples above, a seminary chapel where services of prayer and Holy Eucharist are a daily occurrence and an abandoned storefront church that bears the name "Shed," in order to emphasize the distinctness of a space designed for liturgical habituation and another originally designed for capitalist consumption with no noticeable alterations that would bespeak an alternative function, a lack that in many ways reinforces its original design. The Chapel is shaped by the Eucharist; the *Shed* is shaped by consumerism. The question to be raised, which we will deal with in full in the next chapter, is how the character of a space conditions humans to relate not only to that particular space, but also to the whole of their environment, which are continually overlapping. If worship occurs in a space that conveys temporariness, is the worshipper inclined by the space to treat the liturgical action as temporary? Additionally, is the congregation conditioned to keep the act of worship separate from all other forms of activity and spaces within which they live and move, and through which they relate to others? Can my dinner table at home, for instance, participate in the Table of the Lord if there is no table in the place where I offer prayers and sing praises? If the place where I worship is not designed as a *basilica*, as a throne room for the Lord, how am I to connect the act of worship with the act of hospitality demanded of the Christian home? Is the alarm system of a house, we might say, directly linked not simply to the contents in need of protection but to the dominant metaphor of the spaces a person inhabits, whereby even the home becomes a barrier to the outside rather than a space that relates its inhabitants to what is outside? What is lost or opened to the imagination when human action and space do not co-inhere?

SPACES OF CONVIVIALITY

What we have been exploring in relation to the two spaces described above is how the structure of the space itself conditions the worshipper to imagine her relationship to people, places, and things both within and outside the particular gathering for worship. This relationship between the liturgical act and the liturgical space is essential to Christian worship. Severing space from act obfuscates the relationship between the person and a place of worship. A utilitarian space breeds a utilitarian liturgy, inhibiting the worshipper's ability to inhabit the space, as the space temporalizes the embodiment of liturgical action.

At the same time, a beautiful space of worship filled with signs and symbols of the faith does not mean that the action within will automatically elicit a porous relationship between people and place, even if the space itself evokes such porosity. This is perhaps evidenced most clearly in the pilgrim's journey to sacred sites in Israel, where holy shrines are filled not with prayer but with tourists taking selfies, consumer products bought and sold, and all manner of people and activities who, in a similar way to that of the warehouse church, have separated the space from the liturgical action. The once holy shrine of pilgrimage is reconstituted by religious paraphernalia and media activities by religious and non-religious alike who desire little more than to say that they have visited the site or seen the relic. It is important to note that one's *habitus* can help a person to see through the consumerism run amuck and find amidst the chaos the presence of God; however, without a robust sense of the holy based on one's rootedness in the habits of faith, it is all but impossible.

How might we speak of the language of ecclesial space? What should be abundantly clear at this point is that, following both Martin Heidegger and most especially David Jones, a space is created by certain forms of action, all the while recognizing that space, upon a building's completion, allows for certain movements or at least favors certain activities over others. This should not be seen as limiting but, again, following Jones's articulation of *ligare*, as bound for freedom, connected for the purpose of sustaining the life of the body. Space and action hereby constitute a language. This language is not so much spoken by the human; rather, this language speaks the human into being and, for our purposes, speaks the worshipper into worshipping. This language is inseparable from the words spoken, yet it is the language of the space and actions of the liturgy that make the words intelligible and, we might say, inhabitable. This language sustains the ligaments of the ecclesial body to which the worshipper is bound, and without this connective tissue that gives life to the words of prayer and hymns of praise, the worshipper's spiritual muscles are likely to atrophy, disconnecting her from the corpus. In other words, without the language of interwoven space and action, what is spoken and done by the worshipper will serve not to relate her to people, places, and things but rather to sustain the fictional divisions of society's homogeneous structures.

In his *Tools for Conviviality*, Ivan Illich describes how this plays itself out in the relationship between humans and tools. Illich seeks to reconstruct the human imaginary to comprehend tools as intrinsic to how one relates to others within the social body.[33] Tools have a way of bringing the social body together in closer proximity; however, they can also serve to distance the social body in ways unforeseen. Take, for instance, the automobile. The purpose of the automobile is to decrease the space and time between two points; however, the "watershed" of transportation served only to create more distance and use more time both in production and traffic, reducing society to a virtual enslavement to the car.[34] The greater issue, however, as Illich points out, is how tools of industry have ceased to be an extension of the human, enhancing each person's range of freedom, but now "work" for them, as money "works" in capitalism, reducing the human to a spectator or at best manipulator of machines, limiting the human to a mere consumer-slave.[35] Working through Illich's description of how tools connect or disconnect the human to her environment, we will see how this dynamic affects a person's overall relation to space and action.

We find a helpful analogy in Kurt Vonnegut's *Player Piano*. In *Player Piano*, society is divided essentially into two classes: engineers and "Reeks and Wrecks." Paul, an engineer in this industrial, machine-governed society, becomes involved in a pseudo-revolution with the usual suspects. Coming to realize the all-pervasiveness of machines in society that sustains class divisions and limits the range of human freedom, severing the ligaments, as it were, Paul enlists those who have been abused by machinery. Paul is in turmoil, however, because it may mean the end of his marriage. His life as an engineer, in a family of engineers, is profitable and Paul is in line for top posts in the country, a beautiful home, family, everything a bourgeois man could ever want. Consistently wrestling with what he has to lose,

---

33 Ivan Illich, *Tools for Conviviality* (New York: Harper and Row Publishers, 1973), 20.
34 Ibid., 7–8.
35 Ibid., 10–11.

Paul goes on to sacrifice all for the ideal of a human flourishing that involves living a life where work is done with his own bare hands, perhaps even farming (*bauer*, to make the connection with Heidegger). The revolution takes place; all the machines are smashed. But what happens next leaves Paul in utter turmoil. The people have risen up and knocked down the reigning powers of the machine. However, when the machines that worked for, not with, individuals have been broken into pieces, because of the all-pervasive impact machines have had on the human imaginary the only thing the revolutionaries can think to do next is to repair the machines. The force of the machine on perceived human flourishing has been too overwhelming to overturn, and once shattered the only thing left to do is to put the pieces of the machines back together. The revolution fails because there is no alternative tool or retooling, only the destruction of tools, which only mimics what the tools of the machine have done to its users.

John Ruskin's imperative rings true, "You must either make a tool of the creature, or a man of him. You cannot make both."[36] That is, either the human will be a slave to do the work of another or she will be an artist who makes her way in the world as a creator. Illich's argument is not to hereby do away with tools or machines or to demonize them in any way. He realizes that tools are essential to social relations. Nevertheless, the meaning of a tool does not simply reside in its use; rather, the tool itself bears a sort of implicit imaginary.[37] It is something along the lines of the adage, "To a man with a hammer everything is a nail." While the hammer can be used for many things, it nevertheless *desires*, in the Aristotelian sense, to pound and be used for pounding, whether it is a nail or the head of an enemy. It is simple enough to say that while a tool's function can be reoriented, as in the case of turning swords into plowshares or spears into pruning hooks,[38] nevertheless, without reconstituting such tools, the sword and spear can only be imagined as weapons of death and destruction.

36   John Ruskin, *The Stones of Venice* (London: Smith, Elder and Company, 1867), 161.

37   Marshall McLuhan, *Understanding Media: The Extensions of Man* (Cambridge: MIT Press, 1994), 41–47.

38   Isaiah 2:4.

A convivial reconstruction is necessary, then, a "re-tooling" if you will. Illich contrasts conviviality with industrial productivity. Whereas industrialism enslaves the human to machinery, reducing the individual to a consumer of goods over which she has no control in fashioning or producing, conviviality promotes a social freedom of interdependence for each (*ligare*), which seeks to satisfy the needs of human flourishing in society while enjoining the individual to its governance.[39] That is, conviviality will free the human to fashion goods reciprocally with the whole of society, binding differing cultures together in an economy akin to a gift economy, though Illich does not make this explicit reference. A convivial restructuring of human society is contingent upon a reconstituting of tools whereby each person is able to defend her liberty and offer a careful analysis of the inherent nature of tools as means.[40] The convivial tool, then, will be an extension of the human — especially in the sense of tools as intrinsic to social relations — in a way that increases human flourishing on the whole and does not remove the productive action from the energy of its user. A convivial tool will often reduce the amount of human energy needed for creating; however, it must not eliminate human action. For instance, a standard vacuum cleaner enables a person to clean the carpets with minimal human energy; however, a robotic vacuum requires one only to push the button to turn it on. The robotic vacuum hereby promotes the uncleanness it is designed to remove, for the cleaning process is removed from human action.[41] Cleaning is transformed by the robotic tool into something machines do, but not humans. Analogies will forever breakdown in this regard, for carpet itself may not promote conviviality, as it creates a further dependency on electricity and more machines to maintain it. Nevertheless, the point is that convivial tools must increase the dignity of human activity, even if it lightens the exertion of human energy.

39 Illich, *Tools For Conviviality*, 11.
40 Ibid., 24–25.
41 One can see this embellished in the Amazon series *Humans 2.0*, where AI Robots fill the role of maids and much more, separating the inhabitants of the home from the actions involved in actually inhabiting the home. This is "intended" to provide more time for a family to be a family, when in actuality it deprives the family from essential movements that allow a person to dwell in the home.

Inasmuch as a tool reduces the human to a passive spectator or eliminates her involvement in creative actions, the human ceases to have a telos. By becoming a means, she ceases to *mean* anything. To state the matter plainly, a convivial tool gives life by enhancing human action, a non-convivial tool takes life away by eliminating human action. Movement itself does not imply life, however; rather, it is volitive movement *toward* that manifests life. It is *aiming at* and an increasing awareness both of one's aiming and that at which a person aims.

Certain tools may be inherently destructive, says Illich, inasmuch as they increase human exploitation, dependence, or impotence, robbing rich and poor of conviviality.[42] Take a gun, for instance. The inherent logic of the gun is to inflict violence, even if not to kill. It is designed to penetrate its object with a violent force. Even if used for defense or skeet shooting, one cannot escape its inherent logic. Not all tools used violently, however, bear this necessary logic. One may recall Orville Wright's comment in 1917 about the airplane he and his brother were constructing — a flying tool:

> When my brother and I built and flew the first man-carrying flying machine, we thought that we were introducing into the world an invention which would make further wars practically impossible....

This is obviously not what the airplane provided for modern warfare. It did not eliminate war but has and continues to make war more and more possible, especially with the invention of drones. It is for this reason that a careful analysis of the basic structure of tools is requisite. What are the "structuring structures" that lie within the social body that constitute the tool *as*?[43] The logic of capital and industry construe the tool as an end rather than a means, as modern warfare did with the man-carrying flying machine, which inverts the relation of tool and user such that the human becomes the means — the medium between consumable objects. That is, the human becomes a tool. Tools

---

42   Illich, *Tools For Conviviality*, 26.
43   Pierre Bourdieu, *The Logic of Practice* (Stanford: Stanford University Press, 1990), 53.

become ends when they begin to *work*, as Illich notes this transition in the English language at least since 1600.[44] The human thus transitions from a fashioner of tools for her work, whereby her exertion and what she produces are situated within the logic of herself as end, to become the means to the end that is the tool, separating the human from both action and what is produced by it. This exploitation of the individual renders the human impotent and utterly dependent on the tool, the *work* of which eternally suspends her from what is produced.

The efficient tooling of society leads the human into a whole new set of relations between her tools and others. Men and women go from *working with* their tools to *powering* their tools with human energy, and then begin *operating* tools with "abstract" power. Human action has since nearly been replaced altogether by machines. Engineers, as seen in Vonnegut's *Player Piano*, have developed machines that increasingly reduce the number of operators needed for their production. Greater mechanical power reduces the need for human power, which relegates human labor to jobs within cubicles that serve primarily to analyze the working of the machines and how to develop newer machines that require fewer and fewer operators and analysts. This continuous drive toward efficiency, whereby efficiency means increased speed and greater productivity apart from human touch, reduces the individual to the tool of which Ruskin prophesied (of course by his time it was already too late).

The freedoms that individuals once had have largely been reduced with the rise of technologies designed to create greater freedom. Illich discusses the everyday peasant in Mexico during the early twentieth century, and how he would earn a living by walking his pig to the market to attain the necessary sustenance for daily life. No transport or packaging was needed, just a man and his pig and perhaps a rope around its neck. The automobile could not compete with the bicycle or foot within the city.[45] In the 1940's and 50's, however, funds were pumped into building new roads to create swifter means of

44   Illich, *Tools For Conviviality*, 30.
45   Ibid., 36.

commerce.[46] The consequence was that it created a new economy where the peasant could no longer bring his pig to market, thereby becoming reliant on industrially packaged commodities and bus transport to get him to and fro. The peasant now pays taxes for the roads that have eliminated his means of money making, all the while supporting and sustaining monopolies that promise to one day bring those same benefits of progress home to him.

Illich's point here has little to do with the particular peasant and his piggy going to market in Mexico; rather, it is a matter of the material forces that reconstitute human society, limiting human freedoms and forcing the individual into a labor force that she serves only for the sake of consuming the goods of the same market that enslaves her, all with the promise that her cooperation will be met with the fruits of this market. What we find in Illich's description is a particular construal of language, space, and time. Language, space, and time cease to be tools in the convivial sense of their use toward human ends; rather, the linguistic shift occurs with the transition from space and time as creative human activities to become products for consumption — space and time as that within which products are produced and consumed but are in no way connected to the people and actions of producing. Human labor situated within the new categories of space and time can only be abstracted from individuals for the sake of buying and selling in a system of production.

The logic of production is the linguistic evacuation of time and space from human action that situates human action within abstract time and space. (The reader should recall here our description of the *Shed*.) It is at once for the commodification of human action as purchasable labor as well as for the commodification of time and space as the same. Time and space abstracted from human creative action reduces each, and everything within both, to something that can be measured universally, specifically measured by monetary valuation. Time and space cease to be bound up together with human action as that which measures and

---

46 It is important here to make the connection that Heidegger makes between building and dwelling. The road systems in Mexico City were explicitly designed to alter the economy. In so doing, it devastated the existing economy and dislocated local farmers in favor of a form of production that severs the ligaments of the corpus.

creates life and now serves to house human creativity *as* productivity, construing human action as measurable only within the *body-schema* of the marketplace.[47] This, however, is the linguistic fictionalization of how the human subject relates to her world. To exist as body-mind means that the human inhabits time and space, not that she is *in* time or space.[48] The linguistic dislocation of human action from time and space proffered by the logic of production, by alienating human action from time and space, severs the mind from the body. The body does not inhabit space and time in a permeable relation with the whole of human society; rather, the body becomes productively measured within time and space, separating thought from action, suspending both from the present by removing each from its history or future. It is an ontological reduction of the human to a being *in-itself*, and likewise that of time and space. This fragmenting disassociates the multitude of relations that exist *in-the-between* of human existence. It is a radical division between subjectivity and objectivity,[49] such that there is only absolute polarity between all things, lacking any sense of mutual dependency or "intervolvement," to use Merleau-Ponty's language.

What then does this make of the man and his pig in the market? The pig, once a means of relating man and market, now packaged as bacon in the refrigerator section of the grocery store, has been removed from the peasant and no longer connects him to the plethora of relations once shared. The man is now a consumer *in-himself*, relating only to packaged goods on the shelf, but not to those who once bargained and bartered for his pig. He exists autonomously, relating only to the market as consumer, abstracted from all relations that do not involve the consumption of like products.[50] He is a tool (means) of the market

47 I am nuancing here Merleau-Ponty's use of "body schema" to show that the conditions of reality, materially imposed on the human as a body-soul, construe the human imaginary to comprehend her particular "being-in-the-world" as existing in an intemporal time and abstract space from which she remains eternally detached. See Merleau-Ponty, *Phenomenology of Perception*, 112–70; Bourdieu, *The Logic of Practice*, 80–111.

48 Merleau-Ponty, *Phenomenology of Perception*, 117.

49 We will deal with this divide further in the next chapter.

50 Below it will be shown how this directly relates to the liturgical participant and her extraction from baking bread for Eucharist and participating in its procession in the offertory.

(end). He now possesses market-time that he sells to the market as body labor, which he exchanges in the market for the consumption of goods that he, in many cases, has *produced*. The abstraction of time and space from human action nevertheless *works* on the body's practical sense of its inhabiting the world. The human is disciplined to inhabit neither space nor time, but to remain *in-herself*, autonomous — which leads to a schizophrenic relation to herself as a mind who has a body and not as a body-mind whole. The only possible shared relation with the other, here, is as a non-involved, non-permeable, self-enclosed entity who relates to the other as a mutual consumer of identical products. This particular *state of mind* as that which transcends its body is only possible within a social order that disposes the body to relate to its mind in this partic- ularly abstract way.[51] The body is conditioned by social mechanisms to recall certain ideas and thoughts that the subject is no less conditioned to think of as mere thoughts, capable of abstracting from the conditions at work on the body. Perception, here, is not the totality of perceiving found in Maximus or Merleau-Ponty; rather, perception according to the logic of production has to do with the mind stepping outside of the bodily experience to "re-frame" people, situations, events, etc., as affect- ing only one's disembodied thought processes which can be overcome by simply "thinking" of the matter differently. Thinking is here reduced to a sort of transcendental cognition, not as inhabiting time and space in a mutually permeating relation of being and becoming.

Returning once again to the man and his pig, the product-construed imaginary that now conditions his being-in-the-world limits the free- dom of his abstract mind to the *habitus* of the market that delim- its his actions.[52] He is forced to buy back his body by a period of

51 Bourdieu, *The Logic of Practice*, 66–79.

52 "Everything takes place as if the *habitus* forged coherence and necessity out of accident and contingency; as if it managed to unify the effects of the social necessity undergone from childhood, through the material conditions of existence, the primary relational experiences and the practice of structured actions, objects, spaces and times, and the effects of biological necessity, whether the influence of hormone balances or the weight of the visible characteristics of physique; as if it produced a biological reading of social properties and a social reading of sexual properties, thus leading to a social re-use of biological properties and a biological re-use of social properties" (ibid., 79).

enslavement if he wishes to reunite it to his mind. Such a reunion remains unimaginable, however, or at best infinitely suspended. This is very much akin to Marx's critique of capitalism. The consumer market system of the bourgeoisie is an economic enslavement that isolates the human from herself by the commodification of the end of her labor. The human's productive actions cease to relate to her as their producer when the product is exchanged in the market with no regard for the person as its producer. The producer has become a laborer; she works but she does not create. This alienation of the producer from her product nullifies the production as a transubstantiating force that endows the completed product with the life-energy of its producer. It is the isolation of both producer and the thing produced, which serves also to abstract the very actions involved in the production from their actor.

A person's actions, as purchasable, are not one's own but are owned by the one who pays for the actions to be enacted, and because the actions are bought and sold in the market, that which is produced by the actions bear no attachment to their producer and are commodified in like manner. When the human (producer) is separated from her actions (production) she becomes, as Marx contends, less than human. Marx understands production to be that which makes humans human.[53] It is *the* fundamental activity whereby the human comes to realize her selfhood. Self-illumination is in the act of creating, for what is created by her action retains a residue of her nature to such an extent that the products of human action are "mirrors from which [human] essence shines forth."[54] The reciprocal relation between producer, production, and product is essential for the sort of self-actualization of the human that Marx tirelessly presses toward. It is this self-actualization that remains suspended from the man and his pig. The *habitus* of consumerism only makes possible the free production of thought, perception, and action inherent to the particular

---

53   Allen W. Wood, *Karl Marx* (New York: Routledge, 2005), 31.

54   This directly aligns with David Jones' articulation of "man-the-artist." See David Jones, *Epoch and Artist*, 143–79.

conditions of its own production and no others.[55] A man with one pig is forced to domesticate it as a pet, or at best slaughter it himself for his own consumption. If he is to sustain himself through the consumer market he must manufacture pork in bulk, contract with meat packers, who then contract with grocers to purchase bacon and ham as packaged goods for resale. Bartering with one's pig in the market is no longer possible.

This slight detour helps to call our attention to how spatial restructuring reconstitutes language, making certain actions and relationships possible and others not, conditioning the human to perceive her environment as a dweller or occupant, but not both. The structure of liturgical space and the liturgical actions they inhabit and are inhabited by are inseparable from the structuring of the sensibilities of those who worship in a space. The posture a space conditions me to assume is the language that space speaks in me, to which I give words, and through which I understand my relationship with God and others. To recognize space and action as the structure of a language is crucial for understanding how the words I speak acquire meaning, as they are always relative to this conditioned linguistic.

TERROIR AND LEITOURGIA

Terroir in French has to do specifically with wine making, yet in a deeply cultural sense of the taste of a place, *gout de terroir*. For this reason, it is actually illegal to label a wine with the name Burgundy if it is not from Burgundy, France. Burgundy is at once the wine and the place; the two are inseparable. The *gout de terroir* draws the deep connection that the soil and the hands that work it are inseparable from the taste of the wine. In other words, the wine — its fullness of taste and heightening of the senses — cannot be separated from any of the environmental circumstances within which it is produced. In like manner, Christian liturgy is inseparable from the space and people intervolved in the action, all of which are intervolved in what we might call the *grammar of God*. We might even go so far as to call

---

55 Bourdieu, *The Logic of Practice*, 55.

it the *gout de Dieu*, as it is in, by, and through the Eucharistic space that the worshipper learns what it means to *taste and see that the Lord is good*.[56] The taste of the place, the smell, the touch, the sights and sounds of the *kyriake oikia* are all a language that conditions perception in the worshipper as she is spoken into being through them and called to attention by them, as the unspoken language demands not words but, perhaps, silence.

"If we hope to understand the life which happens in a building or town," writes Christopher Alexander, "we must therefore try to understand the structure of the space itself."[57] Alexander's statement demonstrates that any account of human flourishing must first account for the inhabited spaces of humans and how these structures pattern human behavior and relations. "There is no aspect of our lives," he writes,

> which is not governed by these patterns of events. And if the quality without a name can come into our lives at all, it is clear that it depends entirely on the specific nature of these patterns of events from which our world is made. *And indeed, the world does have a structure, just because these patterns of events which repeat themselves are always anchored in the space.*[58]

These *patterns of space*, as Alexander describes them, are the characteristics of a place that pattern our relationships, which are themselves the structure of our relationships, incapable of being divorced from the physical structures of our environs. I cannot walk out of the front door of my home without being reminded that I am the priest of Saint Michael's Church in Geneseo, New York. Why? Because before me as I exit the space of my home is another space where I celebrate Eucharist and lead the faithful in prayer. The pattern of the walkway conditions me to take notice of this house of prayer, the faithful who lie in wait in the garden, whose prayers are inscribed in the walls of the church, and the many obligations relative to the people who inhabit this space

56 Psalm 34:8.
57 Alexander, *The Timeless Way of Building*, 74.
58 Ibid., 69, italics original.

with me. As I stroll down the sidewalk I am immediately aware that I live in a valley where gusts of wind stride across it, often striking my face with frost in the winter. As I pass storefronts, cafés, and bars, I wave to those inside, many of whom are parishioners and many of whom otherwise still consider me their priest. I am related to those in our village through these structures, for better or for worse, and through these patterned relationships I understand who I am and, as a Christian, who God is. And it is the *gout de terroir* that is Geneseo, New York, and more pressingly Saint Michael's Church, that cannot be neatly separated from my sense of language. These structures and the actions that occur in them are the patterns of my language, speaking me into being in such ways that words can only begin to describe.

CONCLUSION

What I have tried to show in the above is the rootedness of language in space and action, structuring structures that pattern our movements and, thereby, our relationships. To be, following Heidegger, *is* to dwell. And, liturgically speaking, to be is a matter of the indwelling of Christ in the worshipper and the worshipper in Christ, a eucharistic patterning that speaks the Christian into speaking, as it were, forming the faithful in the language that is Christ, whose incarnate action is an unconfused union with all things human.

Liturgical space speaks itself in the worshipper, and through the action of Christ in sacred liturgy the human is made to know herself in relation to the patterning of Christ's self-offering. A space of worship that does not reinforce the pattern of cruciform, liturgical action is a space that fights against the very structuring that gives meaning to the scriptures and prayers invoked in the liturgical actions of a church.

In the final chapter, I will tease out this relationship between language, space, and human action, delving into the medial nature of language, in an effort to show how various patterns of speech condition relationships between people, places, and things.

4

The Grammar of God

The forms and materials which the poet uses, his images and the meanings he would give to those images, his perceptions, what is evoked, invoked or incanted, is in some way or other, to some degree or other, essentially bound up with the particular historic complex to which he, together with each other member of that complex, belongs.

David Jones

That which mediates my life for me, also mediates the existence of other people for me. For me it is the other person.

Karl Marx

Whoever does not love does not know God, for God is love.

1 John 4:8

INTRODUCTION

What is often misunderstood about liturgical action, specifically as it regards Christian liturgy, is that it is neither performative nor initiative. That is, it is not a performance before God to somehow please God or curry favor, nor is the Christian to understand herself as one who initiates contact with God. As outlined in the first chapter, this is a gross misrepresentation of liturgy that stems from a mistranslation and misunderstanding of the word and meaning of *leitourgia*. Any claim that liturgy is instigated by, or an experience simply to be taken in or enjoyed by, humans reduces liturgical action to a temporary, flattened affair that has little or nothing to do with God, save the gross objectification of the same. Such a reduction bears an implicit, disenchanted anthropology, a conception of humanity that is biological at best and animalistic at worst. Liturgy, however, does not originate in human action, even though it implicates humanity in its activity and elicits human participation. Liturgy is the creative agency of God who in Christ has gathered human nature into divine reciprocity, a reciprocity that is without beginning or end. The human's participation in this eternal action is medial by nature. That is, the human is caught up in the divine self-relation of Father, Son, and Holy Spirit. Liturgy hereby names the self-relation of eternal reciprocity that God himself is. To worship, therefore — to participate in the liturgical action — is to be involved in an action that begins outside of human agency yet implicates the human in divine agency. In short, liturgy for the human is a medial matter.

To say that something is medial is to suggest that it operates in the middle, *in-the-between*. In what follows, we will explore the medial nature of liturgical action, examining how Christian Liturgy displaces the agency of the subject involved in the act of worship. Liturgy is hereby understood as an intransitive activity, in the sense that it has no defined object.[1] Accordingly, we will examine the nature of liturgy as an action that *precedes* and *proceeds from* the human, involving the worshipper in the procession and return of God from and to himself in the Liturgy Christ *is*. Using the grammatical category of the middle voice as a window into divine-human *intervolvement*,[2] we will see how it is the singular agency of Christ that makes the human's participation in the act of worship possible. Because Christ is Liturgy *par excellence* — he himself the action of all prayer and praise whose beginning and end is God — human action, especially as this regards the act of worship, is always and only participation. Human action is an *involvement* in the action Christ *is*.

---

1   We will explore this notion of intransitive activity further below in relation to David Jones's *Art and Sacrament*.

2   I borrow this word from Merleau-Ponty, with direct reference to his understanding of the *body schema* that refuses any clear division between mind and body, and the involvement of the body-mind in the world, i.e. as intervolved. Maurice Merleau-Ponty, *Phenomenology of Perception* (New York: Routledge, 2002), 94. In the conclusion, I point beyond the notion of "intervolvement." Intervolvement is a useful term; however, with regard to the movement of creation within divine action "intra-volvement" bears witness to the unconfused proximity between God and creation. See Conclusion below.

The Grammar of God

LANGUAGE AND PERCEPTION

To understand human activity requires an acknowledgement, to one degree or another, of the immensity and impossibility of such a project, a kind of *kata-apo-phatic* exercise. That is, human action is so varied and complex, incorporates numerous actors with varying degrees of involvement, is situated within multiple and often overlapping contexts and environments, engages the present with both past and future events, and is infinitely problematized by linguistic formulations in attempts to account for it. Confessing this multivalent complexity does not, however, prevent us from understanding human action. On the contrary, it is such an acknowledgement that makes any intelligible account of action possible. Before confessing the immensity of this problematic, one must acquire the grammar necessary to speak, or confess, as it were. A grammatical rubric is essential because linguistic use can impair or enhance one's vision of the above complexity. In other words, the very structure of language can suspend a person from perceiving the density of human activity.

A person's *habitus*[3] can enable (and has enabled) persons to understand human activity as reducible to an actor and an object. In the sentence, *I* walked the dog, the pronoun "I" occupies the position of subject; "walked" is the verb; "dog" is the object. Implicit in the very structure of the sentence is a subject-object bifurcation, whereby a subject performs an action *on* an object. Anyone who has ever walked a dog, even (or especially) a small dog, already knows that this statement is not exactly true, yet neither is it more true to say: The *dog* walked me. Once again, the implication of the sentence structure is that the subject performs an action *on* an object. In each instance, there is an active subject and a passive object. Whether "I" am or the "dog" is performing the action, or whether the "dog" or "me" is the object, the action remains external to the subject and object, reducing each to mere subjectivity or objectivity. Reworking the sentence structure can avoid this subject-object duality. For example: "We were walking." Or,

---

3 I refer here to the bodily comportment that gives rise to a particular way of perceiving the world, or how meaning is constructed through habituation in and of the world. See Pierre Bourdieu, *The Logic of Practice*, 52–97.

"The dog and I were walking." In each sentence, a direct or indirect object is missing while each subject is sustained. The "walker" is not performing an action on an external "walked." Rather, each is now involved in the act of walking, whereby agency becomes inconclusive. "Were walking" implies that the subjects are *involved* in a process — they are *participants* in an agency within which they act. This action at once implicates them — they are performing an action, yet the action encapsulates them — their subjectivity is situated within the act of walking.

The grammatical distinctions worked through above distinguish between active/passive and active/middle linguistic constructs. "We were walking" is a middle voice construct. The difference, as will be shown below, is relational. With an active/passive construct there is no essential relation between subject and object: the action is external to the subject and works on an object. Whereas the active/middle construct locates subjectivity within the action, and the would-be object become subject is involved in a shared agency — there is no subject-object dualism, yet neither is subjectivity conflated. Agency, not subjectivity, is blurred. Within an active/passive construction there is an essential autonomy for both subject and object. This reified autonomy makes illusory the relational bond created by activity. *Language is perception.*[4] The need for a grammar to account for agentive *involvement* is essential for moving beyond the aforesaid dualism. Subjective autonomy, in other words, is a linguistic construct; grammar is structured by habits of speech, which are socially conditioned and conditioning.

---

4 To say here that "Language is perception" is not to ascribe to the *Sapir-Whorf hypothesis*; rather, it is to allude to the reality that language — the totality of our speech and gestures — is our means of working through the manner of our inherent relatedness with people, places, and things. Language is hereby inseparable from the whole of our involvement with others in the world; therefore, as we will see further below, human perception is contingent upon how we use words and gestures to relate to others, whether people, places, or things. It is not unlike Roland Barthes' argument that we are obliged to "conceive language and discourse no longer in terms of an instrumental and reified nomenclature but in the very exercise of language." In other words, language does not point to something beyond itself. Rather, language is of the thing to which it points and cannot be separated from it. See Roland Barthes, "To Write: An Intransitive Verb," in *The Languages of Criticism and the Sciences of Man: The Structuralist Controversy*, ed. Richard Macksey (Baltimore: Johns Hopkins University Press, 1970), 134–56.

Language, as culturally conditioned, delimits perception, for better or for worse. To alter perception requires an alternative language acquired only through transforming one's habits of speech.[5]

THE MIDDLE VOICE

While much work has been done in hermeneutics and phenomenology to explore the embodied relation between speech and action, insufficient attention has been given to the structure of language with regard to the middle voice in particular and its disappearance. Émile Benveniste is the most well known linguist to have mapped the correlation between the structural loss of the middle voice in a post-Latin world and the disappearance of a medial sense regarding human action.[6] Suzanne Kemmer, more recently, has seemingly exhausted the meaning and importance of the middle voice for grappling with the modern binary of human action,[7] and Philippe Eberhard has summarized Benveniste's work in relation to Gadamer's hermeneutics, which has born much theological fruit.[8] In addition, Wendell Kisner, arguing for a rereading of Hegel in light of Hegel's middle-voice overtones, especially in the *Logic*, has convincingly shown how careful attention to the middle voice provides a much-needed corrective to human relationships in general and human relations with the natural world in specific.[9] The demise of the middle voice from modern language, save remnants in Greek that persist, involves a restructuring of grammar to such a degree that it is nearly impossible to articulate the everyday occurrence of one's *involvement* in the world. That is, speech fights against any attempt to verbalize a desire or action that is at once one's own, while having its origins outside the individual subject. Modern linguistic structures lack

5   For an interesting analysis of how this works, see Sarah Feldman Barrett, *How Emotions Are Made*, 84–111.

6   Émile Benveniste, *Problems in General Linguistics, Miami Linguistic 8* (Miami: University of Miami Press, 1973).

7   Suzanne Kemmer, *The Middle Voice* (Philadelphia: John Benjamins Publishing Company, 1993).

8   Philippe Eberhard, *The Middle Voice in Gadamer's Hermeneutics: A Basic Interpretation with Some Theological Implications* (Tübingen: Mohr Siebeck, 2004).

9   Wendell Kisner, *Ecological Ethics and Living Subjectivity in Hegel's Logic: The Middle Voice in Autopoietic Life* (New York: Palgrave MacMillan, 2014).

the verbal forms necessary to express this participatory relation — apart from the round-about way of *intransitivity* (although, as Kisner has shown, even this runs the risk of reducing agency to a "reflexive agent," rather than agency as "co-emergent" with the process of the action),[10] and because of said limitations, humans are conditioned by the active/passive binary of language, inclining the human subject to misperceive the medial nature of human experience and existence.

For instance, when the worshipper is at prayer in church, even in her own home, a common statement of this might be, "I went to church today," "I received Eucharist today," or "I prayed to God today." Each articulation of the action of going to church, receiving Eucharist, and praying to God is linguistically construed as if the action begins with the worshipper herself. "I," the subject, "went" / "received" / "prayed," verb, "to church" / "Eucharist" / "to God," direct object. There is no grammatical sense that the worshipper is involved in an action already underway, which then incorporates her when she becomes attentive to its movement. This is quite pronounced in more "Evangelical" churches where, in the context of a contemporary service of Holy Communion, parishioners may sit in comfy pews or chairs while trays of "oyster crackers" and grape juice are distributed. The pastor/pastoral leader (mis)quotes Jesus in the Gospels saying, "This is a *symbol* of my body. . . ."[11] The irony of this scriptural mishap is that these churches are often literalists in their treatment of sacred scripture. It is not even a mistranslation of the text, τοῦτό ἐστιν τὸ σῶμά μου (*This is my body*);[12] church leaders actually insert a word that there is no account of Jesus ever saying, altering the very meaning of what is taking place when worshippers gather for this meal. They fear being associated with Roman Catholics to such a degree that they actually manipulate the text.[13]

10   Ibid., 37.

11   The words of institution in the Gospels read: "This is my body." The insertion of the word "symbol" is a theologically deficient rendering of scripture, out of the Protestant fear that the bread and wine would be co-mingled in any way with the flesh and blood of Christ.

12   Matthew 26:26b.

13   One could argue that this scriptural abuse is akin to the work of those involved in the Jesus Movement, where verses of scripture are voted on as to whether Jesus actually said those words. It is always interesting just how much fundamentalists and liberals are really two sides of the same coin.

At the medial end of the spectrum is the *Prayer of Humble Access*,[14] where the faithful, preparing to receive the Body and Blood of Christ, pray to the Father that they be admitted and made worthy "to eat the flesh of thy dear Son Jesus Christ, and to drink his blood, that we may evermore dwell in him, and he in us." This indwelling of Christ in the faithful, which hearkens back to the Gospel of John, the epistles of Paul and, perhaps most importantly, Revelation 3:20 ("Listen! I am standing at the door, knocking; if you hear my voice and open the door, I will come in to you and eat with you, and you with me"), is a recognition that the worshipper does not merely feast on Christ in the Eucharist or some symbolic food; rather, the worshipper herself becomes a house of bread, a table at which the divine feasts, and herself the bread of God. She consumes and is consumed;[15] she enters the household of God and finds herself to be a house of bread; she approaches the table she is become. The indwelling is her life mediated by the gathering—the *ekklesia* (church), the table, and the bread and wine offered from God's own storehouse. One way to say this, however awkward it might strike the modern English-speaker's ear, would be to say, "I was gathered into the offering of the Son to the Father." Shorthand would be modestly simpler: "I participated in the self-offering of God today." And for those within the liturgical community, it might be summed up with, "I participated in liturgy today."[16] Otherwise, we run the risk of reducing the liturgical action to a this-worldly, psychic affair that is little more than a coping mechanism for life.

The average parishioner in the pew would be hard pressed to admit that this reduction is normative. Nevertheless, it is commonplace for the faithful to speak of liturgy in terms of what they "get out of it," whether they love the music, the traditional or contemporary language, or how the pastor/priest is "so casual." While few would admit their reasons are selfish, many if not most are only able to articulate what they like or don't like about a service on any given Sunday. For the liturgical sensibilities

14   See the *Book of Common Prayer* (1979), 337.

15   William Cavanaugh, *Theopolitical Imagination* (New York: T & T Clark, 2002), 77–98. See also Augustine, *De libero arbitrio,* on the radicalized phenomenology of eating which takes place when the worshipper receives the Eucharistic elements.

16   At the end of the day, this can be understood only in a community where liturgy is recognized as the action of God in Christ and not the "work of the people." See chapter one.

of the worshipper to be transformed, and for her perception of worship to become an involvement of heaven and earth in the Christic action, requires not simply faithful habits and practices but also faithful speech.[17] The liturgical participant must learn to speak as one involved in an action that precedes her, yet incorporates her in itself, where God is not an object of her worship, nor she an object of divine love, but involved, incorporated in the eternal self-offering of the Triune God for whom there is no objectivity.

The active/passive grammatical structure reduces human action to an action done (active) *or* an action undergone (passive).[18] In this sense, every verb has an actor *and* patient. The verb in Indo-European languages, however, as Benveniste shows, "has reference only to the subject, not to the object."[19] In most languages, the verb bears with it a signal that reveals or alludes to an objective or goal.[20] To speak of the middle voice, however, is to address the specific morphosyntactic relation of a subject and her action,[21] what Benveniste calls the *internal diathesis*.[22] *Internal diathesis*, as opposed to *external diathesis*, refers to a middle voice as opposed to active voice construct.[23] In the active voice, verbs denote a process that is accomplished outside the subject. In the middle voice, which is the diathesis to be defined by the opposition, the verb indicates a process centering in the subject, the subject is inside the process of the action[24]—inside his or her own action.[25]

Contrary to the active voice, in the middle voice, the subject "is the seat of the process."[26] The subject is at once the center of the action

17 As outlined in chapter 3, speech is born out of the language that is the interwoven-ness of space and habit, i.e. *habitus*.

18 Benveniste, *Problems in General Linguistics*, 146. Benveniste admits that this is putting it "roughly." This shorthand, however, will be expanded below.

19 Ibid.

20 Ibid.

21 Kemmer, *The Middle Voice*, 243.

22 Benveniste, *Problems in General Linguistics*, 145–51.

23 "Voice," here, "denotes a certain attitude of the subject with relation to the process—by which the process receives its fundamental determination." See Benveniste, *Problems in General Linguistics*, 146.

24 Benveniste, *Problems in General Linguistics*, 148.

25 Eberhard, *The Middle Voice in Gadamer's Hermeneutics*, 16.

26 Benveniste, *Problems in General Linguistics*, 149.

and the agent of the process; "he achieves something which is being achieved in him — being born, sleeping, lying [helpless or dead], imagining, growing, etc. He is indeed inside the process of which he is the agent."[27] To be born, for instance, is not just something that happens to me; rather, in being born, I achieve something that is achieved in me. I use this, perhaps exaggerated, example to get at the structure of the middle voice to which Benveniste directs our attention, which is a dynamic relation of mutual subjects involved in a shared agency, in an action that cannot be described in purely active or passive terms. With every mother and child, the mother does not simply give birth, and the child is not simply given birth to. Both mother and child are participants in an action that encompasses both; each is an *effect* which arises in and through being *affected*. In the middle voice, it is possible to conceive an action that is not reduced to a singular agency, whereby an action is imposed on an object.[28] For example, in the birthing of a child, the child is not a mere passive recipient of an action performed by the mother; rather, the child is *involved*, perhaps most notably in restructuring the mother's abdomen, breasts, and feet. In the simplest of terms: the middle voice enables me to recognize that any action I perform, because it affects my relationship with the person, place, or object involved in the act, also affects me. Telling my wife that I love her and kissing her on the lips before I walk out the door each morning is an act that I perform; however, even if she stands completely emotionless to my affection she is not passive. There is no *pure passivity*, for her loving or emotionless response to my affection, whether she is filled with joy or frustration, is a participation in an action that mediates "my act." The kiss never happens in a vacuum; rather, the singular act dwells within a horizon of activity conditioned by our marriage,

27 Ibid. It is important to note that an activity like sleeping is at once something we do and something done to us. It is a process in which we (unavoidably) participate. It is not exactly something I do, because it is in many ways a state of inactivity; yet it is not exactly something done to me, as I am the one sleeping. It is medial because sleep is happening to me *and* it is I who sleeps. One way we might speak of this, as will be revisited later, is as an active-passivity. I actively undergo that which happens to me.

28 Philippe Eberhard, "The Medial Age or the Present in the Middle Voice," *International Journal of the Humanities* Vol. 3, no. 8 (2005/2006), 127.

each of our sensibilities, our home, neighborhood, village and the town we inhabit at the point of a particular encounter on a particular day, which may be gloomy or sunny, cold or hot, all of which mediate our relationship and background the particular act in question. I may have said something hurtful; she may have slept poorly; our children may have stormed out the door to school without saying goodbye; any and all of which provide context for whatever happens next, which is to suggest that reducing human action either to active *or* passive relieves an action of its humanity, for humanity is inherently relational. Only the middle voice can account for the complexity involved in human action.

What is important to emphasize is how the middle voice, the *internal diathesis*, focuses on the subject's relation to the verb.[29] The subject is inside the process. The middle voice appears at first to blur the line between active and passive. "The process happens to the subject who is within it."[30] Yet as Benveniste points out, the middle voice is not a hybrid. Rather, it exposes a fundamental attitude of the subject's relation to the verb in opposition to the active voice.[31] In the middle voice, the action "envelopes the agent," while the agent remains "immersed in the action."[32] In this sense, the action precedes the subject of the act. Because the subject is neither primary to nor external from the act, subjectivity itself cannot be individuated. The subject is inherently *related*. She is related to her action and the other in such a way that there can be no clear boundary between the subject and anything that might otherwise be termed object. The nature of each is inseparable from their mutual *involvement* in the act in question.

Invoked above is the need of the middle voice for understanding not only human action but what it means to be human altogether. Using the middle voice as a kind of hermeneutic key enables us to conceive an action without necessarily establishing an object in the

29 Eberhard, *The Middle Voice in Gadamer's Hermeneutics*, 15.
30 Ibid.
31 Benveniste, *Problems in General Linguistics*, 146. See also Eberhard, *The Middle Voice in Gadamer's Hermeneutics*, 31.
32 Roland Barthes, "To Write: An Intransitive Verb," in *The Structuralist Controversy: The Languages of Criticism and the Sciences of Man*, eds. Macksey and Donato (Baltimore: John Hopkins University Press, 1970), 152.

process. That is, seeing through the middle voice reveals the dynamism of human action as multivalent and interwoven with the plethora of subjects involved, all the while sustaining the difference of each subject internal to the process of a verb. As Benveniste has argued, the elimination of the middle voice displaces subjectivity, redefining the origin of an action such that the subject is now the singular cause of an action that originates with her, and is performed by her on an object.[33] There is a perceptive shift woven into the syntactical movement away from the middle voice. Accordingly, the subject now ontologically precedes the verb, which, in addition to undermining the complexity of human action, has tremendous ethical implications. When the individual actor/agent becomes the origin of her action, culpability is now singularly attributable to a specified subject. Apart from a causal chain of events, there is no articulable inducement for an individual's action because she is not part of a process that encompasses her activity, as in the middle voice; rather, she is become her own origin — "the master of her own destiny."

The ethical ramifications of this are significant. If my action originates with me it must be the case that culpability for my action resides with me, the actor-agent. If I grow up in poverty with parents who are addicted to narcotics, living in Section 8 housing, does this have an effect on my actions and decisions? Any thoughtful person would answer yes to this question. However, in the ordinary, day-to-day orchestrations of society, whether in the realm of education or the workplace, especially in America, this background is functionally denied. That is, the person, whether a child or adult, is treated as one who has the same opportunities as everyone else. The child who grows up in poverty, a broken home, malnourished, and in less than adequate living conditions has, according to the prophets of democratic capitalism (or perhaps more fittingly, America's capitalist democracy), the same opportunity as the child who grows up in an upper-middle class home with two parents, well fed, and temperate living conditions. What sets them apart is not their background but the "*choices* they make," the

---

33 Benveniste, *Problems in General Linguistics*, 149.

"*effort* they put into succeeding," or their "psychological state," which is often articulated as existing apart from any material background.

This is especially poignant today with school shootings in America, where politicians like Marco Rubio balk at admitting that guns are involved in gun violence, as if a person can shoot another person with an assault rifle without having an assault rifle. This is a linguistic issue. That is, without a grammatical structure of language that makes bodily comportment a perceptive norm in relation to people, places, and things, i.e., guns, arguing over gun violence will always be reduced to the single shooter (subject) who kills (verb) children (direct object) at a school. To suggest that politicians, gun manufacturers, the NRA, and their supporters are not complicit, to greater and lesser degrees, in each death, is both a linguistic and a moral issue.

Seeing through the middle voice, however, enables us to recognize that human action is social. Human action is cultural rather than individual. Yes, the person who shot and killed the person on the street for money is the one who actually pulled the trigger. It is an action with an objective; this is difficult to deny. Nevertheless, this specific action is inseparable from a whole host of other actions that made the shooting possible, or better yet, imaginable. The shooter obtained a gun from somewhere, which was produced by some company, and was made possible by lobbyists and lawmakers. The fear that led the shooter to use the gun for the purpose of killing another person may have arisen from economic hardship, a stress-filled home, or loss of work in an economy where vying for power—violence—is normative. The need or desire for money is birthed out of a particular culture, whether it is the culture of late-capitalism, gang violence, or some other community of desire. From the lens of the middle voice, one is able to recognize that the shooter and the person who gets shot are part of an action that precedes the event of that particular shooting. A culture of violence, even if momentarily, relates the two persons in a process of activity, as the violent act courses through the shooter, altering the personhood of each. Both die as the trigger is pulled.

When we speak only in active/passive terms, it is easy to fail to understand the complexity of human action as that which always precedes any individual act. Before an action can occur it must be imaginable. Before it can be imagined it must be desired. And, depending on what is desired as an end, any means can be justified in the process. Peering through the middle voice window, however, we realize that there are no tabula rasas. Every action is conditioned and conditioning; every human is conditioned toward certain activities — conditioned to imagine certain behaviors as necessary and normative.

THE LINGUISTIC SUBJECT

We have been discussing at this point the grammatical subject and grammatical agent in relation to the verb. It is important now to clarify what a subject is in relation to the middle voice, in order to move into the medial nature of liturgical action for the subject. What, then, is a subject? Language, says Benveniste, "provides the very definition of man."[34] In other words, it is only through language that we come to speak and understand what it means to be human and, therefore, what it means to be a subject. Subject and person are hereby interchangeable. "It is in and through language that man constitutes himself as a *subject*, because language alone establishes the concept of 'ego' in reality, and *its* reality which is that of the being."[35] We might say, with Benveniste, that "*I*" am a subject when I say, "*I*."[36] Subjectivity, according to Benveniste, is a grammatically temporal designation of the human who says "I" in relation to a "you" at this moment in time.[37] The time at which one is a subject is the time at which one speaks as a subject. There is, therefore, no universal subject, only the particular subject who says "I" at the time of her speaking.

Benveniste arrives at this momentary subjectivity through an articulation of language not as instrumental but, rather, language as "in the nature of man."[38] There is no time, argues Benveniste, at which we can harken back to a human without language, language without a

34 Ibid., 171.
35 Ibid.
36 Ibid., 173.
37 Ibid., 172.
38 Ibid., 170. See also, Heidegger, *Poetry, Language, Thought*.

human.[39] Therefore, language—a natural property of the human—cannot be dissociated from the human as an instrument of her communication; it is not external to the speaker/hearer.[40] To be human is to speak.[41] Communication, then, is always a self-communication, even if it is always *more* than a self-communicating. "I" am always spoken into being by "my" act of speaking; "I" hereby become a subject by referring to "myself" as an "I." It is this that is meant by the aforesaid "language is perception."[42]

How we communicate, both verbally and non-verbally, is always more than mere words or gestures for describing people, places, things, or events. Every word spoken is a gesturing and every gesture performed a speaking, all of which condition the interpretation of the world for the speaker-gesturer. Accordingly, every word that is heard and every gesture witnessed is interpreted according to the language of the hearer-viewer, which may or may not be shared with the speaker-gesturer. Further, communication between two persons—their reciprocal speaking and gesturing, their hearing and viewing—is the formation of a language. The occurrence of a conversation is not merely an exchange of words, nor is it simply the employment of a shared tongue. Even for those whose interlocutors share a common language, conversation is no less a conversion, an *entering-into* the world formed by the present act of communicating. What does this mean? It means that communication is always simultaneously a speaking and hearing *from* and a gesturing and witnessing *to*. It is in this sense that language is the condition of experience—a pre-existing condition, as it were. Again, the human is she who is spoken into being in the act of speaking, "*called into being*," as W. H. Auden puts it, "by other persons, our parents, our siblings, our friends."[43] Accordingly, language is an articulation of the "total behavior" of a person by which she makes herself *present*.[44] Language hereby arises from within the human, by nature,

39 Benveniste, *Problems in General Linguistics*.
40 Ibid., 171.
41 Heidegger, *Poetry, Language, Thought*.
42 See p. 124, note 4.
43 W. H. Auden, *Secondary Worlds* (New York: Random House, 1968) 120, italics mine.
44 Cornelius Ernst, *Multiple Echo* (Eugene: Wipf & Stock, 2006), 106.

in response to that which is other than the human, so as to be present *with* what she is not. The human is her language. It is not external, even though language encompasses the speaker-hearer, gesturer-viewer.

In her work with autistic persons, Phoebe Caldwell discussed the struggle "normal" language users have in communicating with persons who have autism. In order for communication to occur, says Caldwell, each person has to recognize that "we are irrevocably bound to our bodies."[45] Everyone has what Caldwell describes as a sensory filter, which carries with it a certain picture of the world:

> The way in which I perceive, the messages that my senses send to my brain (both those from inside my body as well as those from my surroundings) and the way my brain interprets these, determine my responses to my environment and the people in it.[46]

In other words, my perceptive capacity, which involves not only my own specific body chemistry and conditioning but also the environment within which I am situated, constructs for me what is external to me, in, by, and through which I communicate with others.

In the wonderfully produced TV drama *The Good Doctor*,[47] Shawn Murphy, a young autistic surgeon, struggles to process the numerous social cues and normative communication forms of his colleagues and patients. Because of his autistic condition, as well as having savant syndrome, Murphy is able to see and recognize things that his colleagues cannot. Nevertheless, Murphy struggles to understand the nuances of sarcasm, flirtation, and the cutthroat dynamic pervasive in his hospital environment. His sensory filters are vastly different from those of his fellow residents and superiors. In Season 1, Episode 14, the show begins with a competition that pits two residents against two others in an effort

45 Phoebe Caldwell, *Delicious Conversations: Reflections on Autism, Intimacy and Communication* (Brighton: Pavilion Publishing and Media Ltd, 2012), 40.

46 Ibid.

47 *The Good Doctor*. "She." Episode 14. Developed by David Shore. ABC, February 5, 2018.

to create a modest competition to see which team can properly diagnose, treat, and send patients on their way. Led by Dr Lim, after pulling back the sheet to take a closer look at her patient, Dr Kalu blurts out, "That's a . . ." after which Dr Murphy chimes in, ". . . Penis! She's not a girl. He's a boy," he says. As the dialogue unfolds, Quinn, the transgender child, asks Dr Murphy a question: "How do you know you're supposed to be a boy?" "You're question doesn't make sense," he replies, "I'm not supposed to be anything. I am a boy, biologically, that's all." As the episode continues, Murphy, attempting to understand how the child experiences the world as a girl, begins asking questions: "Do you wear dresses?" Dr Kalu, ever interrupting Murphy in the exchanges says, "Murphy, don't." "Quinn is a boy who thinks he's a girl," responds Murphy, "I want to know why he thinks that." Entertained by his line of questioning, Quinn patiently responds, "Sometimes I wear dresses, but sometimes I wear leggings." "Do you like the color pink?," Murphy asks. Chuckling, Quinn responds, "I'm more of a purple girl." The line of questioning continues with continual interruptions from the more socially adept Dr Kalu, and throughout the entire episode Dr Murphy refers to Quinn as "he" or as "boy." Later, Murphy is alone with Quinn and asks, "What does it feel like to be a girl?" After a moment of silence Murphy follows with another question, obviously due to comments he has received from colleagues, "Are you angry? Was that an inflammatory question?" "I'd rather people ask questions instead of pointing and staring," Quinn responds. "When I used to look like a boy," Quinn continues, "I felt different. The kids at school didn't understand, so they picked on me. I spent a lot of time alone." We later learn that Quinn had attempted suicide. "When my parents let me be me," Quinn goes on, "I felt like I didn't have to pretend anymore. I felt free, like when you're in a pool and you just let go and float." As Murphy considers the scenario he responds, "I'm not a very good swimmer." Later he says to Quinn, "I don't know what it feels like to be anyone but me." "Me too," replies Quinn.

The Good Doctor is one of the best television dramas dealing with communication I have ever seen. Throughout each episode, everyone is learning how to communicate, how their preconceptions of others condition their actions and ability to perceive the world. In the episode discussed above, a drama unfolds between the two teams of doctors where competition drives their relationships. However, Dr Murphy, ever seeing in black and white, continually points out not what he himself has done right but highlights Dr Kalu's good decisions, with no attempt to coopt them as his own. He supports Kalu rather than competing with him, unlike the dynamic unfolding between the other team.

As the episode comes to a close, Dr Murphy returns home and asks his shady neighbor to help him break into the apartment's pool that is locked. Murphy wades in and we find the Good Doctor lying in the middle of the pool. His neighbor asks, "Not going to do no laps or nothing?" "No," replies Murphy. "Then what are you doing?" After a dramatic pause Murphy says quite simply, "Understanding." Murphy goes where words cannot, but does so in a way that is inseparable from speech. Murphy, inasmuch as he is able, attempts to inhabit Quinn's experience of "her" own body, not from the vantage of science but from the seat of "her" own experience of what it means for "her" to be a girl, something Murphy cannot comprehend in his body. At the close of the episode, Quinn's grandmother, ever troubled by the notion of Quinn being transgender, is entering the hospital room with pink flowers. "Quinn doesn't like pink," Murphy blurts out. Noticing the shock on her face, Dr Kalu says, "I think she'll like these." As the grandmother enters the room, we hear Murphy say, "*She's* more of a purple girl." Kalu recognizes his linguistic transformation as the screen fades to black. Murphy, while incapable of fully understanding Quinn's sensory filter as transgendered, enters into her world of experience and allows her sensory filter to guide him in order to relate to Quinn as she understands herself. As Caldwell points out, understanding comes from internalizing or aligning our movements in order to learn what a person's reality means to her, rather than looking from the outside and making judgments based on our own.[48]

The extreme examples of autism and transgender relations enable us to understand everyday speech more deeply. We are not here concerned with the viability of transgender relations; rather, our concern

---

48 Caldwell, *Delicious Conversations*, 4.

is to highlight how inhabiting the perceptive field of another opens us to see how our own conceptions are conditioned by our own embodied experience, for good or ill. Doing so, Caldwell shows, will "shift us from our own inner cartography into the perceptive world of someone else. Listening with the heart we see and learn to accept different versions of the world we share."[49] Those who live with autism, for instance, live with a damaged filtration system,[50] which often presents itself in physical, repetitive behavior. What often appears to be strange or unusual behavior is actually an attempt by the autistic person to deal with sensory overload.[51] Whereas most people are able to block out "unnecessary" information and focus on what is important in that moment, someone with autism, working with a "damaged filter," may not be able to set aside certain information, causing them to perseverate, which cycles through their mind until the matter is for them resolved, even while most would have already moved on. An autistic child banging on the table due to sensory overload, for example, will not be aided by someone grabbing their arms and preventing them from doing so. What may help them transition, however, is if someone mimics their behavior to show that they are heard. Caldwell offers an example of a patient chewing on a towel to show how this works.

> Janice is elderly and presents as being extremely anxious. She chews a towel repetitively and periodically wanders in an agitated manner. When she sits down on a sofa, I sit beside her and follow her jaw movements, exploring the feeling she is giving herself. Realizing how rhythmic it is, I tap this rhythm on her knee. Her brain recognizes this pattern and she comes out of her withdrawn state and starts to smile and takes an interest in what I am doing. (I have shifted her attention from solitary self-stimulation to an activity we are sharing.) Her relaxation is palpable to all the staff present. She lies back and eventually

49 Ibid., 26.
50 Ibid., 27.
51 Ibid., 27–28.

doses off. Her support staff comment that they have not seen her so relaxed before.[52]

Creating the rhythm that mimicked the chewing on the towel opened Janice to perceive in Phoebe Caldwell someone who could understand her concerns. She recognized that her anxiety was real, confirmed by Caldwell's rhythmic patterning, which enabled her to relax enough to fall asleep. Caldwell's response was an internalizing of Janice's anxiety, rather than a judgmental suppression of how her anxiety had manifested itself. What happens for Janice in the process, as Caldwell shows, is not only the recognition of a pattern but the drawing of her attention to that which is outside herself. This opens Janice to perceive beyond what has been amplified in her internally. Rather than treating Janice as the object of her care, Caldwell inhabits Janice's anxiety. Caldwell will later speak of this in the Eucharistic language of the Gospels, saying with regard to the persons in her care, "They have become in me and I in them." Again, from the *Prayer of Humble Access*, "Grant us ... to eat the flesh of thy dear Son, Jesus Christ, that we may evermore *dwell in him, and he in us.*"[53] Communication is a co-mingling act. It is an action whereby the interlocutors are involved in a movement that is at once central to who they are and yet encompasses them as well.

Working through the examples above allows us to attune ourselves to the experience of others and resonate with their perceptions, however difficult it may be for us to understand.[54] This way, says Caldwell, we can learn about each other, "not just as objects that can be assessed but as living realities to whom we can relate."[55] This is also why Caldwell seems to deviate from the language of science, using — unexpectedly — Meister Eckhart to help make sense of how communication works. What is needed is an incarnate language, a grammatical structure that lacks divisiveness between subjects and objects. In other

---

52   Ibid., 5.
53   *Book of Common Prayer* (1979), 337, italics mine.
54   Caldwell, *Delicious Conversations*, 16.
55   Ibid.

words, a form of communication where words have meaning in relation to, not in abstraction from, the sensory world of our interlocutors.

To return to the middle voice, it is important to reiterate that grammatical structure conditions the meanings we make. The very absence of a middle voice in modern languages establishes a (hidden) division between the subject and her action and, therefore, any other involved in the action of the verb. The linguistic construct of active/passive in relation to the verb disallows a porous differentiation and delimits the human imaginary to see only division. Any articulation, therefore, of an *inter*locutor or *inter*relatedness is always a fighting against one's own language, a groping for words — a stammering, as it were. Grammatical structure is the preexisting condition of speech, to such a degree that my very intuition of the world and the other is already inscribed upon me, even while I experience it as *my own*. It has me before I know it, and I deceive myself into believing thereby that *my* thoughts are *mine*. It might be more correct to say that the world intuits itself in me. This is akin to David Jones's description of a work of art. Art, argues Jones, cannot be understood as self-expression, as if the artist has a self that is separable from the world and others.[56] Rather, my art is a manifestation of the conditioning to which I have been given and to which I give myself. My action, my art, reveals the God or gods to whom I sacrifice and am being sacrificed.

To recognize art and action as that which precedes and proceeds from the subject of the action — the subject as the "seat of [a] process...[who] achieves something being achieved in him"[57] — is to become aware of the "total behavior" noted by Auden that conditions the whole of human perception. Conversation is a helpful analogy in this regard, because what one speaker has to say is always in relation to a hearer and what has already been said, either by the interlocutor or a preceding speaker/author. Merleau-Ponty describes this well in *The Phenomenology of Perception*.

---

56 Jones, *Epoch and Artist*, 143–79.
57 Benveniste, *Problems in Modern Linguistics*, 149.

I precede my thought in the listener. I am not passive while I am listening; rather, I speak according to . . . what the other is saying. Speaking is not just my own imitation, listening is not submitting to the initiative of the other, because as speaking subjects we are *continuing*. We are resuming a common effort more ancient than we, upon which we are grafted to one another and which is the manifestation, the growth of truth.[58]

For Merleau-Ponty to suggest that I go before myself in speaking—that I precede my own thought—is to suggest that my thoughts are thoughts *relative to*, they are not simply *my thoughts*. My thinking and speaking are not other than the relation I share with the totality of my environment and the event of speaking with this particular person right now, along with the totality of her environment that is overlapping with mine, all of which flows through the subjects involved in the act of speaking. At no point am I able to describe myself and my relatedness or un-relatedness to others apart from my own linguistic field of perception. Even to say that, "I have no words," is a verbal admission that my experience is beyond language. It remains perceptive through my linguistically condition field of perception, which is narrower or wider depending on my ability and willingness to enter the sensory world of others.

We have seen thus far that the human is inseparable from her language, and that language, while not limited to mere words, is conditioned by certain normative conceptions that constitute communication. The examples provided by Phoebe Caldwell enable us further to recognize that communication involves a mutual indwelling of subjects within the communicative act, at least if understanding is the goal. By inhabiting the experience of other persons we learn to feel the world as they do. Complete comprehension remains impossible; however, this is how understanding is achieved. Parsing this out as we have above allows us now to return to the middle voice as a lens by which to grapple with human action and agency, which will become increasingly important as we deal with the liturgical participant's role and involvement in liturgy.

---

58   Maurice Merleau-Ponty, *Phenomenology of Perception*, 144.

AGENCY, ACTION, PARTICIPATION

When we speak of agency, we are typically referring to the cause or initiator of an action. The agent, we might say, is the voluntary causer of the action she performs. Jennifer walked the dog. In the structure of the sentence, Jennifer is the agent. Nevertheless, her syntactical agency in the sentence does not account for the dog's holding a leash in its mouth when Jennifer walks in the door of her apartment. According to the structure of the sentence, Jennifer is the agent, even if the dog initiates the walk in actuality. Additionally, the very existence of a dog in Jennifer's apartment presupposes the need for it to be walked. However, it would not be quite right to say that the dog is the agent. We might say that Sally, the dog, brought her leash to Jennifer to go for a walk. Here the agent is Sally, the dog. Sally initiates the walk. Again, the arrangement of the words on the page betrays the unique relationship that exists between a dog and her owner. Even to say that the dog has an "owner," a common claim, runs counter to the experience one has of living in a home with a dog. (All the more problematic is this assertion when the pet is a cat.) When we speak of the middle voice we are concerned with the relationship between the subject and the verb, and because the relation of a subject to her action is not limited to her subjectivity, since the action encompasses all subjects involved in the sentence, the middle voice is able to account for the lived experience of humans going about their ordinary, *intervolved* lives with other people, animals, places, and things. This is also to suggest, which we will discuss further below, that the loss of the middle voice is bound up together with the decay and near loss of any sense of shared or common life. If my action is always caused by me, and the person toward whom I act is always the passive object of my action, then my action, even the most charitable of acts, will always be an act that separates me from another person, distancing me from the other with every active/passive constructed sentence thought or spoken. When verbal subjects have direct objects, human action becomes an *othering act*, rather than a medial one. Action becomes unilateral, directed toward a goal or end external to the actor. We might return to the analogy of Caldwell and Janice above. Had Caldwell stripped the towel from her mouth and restrained Janice's arms and legs, the end result may have been the same with Janice falling asleep, though this time through exhaustion rather than a feeling of calm and relief. In this scenario, Janice would have been the object of Caldwell's care, however uncaring it might have been. However, Caldwell inhabited Janice's sensory world, which opened Janice to what was outside — Caldwell, enabling a mutual indwelling in a common rhythm. Caldwell and Janice became involved in a movement of rest, whereby each became engaged in a single action, mutually inhabited. There is no clear agent or patient; rather, they are actors, intervolved in a mutually indwelling agency.

When agency is inconclusive, as it is with the middle voice, it becomes difficult if not impossible to think of an action that runs in a single direction, that is, from subject to object. By encompassing the multiple relations of a sentence as subjects involved in the act, the middle voice makes possible the integration of the horizons of each subject without sacrificing the distinctness of each. Moving beyond voice and mere sentence structure, the middle voice opens a window into the pattern of relationships, revealing that the pattern of a relationship *is* the relationship. My action, hereby, is not something I do to another; rather, the action is that which conditions my relationship with another person, inseparable from the action I perform, even if I do not initiate or control the action I perform. For it to be *my* action does not mean the action has to originate with me (agent), nor does it necessitate that the action be conditioned by me, but it does mean that I participate in it. This is Benveniste's aforementioned *internal diathesis*. The act does not start with me, per se, but it does include me and I include myself in it by a willed participation.

If we consider the nature of the middle voice in light of Maximus Confessor's description of the *volitive*, as outlined in chapter two, we are able to conceive a relation between agency, action, and subjectivity or personhood as an interconnected web that is porous and malleable, rather than separate and fixed. Ethically speaking, this broadens the spectrum of complicity with regard to human action, both positively and negatively, as the most passive of participants remains a participant in the action as one incorporated or encompassed by it.[59] To do nothing is no longer to be passive; it is to be involved, willingly or unwillingly, in an act of which I may not be an *active* participant, because the action mediates subjectivity whether I like it or not. If we live in a forest that is being clear-cut by an overseas logging company, you may tie yourself to a tree in protest and I may sit idly by watching it happen. In each instance, while your degree of complicity may be lesser than mine, each of us is complicit by virtue of our *being involved* in the act. The action of which neither of us are agents nonetheless relates us to those who perform the act upon the forest, altering each person's relationship with the land and each other by the cultural pattern of the market that devastates the land for profit; the forest is likewise involved and is not strictly passive to the act. We might draw an analogy here to Jesus's discussion of the speck in our neighbor's eye as compared to the log in our own, no pun intended. "Do not judge," says Jesus, "so that you may not be judged. For with the judgment you make you will be judged, and the measure you give will be the measure you get."[60] Relieving myself of complicity in another's action by denying that I have done wrong in the process may condemn me to an even harsher judgment, for there is only one sin — turning away from God. Presuming that another's sin is not also my own, even in a limited sense, is synonymous with withholding forgiveness — the degree to which I will be forgiven. This does not mean ignoring the act; rather, it means confessing the sin as one who has tasted redemption and desires the same for all others. The unwillingness to see my involvement and complicity in an action that does not originate with me, an action I neither will nor actively perform, remains an act that alters my relationship with the world and others, thereby involving me, to greater or lesser degrees depending on my proximity or willed participation, in the act.

59 A humorous example of this can be examined by watching the final episode of *Seinfeld*, where each of the main characters witnesses a man being robbed on the street, videotapes its happening, and laughs about how overweight the gentleman being robbed is, which prevented his getaway. They are complicit in the crime and found guilty in a court of law because they merely observed the event and, therefore, are basically accomplices. See *Seinfeld*, "The Finale," directed by Andy Ackerman (May 14, 1998; Los Angeles: NBC).

60 Matthew 7:1–2.

This may be all the more important for the good and charitable act. While considering the sin of another I may deny all complicity, I am likely also to deny the complicity of others in the good act that I perform. In so doing I situate the agency of positive activity within my own subjectivity, such that the action I perform remains unilateral, a good that I do or perform, with no acknowledgement of another's persuasion, instigation, or involvement. Each functions under the same logic, the logic that an action has a single source, attributable only to the subject/agent of the action.

As discussed above in relation to the middle voice and the reduction to an active/passive vocal structuring of language, we can begin to infer that the grammatical nature of human action or action in general reduces subjectivity, human or otherwise, to either actors whose actions are singular and separating or passive patients who are affected but not affecting, each remaining external to the act. In the simplest of terms, the active/passive construct reduces action to a unilateral direction; it only flows from subject to object, and the object is only ever passive. The difficulty, then, of recognizing the medial nature of human action and action in general is that any articulation thereof fights against the very structure of modern language. It requires continual explanation, an explanation of the middle voice *in* active-passive terms. This suggests that the way beyond such reductionism may very well require a grammatical return to the middle voice, perhaps even leaving behind the passive altogether. If the structure of language limits the field of perception, then any alteration of perception will require not just a rephrasing or reframing of the subject at hand, as many have suggested, but a restructuring of language, so as to account for the fullness of human experience without limiting an individual's experience to a false subjectivity or mere objectification.

Tracing the linguistic field of vision construed by the active/passive structure of modern language has been necessary to delve into the nature of divine agency and human action with regard to the drama of liturgy. In what follows, we will explore how Liturgy, the action of the Son's eternal offering to the Father, mediated by the eternal procession and return of the Spirit, involves a singular agent-action, within which all of creation participates and is incorporated, in greater and lesser degrees of complicity, for the life of the world. The middle voice hereby serves as a hermeneutic key for the mutual indwelling nature of *leitourgia*.

OUR ONLY MEDIATOR AND ADVOCATE

How might our language affect our understanding of liturgical action? Given that it was not until the nineteenth century that *leitourgia* was retranslated as "the work of the people," linguistically reconfiguring liturgical action as something directed toward an object, rather than flowing through the worshipper, how might the middle voice provide access to the medial nature of liturgy, in order that worshippers inhabit the movement of God more deeply and deliberately? The middle voice left everyday grammar long before *leitourgia* was mistranslated by the Presbyterians of Scotland in 1888, and while the cultural influences on Christian liturgies will have to wait for another essay, it is easy to speculate among post-Reformation circles that a shift in liturgical speech followed a move away from Catholic[61] and Orthodox liturgies where sacramental mediation remains.

It is tempting at this point to suggest that a return to the middle voice in linguistics is long overdue, and while I'm not arguing against this, it is certainly beyond the scope of this essay. The purpose, rather, is to recognize how the linguistic patterns of modern languages limit our ability to understand the nature of human action as mediated, and to see in the middle voice of ancient languages a window of perception that opens our imaginations to see action less as something *we do* or something *done to us* and more as that within which *we are involved*. With regard to liturgy in particular, it is to show forth the nature of liturgical action as that within which the Christian lives, and moves, and has her being.

"There is one God," writes Paul in his first letter to Timothy, "there is also one mediator between God and humankind, Christ Jesus...."[62] There is little doubt in the mind of most Christians that Jesus is the

---

61 Within "Catholic" I lump Anglican (and Episcopal) as well as Lutheran and Reformed traditions that carry on the Catholic faith not limited to a belief separate from the body.

62 1 Timothy 2:5.

mediator of the human's relationship with God. But it is uncertain what modern Christians might mean or understand with regard to Jesus and his medial role in creation. If Jesus alone mediates humanity and divinity, what does this mean for human action, especially as it relates to each person's liturgical role? Is Jesus the go-between, as in mediation law, negotiating between us and God to decide who gets to have more custody over the children or whether God gets the vacation home? Or, is Jesus God from God, Light from Light, who in his very Person, as Second Person of the Trinity, *is* he whose substantiating action assimilates human nature to the inter-Trinitarian Liturgy of eternal giving and receiving, proceeding and returning, whereby volitive participation in the act-agency of Christ makes manifest our being recapitulated[63] in Jesus of Nazareth? It is for this reason that translation and diathesis are of utmost importance. To reiterate once more, mistranslating *leitourgia* as "the work of the people" bears an implicit understanding of the divinity of Jesus as less than God. If *leitourgia* is not "the work of the One for the sake of the many," then Jesus is an exemplar of faith but not *Faith Incarnate*. As to diathesis, the linguistic voice of modern languages delimits our ability to recognize and understand the faith of Christ. To apply Charles Taylor's buffered reading of history over the past five hundred years, in the course of human history, well before the Reformation or Enlightenment, the grammatical shift to active and passive voices creates a linguistic buffer that obfuscates any relationality between a subject and her "object." There really is no "object" in the middle voice; objectivity arises with the loss of the middle voice and the arrival of the passive.

The liturgy of the church throughout the centuries has, however, resisted an active-passive dualism, whereby either the worshipper is the object of God's action or God the object of the human's worship. This dichotomous relation may resonate with post-Enlightenment sensibilities, where the worshipper is become the object of God's love; however, if the human in her particularity is a *logos* of the *Logos*—a

---

63 Again note the double meaning. We know our *being* as recapitulated in Christ through volitive participation in *being recapitulated* by Christ, which is an eternal event—we are never not being recapitulated.

portion of God,[64] then such objectification on the part of either God or human is either a reduction to univocity, as aforementioned with Duns Scotus,[65] or the introduction of a division between God and his action. It must be made explicit that articulating that God is separable from his action, or that the union between act and being in fact needs articulating, is the result of an active/passive grammatical dualism, whereby the subject/agent of an action always has an object/patient. The middle voice makes room and accounts for the interconnectedness of agency and action between multiple subjects involved in and related by the action. God is hereby inseparable from, though not identical to, creation. Deism, for example — that a creator-God made the universe yet remains detached from it — is linguistically imaginable only apart from the middle voice. Accordingly, returning to our liturgical focus, by locating agency in Christ, who is the action he enacts, this also situates the worshipper within the action of divine liturgy, gathered as she is into the Triune Economy of self-offering and reception, procession and return, through volitive participation. The action of Christ — who *is* action qua action — is not external to the worshipper. The worshipper exists within the action of God in Christ — *internal diathesis*, recapitulated in Christ who remains the singular agent of all faithful liturgy and yet incorporates all of creation into his self-offering to the Father — inter-Trinitarian worship. All of creation is already involved in the procession and return of God from and to himself in Christ; however, it is volitive participation in the liturgy that makes-manifest the truth of one's *natural nature*.[66] A person cannot know Christ — cannot know as she is known by Christ — apart from volitive participation in the liturgy. This is more than showing up for church. It is giving oneself to *being given*; it is a deliberate and willful involvement in an action that is not one's own, and yet is inseparable from the person (subjectivity) of the worshipper.

The medial nature of worship runs counter to modern sensibilities, where the liturgical gathering so often appears to be a performance

---

64 See chapter 2 above.
65 See p. 34, note 104.
66 Maximus, *Ambiguum 7*, 1084D.

taking place up front or center stage, while those gathered are passive receptacles of spiritual information or biblical interpretation. This can occur in the most traditional Eucharistic churches as in the most modern lights-and-camera assemblies. It is important to be clear as to what mediality and volitive participation are. The infant who is baptized at two weeks of age, is she a volitive participant? The forty-five-year-old son who is mentally handicapped, standing in worship with his hands raised during praise choruses, is he a volitive participant? The elderly woman sitting in the pew, occupying the same pew for the past fifty-nine years, having nearly rubbed away the beads on her rosary, is she a volitive participant? And likewise for the professor, the bureaucrat, the entrepreneur, or the homeless man in the back, and for that matter the priest up front, are they volitive participants? In answering such questions it is important to recall our previous discussion on the nature of grace and faith.

Each of the above participants is involved in the gracious condescension of God in Christ made-manifest in the liturgical action of the church; however, they are involved *in proportion to* their own self-offering. In the midst of this medial understanding of life in christic action is a taking up of one's cross. It is not enough to say that Christ took up his cross and, therefore, I have no cross to bear; rather, medially speaking, in taking up my cross I learn to inhabit the cross of Christ, and in proportion to my own cruciform habituation is the degree to which I am met by grace and recognize the truth of my life hidden in Christ. Accordingly, the baptized infant cannot be said to be less involved, nor less a volitive participant, simply because of her undeveloped faculty of mind, weakness in body, or complete dependence on others. Moses floating down the river as an infant is involved in the saving action of God, and it is Moses's volitive participation in the redemption of Israel that will continue to serve as his inhabiting the saving action of God as he is tossed and turned in the basket, floating downstream. Volitive participation hereby describes a continual and proportional habitation in grace, whereby the human increases in willed likeness to Christ whose image she has always borne. It is always a *catching up with* the creative action of God in Christ, an action continually stirred up within by a whole world that groans for God.[67] Accordingly, the human is always already a participant before becoming a *volitive participant*. A person will know herself as mediated to the degree that she gives herself to being mediated in Christ. It is not a matter of whether one is being mediated; it is always a matter of knowing what mediates one's life and giving oneself to Christ's liturgical mediation, as opposed to worldly forms of mediation.[68]

In Christ, mediation is always a self-mediation. Christ *is* what he mediates; he *is* the act of mediating. All of creation exists within his medial action — all things live, and move, and have their being in Christ.[69] It is notable how Paul describes the medial nature of life in Christ in his letter to the Philippians.

> Therefore, my beloved, just as you have always obeyed me, not only in my presence, but much more now in my absence, work out your own salvation with fear and trembling; for it is God who is *at work in you, enabling you both to will and to work* for his good pleasure.[70]

Paul describes the working out of one's own salvation as an attending to the work of God within each person, which enables volitive participation in the action/work of Christ. Beforehand, Paul has invited the Philippians to "let the same mind be in you that was in Christ Jesus,"[71] going on to describe an inseparability of body and mind. Christ, says Paul, emptied himself, became a slave, humbled himself, was obedient, and even died on a cross; this is why Jesus of Nazareth, who revealed in his body who God is, is to be praised and worshipped.[72] Paul at first appears to offer a litany of exemplary action for all to emulate, yet he

---

67   Romans 8:22–23, "We know that the whole creation has been groaning in labor pains until now; and not only the creation, but we ourselves, who have the first fruits of the Spirit, groan inwardly while we wait for adoption, the redemption of our bodies."

68   See Luke 11:17–24.

69   John 1.

70   Philippians 2:12–13, italics mine.

71   Philippians 2:5.

72   Philippians 2:6–11.

makes clear that it is this divine, obedient, and humble slave, Jesus, who is God, who dwells within each person to enable the human *to work the work of God*. To have the same mind hereby means to increase in awareness of the death and resurrection of Christ through volitive participation, giving one's whole self to being mediated by God.

What Paul describes in relation to working the work of God is analogous to his articulation of the liturgical economy outlined in chapter one. For Christians to let the same mind be in them as it is in Christ suggests, following the verbal relation of the middle voice, that the medial action of Christ is operative in the person. The relation between God and the human is not a tug-of-war between opposing forces with the human in the middle, as shown in the familiar cartoon images of an angel on one shoulder and a demon on the other. We might think more of a magnetic force. The human, as a portion of God, bears a magnetic relation to God, we might say. God in Christ is always present before humanity, drawing all people to himself, as a magnetic force draws another magnet. However, the presence of God can be a force of energy that deters the human, based on his or her likeness to God. As one's volitive participation in Christ increases, likewise does one's attraction to God. The force of God remains stable, whereas the field of the human fluctuates based on habit of life. This magnetic force between God and human is a medial force that precedes the individual subject yet never relieves the subject of her personhood or particularity. Additionally, the compulsion of one's nature as a portion of God to move toward God is what we might call a non-compulsory compulsion. This compulsion is what Maximus Confessor calls the human's "inner condition." It is non-compulsory, however, in the sense that the human's movement requires her to attend to this *inner condition.*

> [T]he Divine is moved to the extent that it creates an inner condition of desire and love among beings capable of receiving them, and it moves insofar as it naturally attracts the yearning of those who are being moved to it.[73]

---

73 Maximus Confessor, *Ambiguum* 23, 1260C.

Following Maximus, it is more appropriate to say not that God moves the human or that the human moves God but that God moves God within humans, and by giving herself to this *inner condition* of divine motion[74] the human willfully enjoins herself to her true self as a portion of Love. Again, not unlike a magnetic force, one's form of life will determine whether the connection between God and human increases or bounces off, as it were. We might even go so far as to say that, magnetically speaking, as a portion of God, when the human idolatrously makes her life as a god separable from God, she attempts to relate to God with the same magnetic force, which causes the shift away from Christ. However, attending to God as a human, humbly acknowledging the principle of one's being as divine, the attraction is direct and strong, and increases with humility. All of this is simply to say that for Christ to be the mediator of humanity with God means that the human is incorporated into the action of Christ — his self-offering to the Father — and is gathered into God's procession and return by the Holy Spirit.

Mediality denotes the condition of one's being in Christ. "It is an activity of a subject encompassed in a common act, which . . . is God's action in Christ. . . ."[75] As to the liturgical economy, there is but a singular agent of creation, the Triune God — a shared agency. God who is *actus purus* — pure power-act — is not other than his action. Agent and action are one in God. To live is to participate in the action of God, to one degree or another. This also suggests that, while volitive participation in the action of God in Christ is the end of humanity, to withdraw from or work against divine action is perhaps best understood as a *non-act*. To turn away from God — sin — cannot properly be called an act, since God is action and, accordingly, action must thereby

---

74 The understanding of moving with God is well presented in the prayer for the Second Sunday in Lent from the *Book of Common Prayer (1928)*: ". . . Give us grace to use such abstinence, that, our flesh being subdued to the Spirit, we may ever obey *thy godly motions* in righteousness, and true holiness, to thy honour and glory. . . ."

75 Philippe Eberhard, "The Mediality of Our Condition," *Journal of the American Academy of Religion*, Volume 67, Issue 2, 1 June 1999, https://doi.org/10.1093/jaarel/67.2.411, 423.

inhabit the agency of Christ, which is the natural motion of humans.[76] This also accords with Augustine's definition of sin as *privation of being*, for while all movement stands in relation to the singular action of God, either toward or away from, to act is to be moved by one's end, God, while a non-act is to reject one's being moved. We might say that volitive participation in liturgy and the life of virtue is to continually align oneself with the action of God in Christ, while turning away from divine action — *non-act* — is that alone which originates in the human. Nevertheless, it is not properly called a human action, for the human is not the origin of humanity, and, although a *non-act*, it cannot but stand in relation to the divine action it rejects. Agency, in this reduced, immanent sense, is idolatry. The singularity of action made-manifest in Christ is the point of reference for all movement. To move away from Christ — *non-action* — remains a movement toward God, for there is only one meaning of action: that which participates in the movement of God from and to himself. All human movement stands in relation to divine action, either as participation or negation.

Recognizing that the inward groaning of our bodies[77] is the *inner condition* of the human's *natural nature* as a participant in the liturgical agency of Christ opens us to the mystery of human action as *naturally* divine. That is, what is properly understood as a human act cannot be divorced from the creative action of God that incorporates, by virtue of her createdness, the human in Christ's self-offering to the Father. The human is by nature mediated. Therefore, to worship — to participate in the liturgy — is to be caught up in the procession and return of God from and to himself. I give myself to being given. It is not a work that I do; it is an action I inhabit that transcends agentive categories of subjectivity.

AN ACTIVE-PASSIVITY

James K. A. Smith's recent work on "secular liturgies" has shown how liturgical formation reaches well beyond the walls of churches, and that as liturgical beings we are conditioned by all manner of

76 Maximus Confessor, *Ambiguum 15*, 1217C–D.
77 Romans 8:23.

desire-instigating habits and patterns that condition how we perceive our relationships with others.[78] It should be clear at this point that what we are exploring here is not only the material practices and tangible forms of liturgical action as they specifically relate to Christian churches and as they have traversed through history, but also the nature of liturgical action as that which precedes and proceeds from a church's, and its individual members', participation in Christ, who in his Person is the revelation of divine action. In working linguistically through the middle voice, showing the medial nature of liturgical action in Christ, we have shown how important is the linguistic voice for describing the liturgical event. Limited to an active/passive grammatical structuring, even speaking in medial terms transgresses the boundaries of modern language because there is no *voice* for so doing. It is necessary to recognize in this that the grammatical shift away from the middle voice in modern languages is a perceptive shift,[79] a shift that long antedates the more philosophical and phenomenological shift following the 16th-century Reformation and scientific revolution described by Charles Taylor,[80] although it would be impossible to claim that either movement or language precedes the other. Rather, as has been suggested, the two are inseparable. The human is her language.

With the loss of the middle voice, however, in the subject's becoming exterior to the process of the verb, the subject becomes synonymous with the agent of the action. Agency hereby grows out of a displaced subjectivity, whereby the subject, whose action is now grammatically externalized with the elimination of the middle voice, becomes the origin of her action, as opposed to a participant in an action happening to her, which does not deny that her action is her own; rather, it is to recognize that one's action is always beyond individuation. In this grammatical restructuring arises a feeling of "self-consciousness." I become self-aware — conscious of myself as my own individualized

---

78   See James K. A. Smith, *Desiring the Kingdom* (Grand Rapids: Baker Academic, 2009); *Imagining the Kingdom* (Grand Rapids: Baker Academic, 2013); *Awaiting the King* (Grand Rapids: Baker Academic, 2017).

79   Kisner, *Ecological Ethics*, 34.

80   Charles Taylor, *A Secular Age* (Cambridge: Harvard University Press, 2007).

self—to the extent that I recognize myself as the origin of my own action—that I am the agent of my action. As a grammatical subject with no middle voice, my subjectivity—my personhood—precedes my action. I become the sole governor of my actions, which hereby originate with me apart from external conditions or conditioning.

One area in which this reified self comes to capture the modern imagination is with the reduction of art to "self-expression." Picasso describes art as a revelatory act, whereby the artist inhabits the canvas with her body and experiences a manifestation of her bodily comportment conditioned by the totality of her relationship to the world.[81] Accordingly, the artist becomes aware of herself as one whose body is interwoven with the fabric of the world, which becomes visible to her, poured out on canvas. This artistic recognition is not a matter of self-awareness or self-expression so much as it is an awareness of one's being expressed.[82] Reducing art to self-expression follows a grammatical reduction of the subject as agent, limiting the origin of one's thinking and being to the immanent and isolated context of a radical subjectivity. In ontological terms, or at least in a scriptural sense, this subjectivism is as ancient as Adam and Eve. It is the sin of idolatry; subjectivism is the reduction of knowledge to a world disconnected from the *Gnosis* that exceeds it,[83] whereby knowledge of a thing or person ceases to be a relational wisdom where each is incorporated in the act of knowing, now become the informational knowledge of consumption. Again, this is as ancient as the world, and it is important to recognize that while articulation proceeds from experience, our experience is captured and interpreted through the grammatical tools available at present. Again, I do not perceive apart from my language.

When the grammatical tool delimits the perceptive experience, it cannot but cloud the nature of that experience, which runs the risk of

---

81   Juhani Pallasmaa, *The Eyes of the Skin: Architecture and the Senses* (Chichester: Wiley-Academy, 2005), 45.

82   Again, note the double meaning. One's *being* is expressed—mediated, by *being expressed*—by the medial act of making manifest one's mutual involvement with the world.

83   I use *Gnosis* here in direct reference to the early Christian use by Irenaeus, for whom *Gnosis* is inseparable from bodily habituation, not following Gnostics who will later deny this natural and mutual indwelling.

actually closing the human off from her experience of the world. This may very well account for the "delay" in human history of the perceived "buffer zone" that Charles Taylor describes long after the arrival of Latin and a reduction to the binary of active and passive voices.[84] While the grammatical loss happened much earlier in human history, it still took some time for it to be *felt*, although there are numerous and gradual shifts occurring well before the scientific revolution. The grammatical reduction of the subject's relation to the verb as either agent (active) or patient (passive), however, makes it possible to reimagine human action as unilateral rather than relational. While it is true that language flows out of experience; it is also true to say that language conditions how we imagine our experience. As the background of the artist conditions her perceptual horizon, which is poured onto the canvas, likewise does the linguistic enculturation of the artist condition her ability to understand what is made manifest in her art. In a world of the buffered self, art is reduced to self-expression.

When the artist-poet David Jones questions the origins of poetry, what calls it into being, he relates it to the squeezing of grapes to make wine or the confluence of sinuses in the skull, where the blood comes together and drains into one of two transverse sinuses.

> [Poetry] involves the employment of a particular language or languages, and involves that employment at an especially heightened tension. The means or agent is a veritable torcular, squeezing every drain of evocation from the word-forms of that language or languages.[85]

Poetry, we might say, like Tolkien's Elvish language, is the thing it expresses. It comes together within the poet as a confluence of worlds, and whether she is a professional writer, an intellectual, or a person who happens to put pen to paper, the poet is involved in an action the agency of which Jones describes as a "deposit," a mythos of which the

---

84 Taylor, *A Secular Age*, 352–76.
85 Jones, *Epoch and Artist*, 117.

poet herself is a product.[86] For Jones, language is the agency of poetry, one's *habitus*—the whole complex of a human's embodied, cultural habituation and habitation—one's haptic sense. Accordingly, poetry arises naturally within each person as a confluence of linguistically embodied worlds—the deposits of enculturation, as it were. Agency, then, is not to be ascribed to the poet herself; rather, the poet is one who gives herself to this confluence within and, like a wine press, squeezes out the worlds of her bodily comportment into poetic verse. This is why it is a gross misunderstanding to call art "self-expression," because it divides the artist from her art, reducing her artistry to the fiction of her imagination, as if she can imagine anything apart from her relationship with the world of her embodiment.

What we have been describing is another turn of the notch with regard to the medial nature of human life, which has been to help us reach the point of recognition that liturgical action is no less a "deposit" of the liturgical worlds inscribed on our bodies, liturgies that long precede our involvement in them, but are inseparable from who we are and how we imagine what worship is. Liturgy, hereby, is not a matter of self-expression. It is not to be governed by the whims of any one individual's sensibilities. Rather, liturgy is the confluence of linguistic worlds which have passed through the torcular of Christ, who is the wine press of God. The church's participation in the action of God in Christ, if it is to be called liturgy, will resemble this gathering of humanity into Christ's body, so to return the human to herself, transfigured into Eucharist, *for the life of the world*. The church, then, should resemble less a gathering of likeminded folk who enjoy similar tastes in spirituality, and more a wine press, which crushes each person as she enters, coalescing each in the chalice of God, mingled with each other in Christ by the Spirit, to become *little christs*, as Chrysostom puts it, assimilated as they are to the Son in proportion to their participation in the sacramental way. It is in this sense that liturgical mediality can be understood as an *active-passivity*, perhaps our best way of pointing toward the middle voice. It is a giving of ourselves to an

86   Ibid.

action happening to us, to an agency that is not our own. Hereby do we become *leitourgia* — the work of God. We become Christ in proportion to our participation in the work of the One, which is for the sake of the many.

CONCLUSION

Trapped as we are in the binary linguistic world of active and passive voices, any description of liturgy as participation in an agency and action that does not originate with the grammatical subject (worshipper) is always going to transgress the boundaries of language, making it difficult to understand. The mistranslation of *leitourgia* as "the work of the people," that is, is always going to seem right, even though viscerally the worshipper *knows* that she is part of more than her own action, with narcissistic exceptions. This is no less the case with the medial nature of ordinary life; it too works against our linguistic structuring of human experience. We often find ourselves stammering for words to explain a situation or event, happenings that fall outside our subjectivity yet involve us as subjects to the point of our personhoods being inseparable from this or that experience.

In a very real sense, an experience has me as much as I have the experience. When I pass a friend walking down the sidewalk, neither of us expecting to meet the other, we are both involved in an experience conditioned by the existence of the village, town or city, the sidewalk, our separate needs to be going to this or that place, the supremely accidental way that we became friends in the first place, which causes us to stop, catch up, and everything in between, as well as a whole host of other factors well beyond our control. But language stifles any such articulation, or at least any non-descript, simple expression. Rather, we say, "I passed John on the street today." Or, "I ran into Susan earlier this morning." *I*, the subject, *passed* or *ran into* the passive objects *John* and *Susan*. The vocal structure of modern languages do not account for John or Susan's subjectivities, except when they are the ones recounting the event. Then John and Susan become the *I*'s and we learn that Tom and Patty are now objects. The grammatical barrier of a single actor and single patient (the same is true for multiple subjects when they share an object or objects) reduces the encounter to something *I* do to someone else, not something that happens to each of us together. Perhaps this could be alleviated with the sentence "John and I ran into each other today." Nevertheless, try saying this aloud and it is easy to hear how awkward it sounds to the speaker's ears. Our linguistic structuring inclines us toward a single perspective from the almighty seat of objectivity, so that even if we open ourselves to the other or an outside, it is always a working against the language we inhabit — the language that inhabits us. The singularity of perception, while there may be a whole host of historical factors involved that move the human toward such a reduction of reality, is a linguistic condition, moving beyond which requires not only a re-enculturation of shared involvement but the grammatical ability to articulate such mutual participation as normative without the need for continuous over-explanation. In other words, it is not enough to rearrange the words of a sentence, i.e., "We passed each other on the sidewalk today." There needs to be a grammatical voice that refuses an either/or reduction.

The language of liturgy offers a unique opportunity for worshippers to inhabit the world more deeply. It is vital, if the worshipper is to perceive liturgical action as a condition of human nature and an involvement in the eternal agency of God in Christ, that the prayers and praises of Christian liturgies bear the marks of the inward groaning of the Spirit, as Paul puts it. This is evidenced in the repetition of Chronicles 29.14 at the offertory, "All things come of thee, O God, and of thine own have we given thee." That the worshipper's only offering is that which God has already given is a middle voice claim. The human has nothing to offer to God that has not first been given by God, so that it might be offered, not because God lacks anything, but so that the human might inhabit the self-offering of God, an eternal movement within the Trinity who has gathered humanity into divine liturgical action. It may not be possible to reinsert the middle voice into modern languages; however, if the human is to inhabit the eternal as a present, though anticipated, reality, speaking and praying in medial terms is the only way for this inner condition to manifest itself and give way to understanding.

CONCLUSION

Toward a Metaxological Liturgy

IMAGINE A LITURGICAL FORM AND EMPHASIS ATTENTIVE to the ordinary, sophianic movement[1] of God in the places inhabited by particular worshippers in their particular communities across the globe. Such liturgies would account for the entanglement of divinity and humanity *with* creation, recognizing that to the degree the faithful align themselves to divine, creative agency, each person becomes co-terminous with divine action. This is the question that pervades the whole of this work. Christ, who is Liturgy—the self-offering of divinity for the good of that which is not itself divine—incorporates creation into divine agency. Through his condescension, Christ unites human nature to divine action *for the life of the world*. Accordingly, liturgy begins and ends in God, where God is the singular agent of an eternal, creative action, gathering created life into uncreated life, assimilating creation to a co-creative process of divine enfleshment. Humans are hereby bearers of an agency that is not our own,[2] inhabitants of an action that precedes yet proceeds from all created life.

As inhabitants of the world, we breathe the air; we are in contact with a particular plot of earth; and we are related to the people, places, and every thing in between, all day every day, all of which in large and small ways *work on*, *affect*, and *throw* us into relationships we may or may not desire — which we may or may not come to desire. We likewise *work on*, *affect*, and *throw* all manner of people, places, and things into being through our mutual habitation. Humanity's primal and natural existence within God, however, is even more tangible and more material than is often imagined. God is inseparable from everything we

---

1   I refer to sophianic movement following the account given in Martin's *The Submerged Reality*.

2   See Rowan Williams, *The Edge of Words* (London: Bloomsbury Publishing, 2014), 111.

161

encounter in the world. God is not the world, yet God is the primary relationship of all that is *being created*—the world included.[3]

All things *live and move and have their being in Christ.*[4] All things dwell in a universe where God is at the center and periphery, whose creative and life-giving procession and return as Trinity is the action that makes all movement possible. For this reason, the movement of created life, humans included, is perhaps best understood as *intra-action*—created action as involvement in divine action. While arriving at human action as "intra-action" through continued contemplation of the liturgical agency of God, I also recognize Karen Barad's use of this term, following Neils Bohr's work in quantum mechanics, to be complementary.[5] I do not intend to flesh out this overlap in this present work; however, the language and discoveries of quantum mechanics are quite helpful in thinking through the complexity of divine-human involvement that resists univocal expression. William Desmond rightly expresses concerns about losing the "inter," as in interaction, intervolvement, etc., for the purpose of retaining the distinctness of persons and God without reducing either to univocal sameness or equivocal separateness.[6] However, as Barad insists, "in contrast to the usual 'interaction,' which assumes that there are separate individual agencies that precede their interaction, the notion of intra-action recognizes that distinct agencies do not precede, but rather emerge through

---

3 Maximus Confessor, *Ambiguum 7*, esp. 1081B–1085A. In order to maintain the intimate relation between divinity and humanity, while at the same time recognizing all things in their particularity, Maximus articulates the natural relationship of the *logos*—the portion of God each human is by nature—with the *Logos* as the intimate bond that unites all things. Humans are related to other humans not because of accidental characteristics shared in the material world; rather, each is related by virtue of the principle of their being—as a *logos* of the *Logos*. It is the divine portion of each person that conditions the relationship, and because each person is related to the *Logos* any discord is first and foremost a discord with God and accidentally with others. As the psalmist writes, "against you only have I sinned" (Psalm 51:4). Communion with God is made-manifest through the peaceful harmony and joy between humans and creation.

4 Acts 17:28.

5 See Karen Barad, *Meeting the Universe Halfway* (Durham: Duke University Press, 2007).

6 See William Desmond, *God and the Between* (Oxford: Blackwell Publishing, 2008), esp. 2–10.

(or, for our purposes, *proceed from*), their intra-action."[7] This accords with the middle voice described in chapter 4, where the subject exists within the action of the verb. Thinking through the creative agency of God, made-manifest in Christ and continually called into being through liturgical action, "intra-action" does not conflate divine and human (univocity), nor does it admit an absolute distance of the two (equivocity); rather, metaxologically speaking, "intra-action" names the relational ontology of beings within Being, whereby the Agent — God, i.e., Being, who is *action qua action* — the primal action of creation, is the primal action of humans. "Intra-action" names a participation in Action (God), whereby humans participate in their *being-created*, increasing in particularity through increased participation, in relation to God and others. Desmond rightly fears the conflation of human identity and personhood being subsumed into the Godhead; however, *intra-action* actually accounts for the intimacy of God and creation without this feared reduction. Humans exist within the action God is, which precedes yet proceeds from humans, proportionate to each person's volitive participation in God's liturgical agency.

Instead of naming an *interaction* between humans and God, the incarnate nature of divine action incorporates humans into a movement toward God that is more than an exchange or engagement between two separate entities (equivocity). It is, rather, an *intra-activity*, whereby humans are *within* and *related by* divine action as a matter of being — as a matter of becoming. Let me be clear that this is not to suggest, as with Duns Scotus, that God and humans exist within Being (univocity); rather, it is to highlight, with Maximus the Confessor, the reality that all movement stands in direct relation to divine action.[8] Indeed, humans are related to all things by divine action. The movement of humans, then, is a movement within, yet unconfused with, divine action — a movement made possible through participation in the procession and return of God from and to God. The extent to

7 Barad, *Meeting the Universe Halfway*, 33, 132–85.
8 Maximus Confessor, *Ambiguum 7*, 1085B–C. For Maximus, whether persons move according to or against the will of God, they are nonetheless preparing themselves to heed the call of God — they are still moving toward God.

which humans attend to this divine procession and return is the degree to which humans can be said to *act*. Inasmuch as a person participates in the liturgical agency of God in Christ will she know herself as known by Christ who is Liturgy—enacted, as it were, by Christ, without becoming other than herself but always more than she is. To do liturgy is to *become* Liturgy—to become Christ through volitive participation in the procession and return of God from and to God.

Particular instances of liturgical action in the world, whether gatherings for Holy Eucharist, the Liturgy of the Hours, the Daily Office, the innumerable forms by which humans come together for prayer, the adoration of nature, contemplation, and much more, are *metaxological*. *Metaxu* names the *between* of two inseparable entities. Simone Weil refers to *metaxu* as a bridge.[9] I prefer to think of *metaxu* as a fence between two homes. A bridge implies a gap between one place and the next, and while a fence is often understood as separating, it actually helps neighbors know how they are connected. We might imagine a fence between the celestial and the terrestrial, with a gate that opens in both directions, enabling a continuous ebb and flow between *worlds*, while recognizing that one is not the other. This fence is a porous and medial distinction that brings each together without confusing what it enjoins. Liturgy is this gate; it is a metaxological movement *between* the celestial and terrestrial—Christ, our only mediator and advocate.

Liturgy as a binding movement *between* divinity and humanity, an unconfused union of agency and activity, also names a materializing of the *Logos* through the *logoi*[10]—an incarnate becoming as the body of Christ, the church, proportionate to a person's participation in this *mattering* of divine action. It is a materializing that transcends what is

---

9   I employ *metaxu* along a similar vein as that of Simone Weil, *Gravity and Grace*, trans. Emma Crawford and Mario von der Ruhr (New York: Routledge Classics, 2002), 145–47. This term has been used most recently by William Desmond in his important work on the *between* of Philosophy and Theology toward a reassessment of Metaphysics. Michael Martin has also utilized this term to account for Divine Sophia as this *between*—*metaxu*. I do not disagree with any of these and find each account quite compelling; however, this particular use is to directly implicate the *between*, *metaxu*, as a gate that swings both ways.

10   See above chapter 2.

perceptible through the senses yet inseparable from sense perception,[11] whereby a person becomes aware of her *natural nature* as a *logoi* of the *Logos*.[12] The body of Christ is made manifest as an incarnate reality in proportion to the participation of the faithful in the deifying movement of Christ in the world.

Crucially, this is to suggest that knowledge is inseparable from the knowing action, the knower, and that which is known. To know God, therefore, is to participate in the self-knowing, liturgical agency of God, whereby humans are known by God through the filial relation of Father and Son, by virtue of the Son's unconfused assimilating of divine and human natures in Christ.[13] A metaxological liturgy will form participants in a transcendental movement that opens worshippers to inhabit the world more deeply. Incarnational, the divine procession and return that is the creative action of Love encompasses and flows through a liturgy's participants, such that who a person is in her particularity continually rises to the surface, and who a person is in her unique relationship with the *Logos* is materialized in flesh. As a *logos* of the *Logos,* as a distinct *portion* of God, each person bears the image of God through their vocation as created, called into being and continually spoken into being through the Incarnate Word. This divine self-communication is the willed embodiment of Christ in the personhood of humans;[14] nevertheless, it is always proportionate to a person's volitive participation in *willing the will of God.* As I receive myself from the *Logos,* whose portion I am by nature, so am I received by Christ to become divine[15]—the way of deification.

Called for above is a liturgical revolution whose form deliberately reorients worshippers to their *natural nature* as bearers of divine

---

11   See p. 66, note 87. See also John of Damascus, *Orthodox Faith,* iii.2–4; see also Rowan Williams, *Christ the Heart of Creation* (London: Bloomsbury Continuum, 2018), 110–13.

12   See above chapter 2.

13   For an exhaustive study of this filial knowing in Christological formulations and their implications for human knowing, see Rowan Williams, *Christ the Heart of Creation,* esp. chapter 1.2.

14   See chapter 2, as well as p. 47, note 14.

15   Ibid.

agency. It is a movement that begins with the feet and charges the senses, mingling the Eucharistic tables of earth with the Table of Heaven, the tables of our dining rooms and kitchens with the tables of our houses of prayer. The liturgical agency of God in the world awaits our participation. While the Eucharistic feast, celebrated throughout the world, "ensures" our encounter with the mystery of the Word made flesh, its sacramental resonance stops at the rail when we *carry on as normal*, stifling the embodiment of God in our midst. How we carry Christ in our bodies, how we inhabit the world as bearers of God's liturgical agency, as a living sacrifice to God, conditions our ability to recognize and enjoy the movement of the Trinity in our midst, and the degree to which we participate in becoming life for the world. Our involvement does not make liturgy happen; it is always under-way. However, by the gracious condescension of Christ, the liturgical movement of God—which is eternally assimilating the world to divine action—is made-manifest when and where we humans align ourselves to the *kenosis* of Christ, extending *koinonia* with God to and for all.

BIBLIOGRAPHY

Agamben, Giorgio. *Homo Sacer*. Translated by Daniel Heller-Roazen. Stanford: Stanford University Press, 1998.

Alexander, Christopher. *The Timeless Way of Building*. New York: Oxford University Press, 1979.

Ambrose. *Hexameron, Paradise, and Cain and Abel*. Translated by John J. Savage. Vol. 42. The Fathers of the Church. New York: Catholic University of America Press, 1961.

———. *Seven Exegetical Works*. Translated by Michael P. McHugh. Vol. 65. The Fathers of the Church. Washington: Catholic University of America Press, 2003.

———. *Theological and Dogmatic Works*. Translated by Roy J. Deferrari. Vol. 44. The Fathers of the Church. Washington: Catholic University of America Press, 1963.

Anderson, Benedict R. *Imagined Communities: Reflections on the Origin and Spread of Nationalism*. London: Verso, 1991.

Anderson, E. Byron. *Worship and Christian Identity: Practicing Ourselves*. Collegeville: Liturgical Press, 2003.

Anonymous. *Meditations on the Tarot: A Journey into Christian Hermeticism*. Translated by Robert Powell. Brooklyn, NY: Angelico Press, 2020.

Aquinas, Thomas. *Summa Contra Gentiles*. Edited by Anton C. Pegis, James F. Anderson, Vernon J. Bourke, and C. J. O'Neil. Notre Dame: University of Notre Dame Press, 1975.

Aquinas, Thomas. *Summa Theologica: Complete English Edition in Five Volumes*. Vol. I–V. Notre Dame: Christian Classics, 1981.

Aristotle. *The Complete Works of Aristotle: The Revised Oxford Translation*. Edited by Jonathan Barnes. Vol. II. Princeton: Princeton University Press, 1984.

———. *The Nicomachean Ethics*. Translated by H. Rackham. Cambridge: Harvard University Press, 1999.

———. *Poetics*. Translated by Stephen Halliwell. Cambridge: Harvard University Press, 1995.

———. *Politics*. Translated by H. Rackham. Cambridge: Harvard University Press, 1944.

Arnaoutoglou, Ilias. *Ancient Greek Laws: A Sourcebook*. London: Routledge, 1998.

Arndt, William, F. Wilbur Gingrich, Frederick W. Danker, and Walter Bauer, eds. *A Greek-English Lexicon of the New Testament and Other Early Christian Literature: A Translation and Adaptation of the Fourth Revised and Augmented Edition of Walter Bauer's Griechisch-deutsches Wörterbuch zu den Schriften des Neuen Testaments und der Übrigen Urchristlichen Literatur*. Chicago: University of Chicago Press, 1979.

Asad, Talal. *Genealogies of Religion: Discipline and Reasons of Power in Christianity and Islam*. Baltimore: Johns Hopkins University Press, 1993.

Atchley, Edward Godfrey Cuthbert Frederic. *Ordo Romanus Primus*. London: De La More Press, 1905.

Athanasius. *The Life of Antony and the Letter to Marcellinus*. Translated by Robert C. Gregg. New York: Paulist Press, 1980.

Auden, W. H. *Secondary Worlds*. New York: Random House, 1968.

Augustine. *Confessions*. Translated by Henry Chadwick. Oxford: Oxford University Press, 1991.

———. *Tractates on the Gospel of John, 11–27*. Translated by John W. Rettig. Vol. 79. The Fathers of the Church. Washington: Catholic University of America Press, 2003.

Balentine, Samuel E. *The Torah's Vision of Worship*. Minneapolis: Fortress Press, 1999.

Balthasar, Hans Urs von. *Cosmic Liturgy: The Universe According to Maximus the Confessor*. San Francisco: Ignatius Press, 2003.

———. *Love Alone Is Credible*. San Francisco: Ignatius Press, 2004.

———. *Studies in Theological Style: Clerical Styles*. Edited by John Kenneth. Riches. Translated by Andrew Louth, Francis McDonagh, and Brian McNeil, C.R.V. Vol. II. The Glory of the Lord. San Francisco: Ignatius Press, 1984.

Barad, Karen. *Meeting the Universe Halfway*. Durham: Duke University Press, 2007.

Barrett, Sarah Feldman. *How Emotions Are Made*. New York: Houghton Mifflin Harcourt Publishing, 2017.

Benedict. *The Rule of St. Benedict in English*. Translated by Timothy Fry. Collegeville: Liturgical Press, 1981.

Benjamin, Walter. *The Work of Art in the Age of Its Technological Reproducibility, and Other Writings on Media*. Edited by Michael William Jennings, Brigid Doherty, and Thomas Y. Levin. Translated by E. F. N. Jephcott, Rodney Livingstone, and Howard Eiland. Cambridge: Belknap Press of Harvard University Press, 2008.

Benveniste, Émile. *Problems in General Linguistics. Miami Linguistic 8*. Miami: University of Miami Press, 1973.

Berry, Wendell. *Bringing It to the Table: On Farming and Food*. Berkeley: Counterpoint, 2009.

Berthold, George C., trans. *Maximus Confessor: Selected Writings*. New York: Paulist Press, 1985.

Bianchi, Enzo. *God Where Are You?* Brewster: Paraclete Press, 2014.

Bishop, Jeffrey Paul. *The Anticipatory Corpse: Medicine, Power, and the Care of the Dying*. Notre Dame: University of Notre Dame Press, 2011.

Bibliography

Blake, William. *The Complete Poetry and Prose of William Blake.* Edited by David V. Erdman. Berkeley: University of California Press, 1982.

Blondel, Maurice. *Action: Essay on a Critique of Life and a Science of Practice.* Translated by Oliva Blanchette. Notre Dame: University of Notre Dame, 1984.

Bloomer, Kent C., and Charles Willard Moore. *Body, Memory, and Architecture.* New Haven: Yale University Press, 1977.

Blowers, Paul M., and Robert Louis Wilken, trans. *On the Cosmic Mystery of Jesus Christ: Selected Writings from St. Maximus the Confessor.* Crestwood: St. Vladimir's Seminary Press, 2003.

Bonhoeffer, Dietrich. *Act and Being.* Translated by Bernard Noble. New York: Harper and Brothers, Publishers, 1962.

———. *The Cost of Discipleship.* New York: Touchstone, 1995.

———. *Ethics.* New York: Macmillan, 1955.

———. *Letters and Papers from Prison.* Edited by Eberhard Bethge. New York: Macmillan, 1972.

Bossy, John. *Christianity in the West: 1400–1700.* Oxford: Oxford University Press, 1987.

———. "The Mass as a Social Institution 1200–1700." *Past and Present* 100, no. 1 (1983): 29–61. doi:10.1093/past/100.1.29.

Bourdieu, Pierre. *The Logic of Practice.* Stanford: Stanford University Press, 1990.

Bouyer, Louis. *Life and Liturgy.* London: Sheed and Ward, 1956.

Bradshaw, Paul F., and John Allyn Melloh. *Foundations in Ritual Studies: A Reader for Students of Christian Worship.* Grand Rapids: Baker Academic, 2007.

Bremmer, Jan N., and Andrew Erskine, eds. *The Gods of Ancient Greece: Identities and Transformations.* Edinburgh: Edinburgh University Press, 2010.

Brooke, Christopher Nugent Lawrence. *Medieval Church and Society; Collected Essays.* New York: New York University Press, 1972.

———. *The Structure of Medieval Society.* New York: McGraw-Hill, 1971.

Brown, Peter. *The Body and Society: Men, Women, and Sexual Renunciation in Early Christianity.* New York: Columbia University Press, 1988.

———. *The Cult of the Saints: Its Rise and Function in Latin Christianity.* Chicago: University of Chicago Press, 1981.

———. *The Making of Late Antiquity.* Cambridge: Harvard University Press, 1978.

Bulgakov, Sergeï Nikolaevich. *The Bride of the Lamb.* Grand Rapids: William B. Eerdmans Pub., 2002.

———. *Philosophy of Economy.* Translated by Catherine Evtuhov. New Haven: Yale University Press, 2000.

———. *Sophia, the Wisdom of God: An Outline of Sophiology.* Hudson: Lindisfarne Press, 1993.

Cabasilas, Nicolaus. *A Commentary on the Divine Liturgy.* Crestwood: St. Vladimir's Seminary Press, 1977.

Caldwell, Phoebe. *Delicious Conversations: Reflections on Autism, Intimacy and Communication.* Brighton: Pavilion Publishing and Media Ltd, 2012.

Calhoun, Craig J., Edward LiPuma, and Moishe Postone, eds. *Bourdieu: Critical Perspectives.* Chicago: University of Chicago Press, 1993.

Callahan, Virginia Woods, trans. *Saint Gregory of Nyssa: Ascetical Works.* The Fathers of the Church ed. Washington: Catholic University of America Press, 1967.

Carroll, Thomas K., and Thomas P. Halton. *Liturgical Practice in the Fathers.* Wilmington: M. Glazier, 1988.

Casel, Odo. *The Mystery of Christian Worship.* Edited by Burkhard Neunheuser. New York: Crossroad Publishing Company, 1999.

Cassian, John. *Conferences.* Edited by Colm Luibhéid and Eugène Pichery. New York: Paulist Press, 1985.

Cavanaugh, William T. *Theopolitical Imagination.* London: T & T Clark, 2002.

Chase, Frederic Hathaway, Jr., trans. *Saint John of Damascus: Writings.* New York: Fathers of the Church, 1958.

Chazelle, Celia Martin. *The Crucified God in the Carolingian Era: Theology and Art of Christ's Passion.* Cambridge: Cambridge University Press, 2001.

Clement of Alexandria. *Stromateis.* Translated by John Ferguson. Washington: Catholic University of America Press, 1991.

Colish, Marcia L. *The Mirror of Language: A Study in the Medieval Theory of Knowledge.* Lincoln: University of Nebraska Press, 1983.

Copleston, Frederick. *A History of Philosophy: Greece and Rome.* Vol. I. New Jersey: Paulist Press, 1946.

Cox, Harvey Gallagher. *The Feast of Fools: A Theological Essay on Festivity and Fantasy.* Cambridge: Harvard University Press, 1969.

Cross, Richard. *Duns Scotus.* New York: Oxford University Press, 1999.

Cunningham, Conor, and Peter M. Candler, eds. *Transcendence and Phenomenology.* London: SCM Press in Association with the Center of Theology and Philosophy, University of Nottingham, 2007.

Cunningham, Conor. *Darwin's Pious Idea: Why the Ultra-Darwinists and Creationists Both Get It Wrong.* Grand Rapids: William B. Eerdmans Pub., 2010.

———. *Genealogy of Nihilism: Philosophies of Nothing and the Difference of Theology.* London: Routledge, 2002.

Cyprian. *The Letters of St. Cyprian of Carthage.* Translated by G. W. Clarke. Vols. I–III. New York: Newman Press, 1984.

Cyril of Jerusalem. *The Works of Saint Cyril of Jerusalem.* Translated by Leo P. McCauley and Anthony A. Stephenson. Vol. II. Washington: Catholic University of America Press, 1970.

Bibliography

Daniélou, Jean, ed. *From Glory to Glory: Texts from Gregory of Nyssa's Mystical Writings*. Translated by Herbert Musurillo. Crestwood, NY: St. Vladimir's Seminary Press, 1979.

Daniélou, Jean. *God and the Ways of Knowing*. San Francisco: Ignatius Press, 2003.

———. *Platonisme et théologie mystique: Doctrine spirituelle de Saint Grégoire de Nysse*. Paris: Aubier, Éditions Montaigne, 1954.

Davis, Leo Donald. *The First Seven Ecumenical Councils (325–787): Their History and Theology*. Collegeville: Liturgical Press, 1990.

Demosthenes. *Orations 50–59: Private Cases in Neaeram*. Translated by A. T. Murray. Vol. 351. Loeb Classical Library. Cambridge: Harvard University Press, 1939.

Desmond, William. *Being and the Between*. Albany: State University of New York Press, 1995.

———. *God and the Between*. Oxford: Blackwell Publishing, 2008.

Dix, Gregory. *The Shape of the Liturgy*. London: Continuum, 2005.

Dmitriev, Sviatoslav. *City Government in Hellenistic and Roman Asia Minor*. Oxford: Oxford University Press, 2005.

Donna, Bernard, trans. *Saint Cyprian: Letters*. Washington: Catholic University of America Press, 1964.

Duffy, Eamon. *The Stripping of the Altars: Traditional Religion in England, c. 1400–c. 1580*. New Haven: Yale University Press, 1992.

Eagleton, Terry. *Reason, Faith, & Revolution: Reflections on the God Debate*. New Haven: Yale University Press, 2009.

Eberhard, Philippe. *The Middle Voice in Gadamer's Hermeneutics: A Basic Interpretation with Some Theological Implications*. Tübingen: Mohr Siebeck, 2004.

———. "The Medial Age or the Present in the Middle Voice." *International Journal of the Humanities,* Vol. 3, no. 8. 2005/2006.

———. "The Mediality of Our Condition: A Christian Interpretation." *Journal of the American Academy of Religion*, Volume 67, Issue 2, 1 June 1999, 411–34, https://doi.org/10.1093/jaarel/67.2.411.

Eliot, T. S. *Notes Towards the Definition of Culture*. New York, 1949.

———. *Four Quartets*. New York: Harcourt Brace & Co., 1971.

Ellard, Collin. *Places of the Heart*. New York: Bellevue Literary Press, 2015.

Ernst, Cornelius. *Multiple Echo*. Eugene: Wipf & Stock, 2006.

Evans, Fred, and Leonard Lawlor, eds. *Chiasms: Merleau-Ponty's Notion of Flesh*. Albany: State University of New York Press, 2000.

Feiler, Bruce. *The Secrets of Happy Families*. New York: William Morrow, 2013.

Feldman, Yael S. *Glory and Agony: Isaac's Sacrifice and National Narrative*. Stanford: Stanford University Press, 2010.

Finney, Jack. *About Time: 12 Short Stories*. New York: Scribner Paperback Fiction, 1986.

Foley, Edward. *From Age to Age: How Christians Have Celebrated the Eucharist.* Collegeville: Liturgical Press, 2008.

Fowl, Stephen E. *Philippians.* Grand Rapids: William B. Eerdmans Pub., 2005.

Frank, Tenney. *An Economic Survey of Ancient Rome.* Baltimore: Johns Hopkins Press, 1933.

Flesher, Paul V.M., and Bruce Chilton. *The Targums: A Critical Introduction.* Waco: Baylor University Press, 2011.

Fretheim, Terence E. *Exodus.* Louisville: John Knox Press, 1991.

Gadamer, Hans-Georg. *Truth and Method.* Translated by Joel Weinsheimer. London: Continuum, 2006.

Galavaris, George. *Bread and the Liturgy: The Symbolism of Early Christian and Byzantine Bread Stamps.* Madison: University of Wisconsin Press, 1970.

Gardner, Percy. *A Manual of Greek Antiquities.* New York: Charles Scribner's Sons, 1895.

Gavrilyuk, Paul L., and Sarah Coakley, eds. *The Spiritual Senses: Perceiving God in Western Christianity.* Cambridge: Cambridge University Press, 2012.

Gillespie, Michael Allen. *Nihilism before Nietzsche.* Chicago: University of Chicago Press, 1996.

Glimm, Francis Xavier., Joseph Marie-Felix Marique, and Gerald Groveland Walsh, trans. *The Apostolic Fathers.* Washington: Catholic University of America Press, 1969.

Grant, Robert M., ed. *Irenaeus of Lyons.* London: Routledge, 1997.

Gregory. *The Book of Pastoral Rule.* Translated by George E. Demacopoulos. Crestwood: St. Vladimir's Seminary Press, 2007.

Gregory of Nyssa. *Homilies on the Song of Songs.* Translated by Richard A. Norris Jr. Atlanta: Society of Biblical Literature, 2012.

———. *The Life of Moses.* Translated by Abraham J. Malherbe and Everett Ferguson. The Classics of Western Spirituality ed. New York: Paulist Press, 1978.

———. *On the Soul and the Resurrection.* Translated by Catharine P. Roth. Crestwood: St. Vladimir's Seminary Press, 2002.

Haidt, Jonathan. *The Righteous Mind.* New York: Random House, Inc., 2012.

Hall, Edith. *The Theatrical Cast of Athens.* Oxford: Oxford University Press, 2006.

Hefele, Charles Joseph. *A History of the Councils of the Church: From the Original Documents, to the Close of the Council of Nicaea, A.D. 325.* New York: AMS Press, 1894.

Heffernan, Thomas J., and E. Ann Matter, eds. *The Liturgy of the Medieval Church.* Kalamazoo: Western Michigan University Press, 2001.

Heidegger, Martin. *Poetry, Language, Thought.* New York: Harper Collins Publishers, Inc., 1971.

Herbert, Arthur Gabriel. *Liturgy and Society: The Function of the Church in the Modern World.* London: Faber and Faber, 1935.

Bibliography

Hinton, David Alban. *Archaeology, Economy, and Society: England from the Fifth to the Fifteenth Century.* London: Routledge, 1998.

Holmer, Paul L. *The Grammar of Faith.* San Francisco: Harper & Row Publishers, 1978.

Holmes, Brooke. *The Symptom and the Subject: The Emergence of the Physical Body in Ancient Greece.* Princeton: Princeton University Press, 2010.

Homer. *The Iliad.* Translated by Augustus Taber Murray. Cambridge: Harvard University Press, 1988.

Hughes, Dennis D. *Human Sacrifice in Ancient Greece.* London: Routledge, 1991.

Illich, Ivan. *Tools for Conviviality.* New York: Harper and Row Publishers, 1973.

Ingham, Mary Beth, and Mechthild Dreyer. *The Philosophical Vision of John Duns Scotus: An Introduction.* Washington: Catholic University of America Press, 2004.

James, Mervyn. *Society, Politics, and Culture: Studies in Early Modern England.* Cambridge: Cambridge University Press, 1986.

John of Damascus. *Three Treatises on the Divine Images.* Translated by Andrew Louth. Crestwood: St. Vladimir's Seminary Press, 2003.

Johnson, Mark. *The Meaning of the Body: Aesthetics of Human Understanding.* Chicago: University of Chicago Press, 2007.

Jones, David. *Epoch and Artist.* London: Faber and Faber Ltd, 1959.

Jungmann, Josef A. *Liturgical Worship.* New York: Frederick Pustet, 1941.

———. *The Mass of the Roman Rite: Its Origins and Development (Missarum Sollemnia).* Translated by Francis A. Brunner. Vol. II. New York: Benziger Brothers, 1955.

———. *The Place of Christ in Liturgical Prayer.* Staten Island: Alba House, 1965.

———. *The Sacrifice of the Church; the Meaning of the Mass.* Collegeville: Liturgical Press, 1956.

Justin Martyr. *The First and Second Apologies.* Translated by Leslie W. Barnard. New York: Paulist Press, 1997.

Juvin, Hervé. *The Coming of the Body.* Translated by John Howe. London: Verso, 2010.

Kavanagh, Aidan. *On Liturgical Theology: The Hale Memorial Lectures of Seabury-Western Theological Seminary, 1981.* Collegeville: Liturgical Press, 1992.

Kemmer, Suzanne. *The Middle Voice.* Philadelphia: John Benjamins Publishing Company, 1993.

King, Archdale A. *Liturgies of the Past.* London: Longmans, 1959.

———. *Liturgy of the Roman Church.* London: Longmans, Green and Company, 1957.

Kirchgässner, Alfons. *Unto the Altar: The Practice of Catholic Worship.* New York: Herder and Herder, 1963.

Kisner, Wendell. *Ecological Ethics and Living Subjectivity in Hegel's Logic: The Middle Voice in Autopoietic Life*. New York: Palgrave MacMillan, 2014.

Klauser, Theodor. *A Short History of the Western Liturgy: An Account and Some Reflections*. Oxford: Oxford University Press, 1979.

Kleist, James A., trans. *The Epistles of St. Clement of Rome and St. Ignatius of Antioch*. Edited by Johannes Quasten and Joseph C. Plumpe. New York: Newman Press, 1946.

Krautheimer, Richard, and Slobodan Ćurčić. *Early Christian and Byzantine Architecture*. New Haven: Yale University Press, 1986.

Kunzler, Michael. *The Church's Liturgy*. London: Continuum, 2001.

Latour, Bruno. *Pandora's Hope: Essays on the Reality of Science Studies*. Cambridge: Harvard University Press, 1999.

Lear, Jonathan. *Aristotle: The Desire to Understand*. Cambridge: Cambridge University Press, 1988.

Lefebvre, Henri. *The Production of Space*. Translated by Donald Nicholson-Smith. Oxford: Blackwell, 2005.

Leo the Great. *Letters*. Translated by Edmund Hunt. Washington: Catholic University of America Press, 1963.

Levenson, Jon Douglas. *Abraham between Torah and Gospel*. Milwaukee: Marquette University Press, 2011.

Lossky, Vladimir. *In the Image and Likeness of God*. Edited by John H. Erickson and Thomas E. Bird. Crestwood: St. Vladimir's Seminary Press, 1974.

Louth, Andrew. *The Origins of the Christian Mystical Tradition: From Plato to Denys*. Oxford: Oxford University Press, 2007.

Louth, Andrew, trans. *Maximus the Confessor*. New York: Routledge, 1996.

Lubac, Henri de. *Catholicism: Christ and the Common Destiny of Man*. Translated by Lancelot Shepherd and Elizabeth Englund. San Francisco: Ignatius Press, 1988.

———. *Corpus Mysticum: The Eucharist and the Church in the Middle Ages: Historical Survey*. Edited by Laurence Paul Hemming and Susan Frank Parsons. Translated by Gemma Simmonds and Richard Price. London: SCM Press, 2006.

———. *The Mystery of the Supernatural*. Translated by Rosemary Sheed. New York: Crossroad Publishing Company, 1998.

Luibhéid, Colm, and Paul Rorem, trans. *Pseudo-Dionysius: The Complete Works*. New York: Paulist Press, 1987.

MacIntyre, Alasdair. *After Virtue: A Study in Moral Theory*. Notre Dame: University of Notre Dame Press, 1984.

———. *Dependent Rational Animals: Why Human Beings Need the Virtues*. Chicago: Open Court, 1999.

Bibliography

——. *Whose Justice? Which Rationality?* Notre Dame: University of Notre Dame Press, 1988.

Macksey, Richard, and Eugenio Donato. *The Structuralist Controversy: The Languages of Criticism and the Sciences of Man.* Baltimore: John Hopkins University Press, 1970.

Martin, Michael. *The Submerged Reality: Sophiology and the Turn to a Poetic Metaphysics.* Brooklyn: Angelico Press, 2015.

Marx, Karl, and Friedrich Engels. *Economic and Philosophic Manuscripts of 1844.* Translated by Martin Milligan. Amherst: Prometheus Books, 1988.

Mauss, Marcel. *The Gift: Forms and Functions of Exchange in Archaic Societies.* New York: Norton, 1967.

Mawson, Andrew. *The Six Factors of Knowledge Worker Productivity.* Muscateen: Allsteel.

Maximus. *On Difficulties in the Church Fathers: The Ambigua.* Volumes I & II. Translated by Nicholas Constas. Cambridge: Harvard University Press, 2014.

Mazza, Enrico. *Mystagogy: A Theology of Liturgy in the Patristic Age.* New York: Pueblo Publishing Company, 1989.

McGilchrist, Iain. *The Master and His Emissary: The Divided Brain and the Making of the Western World.* New Haven: Yale University Press, 2009.

McLuhan, Marshall. *Understanding Media: The Extensions of Man.* Cambridge: MIT Press, 1994.

McNeill, John T., and Helena M. Gamer, eds. *Medieval Handbooks of Penance: A Translation of the Principal "libri Poenitentiales" and Selections from Related Documents.* New York: Columbia University Press, 1990.

Melchior-Bonnet, Sabine. *The Mirror: A History.* New York: Routledge, 2001.

Menzies, Allan, ed. *The Gospel of Peter, the Diatessaron of Tatian, the Apocalyspe of Peter, the Visio Pauli, the Apocalypses of the Virgin and Sedrach, the Testament of Abraham, the Acts of Xanthippe and Polyxena, the Narrative of Zosimus, the Apology of Aristides, the Epistles of Clement (Complete Text), Origen's Commentary on John, Books I–X, and Commentary on Matthew, Books I, II, and X–XIV.* Vol. IX. Ante-Nicene Fathers. Peabody: Hendrickson Publishers, 1999.

Merleau-Ponty, Maurice. *Phenomenology of Perception.* Translated by Colin Smith. London: Routledge, 2002.

——. *The Primacy of Perception.* Edited by James M. Edie. Chicago: Northwestern, 1964.

——. *Sense and Non-sense.* Translated by Hubert L. Dreyfus and Patricia Allen Dreyfus. Evanston: Northwestern University Press, 1964.

Meyendorff, John. *Byzantine Theology: Historical Trends and Doctrinal Themes.* New York: Fordham University Press, 1979.

——. *Christ in Eastern Christian Thought.* Washington: Corpus Books, 1969.

————. *Imperial Unity and Christian Divisions: The Church, 450–680 AD*. Crestwood: St. Vladimir's Seminary Press, 1989.

Michel, Virgil George. *Christian Social Reconstruction: Some Fundamentals of the Quadragesimo Anno*. Milwaukee: Bruce Publishing Company, 1937.

Migne, Jacques Paul, ed. *Patrologia Graeca*. Paris, 1857–1886.

————. *Patrologia Latina*. Paris, 1844–1864.

Milavec, Aaron, trans. *The Didache: Text, Translation, Analysis, and Commentary*. Collegeville: Liturgical Press, 2004.

Méndez, Montoya Angel F. *Theology of Food: Eating and the Eucharist*. Chichester: Wiley-Blackwell, 2009.

Mondzain, Marie-José. *Image, Icon, Economy: The Byzantine Origins of the Contemporary Imaginary*. Stanford: Stanford University Press, 2005.

Moore, Sebastian. *The Crucified Jesus Is No Stranger*. New York: Paulist Press, 1977.

Mueller, Mary Magdeleine, trans. *Saint Caesarius of Arles: Sermons*. Vol. III. Washington: Catholic University of America Press, 1973.

Neusner, Jacob. *The Four Stages of Rabbinic Judaism*. London: Routledge, 1999.

Noort, Edward, and Eibert J. C. Tigchelaar, eds. *The Sacrifice of Isaac: The Aqedah (Genesis 22) and Its Interpretations*. Leiden: Brill, 2002.

O'Donovan, Oliver, and Joan Lockwood O'Donovan. *From Irenaeus to Grotius: A Sourcebook in Christian Political Thought, 100–1625*. Grand Rapids: William B. Eerdmans Pub., 1999.

Ong, Walter J. *Orality and Literacy: The Technologizing of the Word*. London: Methuen, 1982.

Origen. *The Song of Songs: Commentary and Homilies*. Translated by R. P. Lawson. Edited by Johannes Quasten and Joseph C. Plumpe. Ancient Christian Writers ed. Vol. XXVI. New York: Newman Press, 1956.

Pabst, Adrian and Christoph Schneider. *Encounters Between Eastern Orthodoxy and Radical Orthodoxy*. New York: Routledge, 2009.

Palazzo, Eric. *A History of Liturgical Books: From the Beginning to the Thirteenth Century*. Translated by Madeleine Beaumont. Collegeville: Liturgical Press, 1998.

Pallasmaa, Juhani. *The Eyes of the Skin: Architecture and the Senses*. Chichester: Wiley-Academy, 2005.

Papanikolaou, Aristotle. *Being with God: Trinity, Apophaticism, and Divine-human Communion*. Notre Dame: University of Notre Dame Press, 2006.

Parker, Robert. *On Greek Religion*. Ithaca: Cornell University Press, 2011.

Pickstock, Catherine. *After Writing: On the Liturgical Consummation of Philosophy*. Oxford: Blackwell Publishers, 1998.

Plato. *Timaeus*. Translated by Robert Gregg Bury. Cambridge: Harvard University Press, 1981.

Pulleyn, Simon. *Prayer in Greek Religion*. Oxford: Clarendon Press, 1997.

Bibliography

Ratzinger, Joseph. *The Spirit of the Liturgy*. San Francisco: Ignatius Press, 2000.

Roberts, Alexander, and James Donaldson. *The Apostolic Fathers with Justin Martyr and Irenæus*. Vol. I. Ante-Nicene Fathers. Peabody: Hendrickson Publishers, 1999.

———. *Fathers of the Third and Fourth Centuries*. Vol. VII. Ante-Nicene Fathers. Peabody: Hendrickson Publishers, 1999.

Rordorf, Willy, ed. *The Eucharist of the Early Christians*. Translated by Matthew J. O'Connell. New York: Pueblo Publishing Company, 1978.

Ruskin, John. *The Stones of Venice*. London: Smith, Elder and Company, 1867.

Russell, Norman, trans. *Cyril of Alexandria*. London: Routledge, 2000.

Schaff, Philip, and Henry Wace, eds. *Select Writings and Letters of Gregory, Bishop of Nyssa*. Translated by William Moore and Henry Austin Wilson. Nicene and Post-Nicene Fathers ed. Vol. V. Peabody: Hendrickson Publishers, 1999.

Schaff, Philip, Henry Wace, and W. Sanday, eds. *Hilary of Poitiers, John of Damascus*. Translated by Edward William Watson and Leighton Pullan. Nicene and Post-Nicene Fathers ed. Vol. IX. Second Series. Peabody: Hendrickson Publishers, 1994.

Scharlemann, Robert P. *The Reason of Following: Christology and the Ecstatic I*. Chicago: University of Chicago Press, 1991.

Schmemann, Alexander. *For the Life of the World: Sacraments and Orthodoxy*. Crestwood: St. Vladimir's Seminary Press, 1973.

———. *Introduction to Liturgical Theology*. New York: St. Vladimir's Seminary Press, 1966.

Scotus, John Duns. *Duns Scotus on the Will and Morality*. Translated by Allan Bernard Wolter. Washington: Catholic University of America Press, 1986.

———. *Philosophical Writings: A Selection*. Translated by Allan Bernard Wolter. Indianapolis: Hackett Publishing, 1987.

Senn, Frank C. *New Creation: A Liturgical Worldview*. Minneapolis: Fortress Press, 2000.

The Seventh Seal. Directed by Ingmar Bergman. Stockholm, Sweden: Svensk Filmindustri, 1957. DVD.

Simson, Otto Georg von. *Sacred Fortress: Byzantine Art and Statecraft in Ravenna*. Princeton: Princeton University Press, 1987.

Smith, James K. A. *How (Not) to be Secular*. Grand Rapids: Wm. B. Eerdmans Publishing Co., 2014.

———. *Desiring the Kingdom*. Grand Rapids: Baker Academic, 2009.

———. *Imagining the Kingdom*. Grand Rapids: Baker Academic, 2013.

———. *Awaiting the King*. Grand Rapids: Baker Academic, 2017.

Stanislavsky, Konstantin. *Creating a Role*. Translated by Elizabeth Reynolds Hapgood. New York: Theatre Arts Books, 1961.

Straw, Carole Ellen. *Gregory the Great: Perfection in Imperfection*. Berkeley: University of California Press, 1988.

Taylor, Charles. *A Secular Age*. Cambridge: Belknap Press of Harvard University Press, 2007.

Tenney, Frank. *An Economic Survey of Ancient Rome: Rome and Italy of the Republic*, vol. I. Baltimore: Johns Hopkins Press, 1936.

Thompson, Bard, comp. *Liturgies of the Western Church*. Cleveland: Meridian Books, 1961.

Thunberg, Lars. *Microcosm and Mediator: The Theological Anthropology of Maximus the Confessor*. Chicago: Open Court, 1995.

Thurian, Max. *The Eucharistic Memorial*. Richmond: John Knox Press, 1960.

Tierney, Brian. *The Crisis of Church and State: 1050–1300*. Toronto: University of Toronto Press, 1988.

Turcescu, Lucian. *Gregory of Nyssa and the Concept of Divine Persons*. Oxford: Oxford University Press, 2005.

Underhill, Evelyn. *Worship*. New York: Harper, 1957.

Voegelin, Eric. *The New Science of Politics, an Introduction*. Chicago: University of Chicago Press, 1952.

Vonnegut, Kurt. *Player Piano*. New York: Delacorte Press, 1952.

Walton, John H. *Ancient Near Eastern Thought and the Old Testament: Introducing the Conceptual World of the Hebrew Bible*. Grand Rapids: Baker Academic, 2006.

———. *The Lost World of Genesis One: Ancient Cosmology and the Origins Debate*. Downers Grove: IVP Academic, 2009.

Weil, Simone. *Gravity and Grace*. Translated by Emma Crawford and Mario von der Ruhr. New York: Routledge Classics, 2002.

Williams, Rowan. *Eucharistic Sacrifice: The Roots of a Metaphor*. Nottinghamshire: Grove Books, 1982.

———. *The Wound of Knowledge*. Oregon: Wipf and Stock, 1998.

———. *The Edge of Words*. London: Bloomsbury Publishing, Plc., 2014.

———. *Christ the Heart of Creation*. London: Bloomsbury Continuum, 2018.

Wilson, Peter. *The Athenian Institution of the Khoregia: The Chorus, the City, and the Stage*. Cambridge: Cambridge University Press, 2000.

Wood, Allen W. *Karl Marx*. New York: Routledge, 2005.

Wybrew, Hugh. *The Orthodox Liturgy*. Crestwood: St. Vladimir's Seminary Press, 1989.

Yarnold, Edward, trans. *Cyril of Jerusalem*. London: Routledge, 2000.

Zajonc, Arthur. *Catching the Light: The Entwined History of Light and Mind*. New York: Bantam Books, 1993.

ACKNOWLEDGEMENTS

MY INTEREST IN LITURGICAL THEOLOGY BEGAN when I was an undergrad at Trevecca Nazarene University, where I unexpectedly discovered the writings of the Church Fathers, notably Maximus the Confessor. This led to further research and investigation at Duke Divinity School, Nashotah House Theological Seminary, and the University of Nottingham. I am grateful to my mentors and conversation partners along the way: Henry Spaulding, Steven Hoskins, Schuy Weishaar, Carson Walden, Stanley Hauerwas, J. Warren Smith, James K. A. Smith, Michael Budde, D. Stephen Long, Catherine Pickstock, Simon Oliver, Conor Cunningham, Frank Valdez, Hugh Cruse, Bill Duryea, Elizabeth Bass, Richard Eatman, John Feeney, Garwood Anderson, Steven Peay, Thomas Holtzen, Isaac Slater, Prince Singh, Kyle Bennett, Harris Bechtol, and especially to John Milbank who facilitated this work in its original stage.

This work would not have been possible without the generous support of Susan Keefe (1954–2012). Her direction of my studies at Duke Divinity School, her friendship, and her fruitful criticism of my work during my time at both Duke Divinity School and the University of Nottingham will never be forgotten. She is the most selfless person I have ever known, and her life is a true participation in Christ the Liturgy.

Last, but not least, I thank Amanda and Wyles and Aydah. They have endured the most from my research and writing and all the time away from home it has caused. I am eternally grateful to Amanda for her faithful encouragement and support and to Wyles and Aydah who constantly distracted me to help me realize what I am really writing about. I am also grateful to my parents Bill and Fay Daniel, and to my in-laws, Jim and Kathy Kelley, who have been a constant source of encouragement, more so than perhaps they will ever know.

INDEX OF
SCRIPTURE REFERENCES

Gen			*Lk*			*Gal*	
1:26	44		2:30–32	54		2:19–20	32
12:1	49		2:35	54		11:20	18
22	22, 24		11:17–24	150			
22:5	24		11:32	54		*Eph*	
			11:33	54		1:7–10	31
Lev			11:34–36	53		2:19–3:2	32
3:5	11		11:37–41	54		4	32
			11:39	54		3	37
1 Chr							
29:14	23, 159		*Jn*			*Phil*	
			1	150		2:5	150
Ps			6:51	2		2:6–11	150
33:9	27					2:12–13	150
34:8	27, 119		*Acts*			2:17	7
51	9		17:28	162		2:25	7
51:4	162					2:30	7
			Rom			3:10	19, 25
Isa			8:22–23	150		3	30
2:4	110		8:23	153		4:15	14
			8:32	18			
Jon			13:6	32		*Col*	
1:9	53		15:14–16	7		1	35
4:6–11	54		15:27	14			
						1 Tim	
Matt			*1 Cor*			2:5	146
4:1	18		4	30			
5	27		9	30		*Heb*	
6:19–21	54		11:21–22	8		1:10	11
6:21	54		15:14	36		10	2, 50
6:22–23	53					13:15	26
6:24	54		*2 Cor*				
7:1–2	144		4:8–12	35		*1 Jn*	
7:23	75		9:11–12	13		1:3	18
25:37–40	13		13:13	14, 18		4:8	84, 121
26:26	126						
						Rev	
						3:20	127

SUBJECT INDEX

Abraham and Isaac, 22–25, 49

action: active-passivity, 143, 173; *actus purus*, 50, 73, 152; and agency, 2, 74, 88, 121–9, 141–66; of Christ, 17, 27, 30, 34, 43–4, 48, 75; divine, 20, 33, 35, 45, 47–8, 50, 78, 82, 84, 102, 122, 152–4, 161–6; *esse actus purus*, 50; habitual, 38, 116; human, 3, 20, 33–4, 46, 48, 56, 63, 74, 107, 111–66; as internal principle, 74; liturgical, 2–5, 8, 13, 17, 26–39, 43, 49, 81, 85, 92, 105–8; 121–2, 127, 133, 146, 149, 154, 159, 161–6; and office, 3–11, 19, 30–1; and production, 109–18; sacramental, 106; sacrificial, 6, 9–10, 19, 30; as self-knowledge, 63, 81, 115; and space, 108, 109, 116–20; and virtue, 56, 60, 63, *see also* agency

Agamben, Giorgio, 88

Alexander, Christopher, 87, 97, 119

Ambrose of Milan, Saint, 18

analogia entis, 26, 34

Aquinas. *See* Thomas Aquinas

Areopagite, Pseudo-Dionysius, 85

Arnaoutoglou, Ilias, 5

Aristotle, 4, 5, 56, 62, 75; *Nichomachean Ethics*, 5, 75; *Politics*, 4

Art: *ars*, 102; as sacrament, 102, 122; "man" as artist, 103; as manifesting the human condition, 140, 155–7

assimilate, 1, 12, 17, 19, 22, 28, 30–1, 34, 38, 75, 79, 81, 85, 147, 157

Athanasius, Saint, 55, 79, 80

Auden, W. H., 134, 140

Augustine of Hippo, Saint, 47, 72, 127, 153

Balthasar, Hans Urs von, 49

Barad, Karen, 162–3

Barrett, Sarah F., 88, 125

Barthes, Roland, 124, 130

Basil the Great, Saint, 55, 75

basilike, 102, 107

bauen, 101, 110

Being, 3, 34, 63, 70, 83–4, 163

being-known, 35, 49–51, 72–8, 80–2

Benveniste, Émile, 125, 128–34, 140, 143

Bernard of Clairvaux, Saint, 13

Bianchi, Enzo, 46, 49

bishop: as Christ, 10–12, 19, 29; as economist, 12; as liturgist, 26–9; *primus inter pares,* 9

Bonhoeffer, Dietrich, 1, 27

body schema, 81, 115, 122

Book of Common Prayer, 42, 84, 127, 139, 152

Bourdieu, Pierre, 112, 115–6, 118, 123

Bremmer, Jan N., 21

Caldwell, Phoebe, 135–43

Camus, Albert, 41

capitalism, 106, 109, 117, 131–2

Casel, Odo 3, 82

Cavanaugh, William T., 127

Chesterton, G. K., 102

Chilton, Bruce, 24

christotokos, 19, 45

Chrysostom, Saint John, 10, 34, 157

Clement of Rome, Saint, 9–12

Coakley, Sarah 64–6, 68

conviviality, 107, 109, 111–4

Cunningham, Conor, 56, 83

Cyprian of Carthage, Saint, 19

Cyril of Alexandria, Saint, 26–7, 80–2

Danckert, James, 91

Daniélou, Jean 64–6

deification, 27, 60, 165

De Bérulle, Pierre, 71
Demosthenes, 5
Descartes, René, 58
Desmond, William 162–4
diathesis, 128, 130, 143, 147–8
Didache, the, 27, 28
Divine Sophia, 72, 161, 164
Dmitriev, Sviatoslav, 3, 5
Dreyer, Mechthild, 83–4
Duns Scotus, Joannes, 34, 83–4, 148, 163

Eberhard, Phillipe, 125, 128–30, 152
Eckhart, Meister, 139
economy: of creation, 10; divine, 8, 10, 24–5, 30–4, 37, 39, 102, 148; gift, 15, 111; as household, 11; Jesus as, 38; liturgical, 8, 11–2, 19, 30–4, 82, 151–2; political, 102; *see also oikonomia*
ekklesia, 8, 102, 127
Eliot, T. S., 17
Ellard, Collin, 91
equivocity, 163
Ernst, Corrnelius, 134
Erskine, Andrew, 21
erotic-knowing, 49–50, 73, 77–9, 85
Eucharist: and becoming, 127, 157; celebration of, 38, 99–100, 164; Christ's offering, 33; gathering of, 37; and offering, 26–7, 33, 115; and language, 139; receiving, 33, 126–7; liturgy of, 26, 37, 42; patterning of, 120, 149; sacramental action of, 106–7; and space, 119; as sacrifice, 23, 26, 28; table of, 166
eudaimonia, 5

Feiler, Bruce, 98
Feldman, Yael, 23
Flesher, Paul V. M., 24

Gadamer, Hans George, 64, 137–8, 142, 144, 190
Gavrilyuk, Paul L., 64
gaze: as bodily comportment, 54–5, 59, 62–3; toward Christ, 47, 54–5, 60; of God, 54; and mirrors, 57; mutual, 60; object of, 53, 55–7, 61; of virtue, 60; *see also* image and likeness
gift, 5, 6, 81, 86, 122, *see also* economy
Gnosis, 66, 155
Gnosticism, 36–7, 39, 155
Gregory of Nazianzen, Saint, 55, 75
Gregory of Nyssa, Saint, 43, 46–51, 55–71, 75, 83

habitus, 108, 116–7, 123, 128, 157
Haidt, Jonathan, 89
Hall, Edward T., 87
Hamilton, Diane, 96
Hebb, Donald, 91
Heidegger, Martin, 101–2, 105, 108, 110, 114, 120, 133–4
Holmes, Brooke, 20–1
Homer, 21
homo liturgicus, 46
Hume, David, 53

Ignatius of Antioch, Saint, 3, 11–2, 17, 19, 36–7, 45
Illich, Ivan, 109–14
image and likeness, 29, 44–8, 52, 60, 66, 85, 149
imago Dei, 29–30, 45–6, 52, 61–3, 71, 74, 79, 165
Incarnation, 28, 31–2, 37, 47, 73–4, 99, 165
Ingham, Mary Beth, 83–4
intervolvement, 115, 118, 122, 142–3, 162
intra-action, 162–3
intransitive, 122, 126
Irenaeus of Lyons, Saint, 3, 16–7, 26–33, 71, 74, 155

Subject Index

John Chrysostom, Saint, 10, 34, 157
John of Damascus, Saint, 55, 69–70, 75–9, 165
Jonah, 53–4
Jones, David 102–4, 108, 117, 121–2, 140, 156–7

Kant, Immanuel, 53, 56
Kemmer, Suzanne, 125, 128
kenosis, 17, 27, 79, 183, *see also koinonia*
Kisner, Wendell, 125–6, 154
know yourself, 49, 59–60
koinonia: in Christ, 14, 17–9, 25, 30, 37; as gift, 14–6, 18; economy of, 15, 34; and offering, 18, 33; and human telos, 19; and kenosis, 25, 166; and reciprocity, 15
Kunzler, Michael, 3
kyriake oikia, 102, 119

language: as concealing meaning, 101–2, 113; as condition of perception, 119–20, 123–34, 146, 154–6; and space, 1, 108, 114, 118, 120; speaking and spoken by, 108, 118, 159; and subjectivity, 133–41, 158; structure of, 141–5; *see also habitus*
leitourgia, 1- 7, 9–10, 12, 14, 24, 30, 34, 37, 39, 43, 48, 102, 118, 121, 146–7, 158
Levenson, Jon D., 24
lex orandi, lex credendi, 81
ligare, 103, 108, 111
likeness, *see* image and likeness
logoi, 48, 164–5
Logos, 37, 44, 47–8, 74, 147, 162, 164–5
Lord's Supper, 8–9, *see also* Eucharist
Lossky, Vladmir, 66

MacIntyre, Alasdair, 1
made-manifest, 31, 38–9, 44–7, 53, 68, 149, 153, 162–3, 166

Martin, Michael, 72, 161, 164
Marx, Karl, 117, 121
Mauss, Marcel, 14–5
Maximus Confessor, Saint, 20, 30, 32, 38, 43–50, 65, 71–7, 116, 143, 148, 151, 153, 162–4
McLuhan, Marshall, 110
Melchio-Bonnet, Sabine, 57–8
Merleau-Ponty, Maurice, 49, 115–6, 122, 140–1
Merrifield, Colleen, 91
metaxological, 161–6
metaxu, 164
Meyendorff, John, 50
middle voice, xiii, 46, 48, 121–59, 163
Milbank, John, 71
Moore, Sebastian, 43
mysteries, 17, 19, 27, 31, 36, 63, 100

natural nature, 38, 43–4, 48, 54, 71, 82, 148, 153, 165
Neusner, Jacob, 23
Nin, Anaïs, 41

offering: eucharistic, 26, 33; financial, 3; to Greek gods, 20–1; in Judaism, 22–4; liturgist's role of gathering, 8, 28–30; mediated by priests, 7; of the people, 7, 11, 30, 149; receiving as, 15, 24–30, 38; sacrificial, 7, 8, 12, 14, 25, 30; as self-emptying, 14, 27; servant, 4; the Son/Christ as self-offering, 2, 8, 10, 12–4, 34, 37, 43, 50, 120, 148, 152–3, 159, 161; Trinity as self-offering, 71–85, 128, 145, 148; union with offerer and act of, 3–4, 8–12, 18, 28–31, 50; vicarious, 21; widow's mite, 16; *see also* Abraham and Isaac, *koinonia*
oikonomia, 30–1, 102, *see also* economy
ontology, 2, 163
Origen, 65–6

Pabst, Adrian, 71
Pallasmaa, Juhani, 155
Panofsky, Erwin, 91
Parker, Robert, 20
participation: anagogic relation of, 2–3; in divine goodness, 82; eucharistic, 8; the human made holy by, 27; in Jesus's/Christ's liturgy, 10, 17, 24–39, 47, 122, 129, 154, 158; and intra-action, 163; logic of, 36; ontology of, 2–3; in the sufferings of Christ, 82; and the tree of life, 55–6, 60, 64, 80; in Triune reciprocity, 27, 32, 163; understanding proportionate to, 43, 48–9, 55, 60–3, 71, 80, 82, 157; volitive, 2, 45, 50, 56, 79, 147–53, 163–5; willed, 44, 46, 74, 82–3; 143–4; *see also koinonia*
passion, 36–7, 82
Paul, Saint, 3, 6–14, 25, 30–2, 35–7, 41, 64, 82, 106, 109–10, 127, 146, 150–1, 159
perception: erotic, 49; affected by habits and habitats, 98–9, 140; as linguistic condition, 119, 123–5, 134, 141, 145–6, 159; sense, 50, 65–71, 165; socially conditioned, 116–7; and virtue, 45; *see also* Merleau-Ponty
Picasso, Pablo, 155
Pickstock, Catherine, 35, 83–4
Plato, 5, 55, 66; *Timaeus*, 52
Poetry, 156–7
psychogeographic, 92
Pulleyn, Simon, 20

recapitulate, 2–3, 43–4, 147–8
reciprocity, 2, 15, 17, 19, 22, 27, 50, 57, 68, 73, 77–80, 122
religio, 102–3
resurrection, 28, 30–3, 37, 64–7, 151
Ruskin, John 110, 113

sacrament: action of, 106; church as, 8, 51, 62; and economy, 30; as mediating Christ, 31, 43, 100, 146, 166; habituation in, 48, 157; *see also* mysteries
sacrifice: animal, 21–3; of the Church, 16; Christ as, 10, 12, 27, 30, 38; Eucharist as, 26, 28; and fasting, 13; Greek, 21–2, 24; Hebrew, 22–4, 30; *Hebrews*, 26; of Isaac, 22–3; and *leitourgia*, 7; living, 10, 14, 25, 29, 50, 64, 166; as manifesting God, 140; and offering, 10; of the one, 3; of Paul, 110; of the people, 10; of praise and thanksgiving, 37; as prefiguring Christ, 20; spiritual, 26; unbloody, 28; *see also* economy, offering
Schmemann, Alexander, 81
self-emptying: of God in Christ, 13, 25–7, 31; nature of offering, 14; of the Trinity, 25; willed, 17
Senn, Frank C., 34
sense perception, *see* perception
Shepherd of Hermas, 12–3
Smith, James K. A., 88, 153–4
space: and action, 108–20; affectivity of, 89–107, 118; ecclesial, 99–108, 119–20; and language, 114–5, 118, 128; and time, 109, 114–6
structuring structures, 112, 120
subjectivity, 49–61, 73, 115–6, 123–59, 163
suffering: of God in Christ, 19, 30, 35–7, 82; human, 30, 35–7; of Paul, 35; paticipatory nature of, 35

Taylor, Charles, 88, 147, 154, 156
Tenney, Frank, 4
theotokos, 45
Thomas Aquinas, Saint, 34, 75, 81
thrownness, 89
Thurian, Max, 23

Subject Index

time: assimilated to Christ, 34; gathered by God, 74; and space, 109, 114–6; and subjectivity, 133

Tolkien, J. R. R., 156

Trinity: as erotic-knowing, 50, 71–3, 78; as eternal gift, act of giving, and giver, 15, 159; movement of, 162, 166; and perichoresis, 51; as reciprocity, 2

Underhill, Evelyn, 1

univocity, 35, 83, 148, 163

Voegelin, Eric, 73

Vonnegut, Kurt, 109, 113

Weil, Simone, 164

Weltanschauung, 58

Williams, Rowan, 27, 66, 161, 165

Wilson, Peter, 5

Wittgenstein, Ludwig, 63

Wright, Orville, 112

WILLIAM DANIEL (PH.D., UNIVERSITY OF Nottingham) is rector of St. Michael's Church, Dean for Liturgy and Formation in the Episcopal Diocese of Rochester, and adjunct professor of humanities at SUNY Geneseo, in Geneseo, New York. He is the author of *Inhabited by Grace* (Church Publishing, Inc.), various works of poetry and social commentary, and is a roaster of coffee. You can follow Fr. Daniel at www.williamdaniel.info.

www.ingramcontent.com/pod-product-compliance
Lightning Source LLC
Chambersburg PA
CBHW022007080426
42733CB00007B/511